Charles Olson

Charles Olson

Call Him Ishmael

BY PAUL CHRISTENSEN

Foreword by George F. Butterick

University of Texas Press, Austin & London

To my parents

Due to the lengthy copyright data,
an extension of the copyright
page is given on page 245.

Library of Congress Cataloging in Publication Data
Christensen, Paul.
    Charles Olson, call him Ishmael.
    Bibliography: p.
    Includes index.
    1. Olson, Charles, 1910–1970—Criticism and
interpretation. I. Title.
PS3529.L655Z615   811'.5'4   78-8624
ISBN 0-292-71046-1
Copyright © 1975, 1979 by Paul Christensen

Contents

Foreword

The briefest survey will reveal that until now Charles Olson has not been given the serious critical attention his poetry and poetics demand. Many of the earlier critics, too close in time, were unable to clearly distinguish his contributions to American writing. Most reviewers compared Olson to Ezra Pound only to dismiss him as a Poundian imitator or disciple. James Dickey, for instance, rejected the poems in both *The Distances* and *The Maximus Poems* as "predictable Pound-cum-William-Carlos-Williams constructions." Karl Shapiro wrote haughtily, "Charles Olsen [*sic*] is a disciple of Pound and I like him for that. Pound in the long run is the best modern master, if one needs masters." And Robert Lowell remarked in an interview published in 1971, "Olson's *Maximus* is *Paterson* and the *Cantos*, though woodier," whatever that means. Even George Oppen, ordinarily given to fine discriminations, wrote that "to encounter Olson's work, in spite of the currency of the phrase, is simply not an encounter with a new poetry," because of the "audible presence of Pound" in the verse (this may have been one of the reasons Olson chides Oppen in *The Maximus Poems*). Only Charles Boer's extended memoir gave us the man in all his original dynamic genius and extravagance, his uniqueness, his variability. It was hoped the publication of *Charles Olson & Ezra Pound*, so ably edited by Catherine Seelye, as one of the earliest posthumous volumes, would cause the entire issue to be raised and thoroughly faced, and to some extent that has begun to happen.

Paul Christensen does not face this issue at the greatest possible length or, thank goodness, exhaust himself upon it but saves his strength (real strength) for the larger issue: how does a poet propose to transform the world (if it needs transforming; celebrate it, if that is what is called for)? He discusses Olson in terms of a new awareness, an altered consciousness that Olson's own writings propose and—almost by the straining of syntax alone—require. The title, of course, echoes that of Olson's study of Melville and America, but it also presents the poet himself as Ishmael, Melville's Ishmael, a sole survivor. Survivor of what, it might be asked—the West? modernism? perhaps America itself? Certainly a survivor of the old dispensation or disposition of mind. Olson is both as archaic as Pleistocene man and, as Christensen writes, a "first Westerner of the new consciousness."

This book is not just a mechanical reading through the poems—even with wit and common sense—or the imposition of some ideological or systemic grid on the work to see what it will yield. It is rich in the author's own ideas, with a sense of literary and intellectual history, original scholarship (he has done at least one thing I could not do—identify the old German x-ray technician whose story is alluded to in "The Distances"), and a critical intelligence that is at once sympathetic and usefully precise. All this is present in a style most pleasant and effortless. It is a brisk, sure prose—but not all charm, or charm alone. There is method, orderliness in his approach. He gives us the man, the essential biographical details, then proceeds with the earliest writings, discussing them against the intellectual background of the time, and from there advances to separate "subject categories," a long comprehensive stretch on *The Maximus Poems*, and concludes by placing Olson once more in history, among his contemporaries. He reasons, he weighs, he wrestles. He applauds the risks Olson took. He grapples with them both above and below the surface. He remains self-possessed in the face of undisguised eccentricities.

The writing, then, is characterized by a general orderliness of mind, without the relegating of live ideas to labeled cages and other substitutes for thought. Christensen's judgments are his own, not begged or borrowed. He does not bluff the difficulties. He covers the ground, from the most immediate and obvious—Olson's relationship with his predecessors Eliot, Pound, and Williams, the tradition of the long poem—but also back to Hegel and the Romantics. He is not overly dependent on but faithful to the texts. He uses them in such a way that we are stirred to go back to them in their entirety, back to them as to a favorite hope or home.

Christensen's book is a series of natural balances between proof and faith. And behind all the words is the deeply rooted conviction that Olson's work, wide and sprawling though it may be, originates in a coherent, clear center of concern. Christensen shows us the ways in which Olson's poetry can be judged on its own terms, by its own techniques, as well as according to more commonly traditional ones. The techniques in the verse as practiced by Olson include processual (in Whiteheadian terms), "openness," discovery rather than recovery of form, reward by image, syncopation, incremental associations, paratactic forwarding. It is not unusual to observe that the experimental mode has conventions of its own, that the avant-garde becomes a tradition like any other, a "tradition of the new." Consequently, it is possible to judge a bad "projective" poem from a good one without blindly dismissing all such poetry as antipoetic. Within the new consciousness, within the new conventions, as within the limits of the old, only the most energetic, the subtlest, the largest-hearted survive. It is no different than for the writer of the sonnet or the sestina. At its worst, what in 1950 Olson called "open" poetry leads to vapid looseness, sleepy rambles, pedantic tangle, solipsism, exclusiveness, and other forms of selfishness and decadence. There might even be, in an author's sudden terror of blank openness, a forced apocalypticism. At its best, however, a wholly new and dominant tradition emerges, although one already begun by Whitman, vers libre, and imagism. Its characteristics are triumph, ecstasy, heart change, renewed mind, recovered purpose, keenness of sensation, sensual awakening, and comprehension—not the least bit different from the "old" verse of Arnold or Tennyson. What is different, perhaps, are the risks it takes, the pitching of success or failure on the moment and against the limits of language, the total organicism.

The reoriented consciousness is not hot-eyed mysticism. It is not to lead to automatic writing or astral projection or other attempts at sustained ecstasy. Olson was not so inexperienced. The new consciousness is a polis of the self. It is "a coherence which, for the first time since the ice [always that scope in Olson], gave man the chance to join knowledge to culture and, with this weapon, shape dignities of economics and value sufficient to make daily life itself a dignity and a sufficiency." This is what Olson sought for the poem, to "make daily life itself a dignity and a sufficiency."

Christensen is willing to judge Olson's poems on their own merits rather than solely against the terms of formalist verse. Otherwise, how can he discuss the change of consciousness the writing proposes, how can he dare? He begins to build the principles for understanding and judging this new poetry that has emerged since the Second World War, this postmodernism. He contributes directly to what he calls a "new grammar" for such poetry. And within the new tradition, thanks to his work, it will be seen there are gradations and discriminations enough for any dedicated reader, or seeds enough for the *next* poetic advance.

Olson's is not comfortable poetry, and when it moves it sunders. With its freely wielded lines and disarming syntax, it does violence to complacency and orthodoxy. It dislocates readers either too inexperienced or too set in their ways or, it would be hoped, relocates such readers. A new, positive earth of value is felt under the feet. It is a poetry of belief, a poetics of optimism. Olson begins his "Human Universe" essay, his most accomplished piece of theoretical prose, with the statement, "There are laws." That piece, like the "Projective Verse" essay before it, embodies the very argument it seeks to make. It is equal to its argument, not about it; its form is, indeed, nothing less than the extension of its content. It opens with a denunciation of reason as the major determinant of life, arguing the invention of logic and classification by the Greeks is that which divides us from nature and from ourselves and which has estranged us from all that ought to be most familiar. And, rather than argue it out thoroughly, syllogistically, logically, Olson substitutes the very alternative he has proposed, concluding with a myth itself, the Mayan story of the Sun and the Moon—which wins the day and the case.

Similarly, the "Projective Verse" essay embodies the very principles it propounds, the total energy. It is itself an "energy-discharge"—so that literalists need not turn blue in the face, as X. J. Kennedy once claimed he did, seeking to put Olson's principle of "breath" into practice. Another poet wondered helplessly if a person in an iron lung could ever write "projective verse"!

Many of the early reviews were mocking, rhetorical, in the way some reviewers can get, but also vituperative and almost inexplicably hostile from today's perspective. Louis Simpson, winner of the Pulitzer Prize for poetry and professor for years, rejected Olson as a dull poet of "small feeling." (Paul Christensen knows otherwise.) Simpson writes of the poems in *The Distances*—a volume which includes "As The Dead Prey Upon Us" and "The Lordly and Isolate Satyrs"—that "if Pound did not exist, neither would these poems." Robert Bly, who may have softened his views somewhat in more recent years, declares in a survey of poetry published in 1960 that "the worst book of the year was probably Charles Olson's *Maximus Poems*. This is Babbitt in verse, and it is painful to see intelligent men defend it." (The only more bitter attacks to date have come from Martin Seymour-Smith, Robert Creeley's old English friend from Mallorca days, a character in *The Island* and author of a *Bluffer's Guide to Literature*, who has entries for Olson in two separate books purported to be reference works and guides. His remarks include such amazing statements as "Olson, who was in many ways a good and generous man, had an excellent education . . . which he partially misused" and "[Olson's] influence cannot be stated to have been bad, but it was not good"—though it must be said his odd views in the volumes are by no means limited to Olson.)

It is of course more convenient for some minds to respond that way; it assures their independence and conserves energy for the business of their own creation. And it might be said that the lines of both poets,

Simpson and Bly, opened up in the course of the 1960s, became "Americanized"—as did James Dickey's and Adrienne Rich's—as the cultural wind shifted. Mostly it was "Projective Verse" that gave the trouble. But, then, it should be recalled that, at the very time that essay was being written out in letters to Creeley, a reviewer in *Poetry*—once the bellwether of American poetry—was dismissing William Carlos Williams, that most American of poets, as a "very minor poet"!

Perhaps now that the earth has creaked a little more on its axis—new nations have emerged, old colonial attitudes have been thrown off—Olson can be approached more directly. New assessments can be made, younger readers guided both to an understanding of his accomplishments and to what he hoped to accomplish but fell short of achieving. Paul Christensen has been alert enough to arrive early, and his book is a welcome relief. He has been able to construct a remarkably comprehensive study. His book is a patient, generous, long-sighted introduction to one of our most challenging poets, one who in many ways represents the recent giantism of America more than any of its other poets. It is not only timely but, by its care and passionate intelligence in this boom year (there are at least two other fine books on Olson appearing from the nation's university presses, as well as a scholarly guide to his major poem), it becomes already, automatically, a standard volume in the approach to Olson (and modern poetics at large, for that matter). Standard, then, in both senses: a flutter at the head of the advance, and also a dependable, substantial reference work—a fixed value—to be regularly and widely used.

University of Connecticut   George F. Butterick
April 1978

Acknowledgments

It is a pleasure for me to thank those who joined with me in celebrating the life and work of a great poet: I owe these friends and counselors my deep gratitude for giving me insight into my subject, discipline to think clearly, and support and encouragement to raise the result far above my own standards. I have not achieved all I set out to do, but where I have understood and followed their advice, I am proud of what I have written.

I wish, first of all, to thank my mentor and friend Daniel Hoffman for his constant faith in me and for his help in shaping the argument and the scope of this work. I owe what thoroughness I bring to this study to his own care for intensity and completeness of thought. His counsel to me was all the more fruitful because I wrote about a poet and a new direction of poetry which were foreign to his sympathies; my advocacy was never allowed to remain easy or loose or vague. And I feel tempered by the fire of this wise and compassionate critic of our literature. I owe another debt to my friend John Moffett, who talked late into the nights with me about the social reality transmuted in literature. From him I received an education in Marxist interpretation which altered and clarified the literary realm around me.

And from Donald Allen and George Butterick I have received expert knowledge about my subject. Allen patiently examined an earlier draft of this study and guided me toward greater accuracy in many details. George Butterick, curator of the Literary Archives of the University of Connecticut Library, gave me an exhaustive tour of the Olson papers and other files of the archives over a period of several weeks and then subjected my draft to wonderful scrutiny, from which I rewrote and greatly improved this study. All Olson scholars are indebted many times over to these inexhaustible spirits.

It was my good fortune to have had Clyde L. Grimm, Jr., prepare the text of this study for publication; he brought an exquisite craftsmanship to my work, and in many places I felt as though my prose had been the uncut stone from which he chipped out many good forms that might otherwise have remained indifferently submerged in my argument. I lament the passing of *il miglior fabbro*, for this was the last manuscript he was to prepare before his untimely death.

For close readings of later drafts and for many stylistic corrections and graces, I am indebted particularly to Karl E. Elmquist, a man too gracious to accept any other thanks but these. I am also grateful to Richard Hauer Costa, another colleague, who read a chapter and made a number of good suggestions which I have incorporated here.

I should also like to mention the support and encouragement of several others who helped me bring this study to publication. I am flattered by the kind and supporting attitude of Prof. Archibald Hill, who assisted me in having this book considered for publication. And I wish to thank Prof. David H. Stewart, head of the English Department, and Prof. W. David Maxwell, Dean of the College of Liberal Arts, Texas A&M University, for reducing my teaching schedule, which allowed me time to prepare a final draft of this work.

Much of my research about Olson took place in the reading room of the Humanities Research Center at the University of Texas at Austin, where I was assisted by a very competent staff. I especially thank David Farmer, the Assistant Director of the HRC, Sally Leach, and Ellen Dunlap for granting me certain privileges and attention that made my research a pleasure. And I feel a similar high regard for the Literary Archives at the University of Connecticut at Storrs, where I sat each day among heaps of Olson's manuscripts and books, looked after by George Butterick.

Others who have given me support at different stages of this study include Linda W. Wagner, who read a draft of this study and spirited me on with her comments; Greg Kuzma, who in publishing an essay I wrote on Olson encouraged me to rewrite and incorporate those ideas here; and Robert Creeley, who showed an interest in my project at its very beginning and some years back gave me his time for what must have seemed very clumsy questions. He is an eloquent apologist of postmodernism and a source for many scholars of this literary epoch. I am pleased to be able to include his name in these tributes.

I am indebted to other Olson scholars as well; with them I feel a keen sense of fellowship, for we are pioneers in a trackless new terrain. I am especially thankful for the work of Albert Gould Glover, whose editorial collaborations with George Butterick and whose dissertation edition of the "Letters for Origin" made my study all the more feasible. I learned much from the brilliant perceptions of Donald Byrd, whose command of the *Maximus* poems inspired me to look more deeply for my own perspective on Olson. And there are others, too, whose voices are all mingled with my own.

In helping me acquire the photographs for this work, I am indebted to Michael Davidson of Special Collections, the Library of the University of California at San Diego, for his energetic cooperation; to Jonathan Williams for materials used here as well as for all his other services to the new poetry through Jargon Press and the Jargon Archives; and to Ed Dorn for coming through with help on very short notice; to George Butterick for the bulk of the photographs on Olson and related figures; to Gerard Malanga for what are now the classic portraits of Charles Olson and Robert Duncan reprinted here; and to the Humanities Research Center, the University of Texas at Austin, for use of the rare photograph of Cid Corman.

I am in the debt of many other good people, especially William Hussey and Ralph Maud, for kindnesses, suggestions, and ideas too detailed to single out in these broad remarks. In the other direction is a help pervading everything I have tried to do: the devotion of my wife, Catherine, who came with me through every hour of my effort to make this study worthwhile.

Charles Olson

1. Charles Olson: An Introduction

> The question, the fear he raises up himself against
> (against the same each act is proffered, under the eyes
> each fix, the town of the earth over, is managed) is: Who
> am I?
>
> —"In Cold Hell, In Thicket"

> . . . particularism has to be fought for anew.
>
> —"Human Universe"

> It is his body that is his answer, his body intact and fought for,
> the absolute of his organism in its simplest terms, this structure
> evolved by nature, repeated in each act of birth, the animal
> man. . . .
>
> —"The Resistance"

The essential Charles Olson lies somewhere under his texts like a root system, a sprawl of interests raying out from an elusive center that produced, over the twenty-five years of his writing life, a puzzling variety of short, precisely worded essays and notes, a collection of plays, a book about Melville, roughly a hundred short poems, and one long poem that runs almost six hundred pages. In the years that have passed since his death in 1970, he has come under increasingly close public scrutiny. Several recent dissertations have analyzed parts of his work and life, interviewers have ferreted out of his closest associates the intimate facts of his friendships, and others have considered his significance as a theorist and educator. The mass of his unpublished writing, purchased by the University of Connecticut, is undergoing the slow process of publication; an archive has been set up at Storrs, his library reconstructed, his notes filed and organized. Reminiscences continue to appear in journals that attend to events in modern poetry, and even the most trivial details of Olson's residence in Gloucester have become part of the restoration process. (For example, the second-story apartment in the ramshackle old clapboard building at Fort Point has been immortalized in published photographs; the window he looked out to sea from in *The Maximus Poems: Volume Three* fills a page in the Olson issue of *Boundary 2*.)[1]

But much of this attention is directed only to specific facets of Olson's work and life. For example, Donald Byrd's dissertation "Charles Olson's *Maximus*: An Introduction," concentrates on the linguistic, philosophical, and historical issues Olson needed to resolve in order to create and sustain the arguments of the first two volumes of his *Maximus* sequence. Byrd's purpose is chiefly to provide a critical introduction to the sequence, though in the process he sheds light on the pattern of Olson's thinking as a whole. In *Letters for Origin, 1950–1956*, edited by Albert Glover, we are confronted with Olson the founder of a new movement in poetry; the letters show us the kind of disciplined and comprehensive attention Olson gave to the work being written in his time, both berating and encouraging the editor of *Origin*, Cid Corman, to continue to gather in new talent. This is an argumentative Olson, theorist of a new poetry, using all his rhetorical skills to make Corman see his ideas and use them. Martin Duberman's *Black Mountain: An Exploration in Community* shows us Olson the educator, applying the principles of his poetic to the teaching of new poets, demanding from their work the kind of absorption with self he expressed in his own poems.

The great variety of essays and notes that Matthew Corrigan collected for the Olson issue of *Boundary 2* ranges from eulogies to close inspections of individual short poems; it documents the initial stages by which an innovative poet's life and work undergo cultural osmosis. According to Corrigan's "Preface," the essays reflect "Olson's status three years after his death. . . . Put another way Olson now seems out of the hands of the avant and into the hands of the middle guard (complete with barbed footnotes); one positive of which is the absence of that awful atavism which tainted the first (the avant) writing on him" (p. xi). The notoriety and controversy that surround a living artist of the avant garde shield him, perhaps, from criticism, but after his death, his work undergoes demystification through the laborious process of steady exegesis. Ezra Pound's *Cantos*, William Carlos Williams' *Paterson*, and T. S. Eliot's "The Waste Land" are at a much more advanced stage of cultural integration; they are now standard texts of this century's poetry.

Olson's work has only just begun to be examined, sifted, tried in the courts of literary journals. Critics have even begun to express judgments of an official character on which of the works are to be deemed "classical." Guy Davenport, for example, perhaps the most distinguished scholar of modern literature yet to take up the work of Olson, has made one such ruling:

> "The Kingfishers" is itself a paradigm of the process of continuity and change which it tracks with a kind of philosophical radar.

This most modern of American poems, the most energetically
influential text in the last thirty-five years, is a resuscitation of a
poetic form worked to death between the late eighteenth and
mid-nineteenth centuries, from the age of Peacock's "Palmyra,"
Shelley's "The Demon of the World" and "Ozymandias," and
Volney's *Les Ruines* to the masterwork of all meditations on
ruins, Melville's *Clarel*.[2]

But judgments continue to differ as Olson's final poems come into print.
Archaeologist of Morning (1973) and the very recent third volume of
the *Maximus* poems are now undergoing the preliminary criticism of
book reviewers and commentators.

In the present study I willingly hazard the risks of attempting to make
a more comprehensive study of the underlying unities which the poems,
essays, letters, and other works subtly, teasingly suggest. My premise that
there is such unity is "conjectural" in the sense that Olson used the
term: its etymology reaches back to the Latin *conjicere*, "to throw together," or toss, as Marcel Duchamp tossed the rods in his studio, allowing them to fall randomly and make a design, from which he fashioned
"The Mechanical Bride," a work of the most deliberate precision. As
Olson wrote to Corman,

                            a man can only express that
         which he knows

                    Now the further difficulty is, we think we know. And
                        that
                    too is a mare's nest: we don't even know until we
                        bend
                    to the modesty to say we have nothing to say. Then
                        we offer
                    our *conjectures* abt what it is we have found to
                        wonder abt. . . . [3]

Given the diversity of Olson's interests and preoccupations as a poet,
we are confronted with the question: do the life and work of this poet
have a design? And if they do, what premise could possibly draw all the
relevant details together and make them meaningful, expressive of a
single, absorbing concern? Olson's enthusiasms encompass such oddments
as Hopi language, Mayan statuary, non-Euclidean geometry, Melville's
fiction, the austere thought structures in Whitehead's philosophy, the
fragmentary remains of the Sumerian and Hittite civilizations, Norse,

Greek, and Egyptian mythology, numerology and the Tarot, the history of human migration, naval and economic history, the etymology of common words, pre-Socratic philosophy, the historical origins of the New England colonies, the development of the fishing industry off the coast of Massachusetts, accounts of the conquest of Mexico, the collapse of the Aztec and Mayan civilizations. The list could be extended. Is there an underlying unity at all? Or do these scattered interests, which seem to enter willy-nilly into Olson's prose and poetry, merely reflect the eccentric learning of the autodidact? Or might they imply a frantic mimicry of the erudition he envied in Pound?

Perhaps a bit of both of these is the answer, but Olson used his knowledge as comfortably as he drew upon his most casual experience. He fashioned his writing out of arcane lore with confidence; the prose emerges from an awesome memory, an almost total recall of his reading. His most difficult poems bear unwieldy structures of detail; they are like the Watts towers of Simon Rodilla that Robert Duncan describes in one of his poems:

> three spires
> rising 104 feet, bejewelld with glass,
> shells, fragments of tile, scavenged
> from the city dump, from sea-wrack, . . .
> . . . built up from bits of beauty
> sorted out—thirty-three years of it—
> the great mitred structure rising
> out of squalid suburbs where the
> mind is beaten back to the traffic, . . .
>
> The poem . . .
> "The poet,"
> Charles Olson writes,
> "cannot afford to traffic in any other *sign* than his one"
> "his self," he says, "the man
> or woman he is" Who? Rodia
> at 81 is through work.
> Whatever man or woman he is,
> he is a tower, three towers,
> a trinity upraised by himself.[4]

If Olson were merely Pound's mimic or a poseur, all the factual minutiae of his poems and essays would be dead weight. Part of the excitement of his best art, however, is the personal possession he takes of his learning; he expresses himself through mosaic patterns of allusion and direct quotation. All the haphazard learning is actually used in the writing; it contributes directly to the forms of his expression. He uses factual data as means of extending the range of his language. The terms and details of other fields of learning complicate and enrich the assertions of his prose. The diversity of his attention is almost a greed for experience, out of frustration with the fact that most of our thoughts arise within the narrow confines of ordinary experience. But Olson's most arcane references are at heart simple parallels to his own ideas. Perhaps the fault of this kind of writing is its tendency toward overelaboration; he often ran the risk of simply adorning his common sense instead of truly illuminating it with analogy. But the intention of all this breadth of reference, while not excusing its worst excesses, at least explains what it is attempting to do: to show a mind that has ventured out beyond its own routines of thought and experience and sought to immerse itself in areas of experience, of the remote past and of other cultures, that Western civilization has deliberately or unwittingly ignored.

We get close to the possibility of a unifying premise when we begin to think of Olson as an American writer who gradually came to reject certain of the tendencies he believed peculiar to Western civilization. There is no easy way to generalize on the nature of his rejection of Western thinking; his sense of the issues involved was entirely too specific for him to fix them into one embracing principle. We are on safer ground to suggest that he rebelled against philosophical discourse that required an abstract language to discover the laws of experience. Such discourse violated a basic integrity of communication for Olson: it assigned meanings to words different from the experience they specifically denoted. In this radical separation of human sign from its object, Olson believed that Western civilization had cut itself off from direct perception and, consequently, from a compassionate understanding of the phenomena of nature. In an introductory note to "A Bibliography on the State of Knowledge for Charles Doria," a student of myth he taught during his years at the State University of New York at Buffalo, he summarizes in a single sentence a long-time concern for the restoration of the particular in language: "Words then are naming and logography is writing as though each word is physical and that objects are originally motivating. This is the doctrine of the earth."[5]

He felt that once Greek philosophy had broken the bond between sign and referent, language began to acquire a logic of its own, distinct from its capacity to express reality. Language was thus allowed to drift from its representational functions, so that new, purely hypothetical conditions could be invented by the manipulation of words. He was fond of observing that the mere syntax of the simple sentence in English implied a contrived reality of cause and effect; worse, it constrained us from rendering what lay beneath the surface of our immediate awareness. Consciousness was thus denied access to its dark underside, the unconscious, the function of which is to renew and restructure awareness by its continuous upheaval of intuition and new content.

Olson was not the first writer to raise these issues about language. The European phenomenologists, led by Martin Heidegger, made a more rigorous criticism of language from the same perspective. Heidegger attacked language especially for its vitiation of what he called Being; Olson's generally equivalent term was Self.

But Olson was not a trained philosopher nor was he particularly aware of the ferment of phenomenological thought in Europe at the time he was writing. Instead, his critique of the drift of language toward a generalized subjectivity was specifically directed toward poetry and the habits of its composition. Literature was the victim of the stagnation of language. A new poetic would have to include a new sense of language as well as a program for new forms and techniques of composition.

Olson's philosophical concerns converge on the remaking of poetry from its language to its most subtle refinements of form. The root of the poem is the word, and the word must be reoriented to its denotative function. The subjectivization of words had robbed them of their clear attachment to the world. Our ability to take the world in through words depends entirely upon the capacity of the words to transmit lived experience. But since the Greeks, Olson argued, the mind had come to hoard the signs of objects and attribute to them private notions of their meaning. The mind, intent to structure experience by increasingly rigid systems, had made words support such structurings, when in fact the real value of words lay in their power to assault structuring through what they told of nature's more changeful processes.

By subjectivizing words, or by suppressing their full weight of denotation, the mind could absolutize nature in terms of its own logical priorities. Hence, the poem, rather than displaying the awesome power of nature, tended to narcissize experience; the poem was not a mirror held up to man in nature but a reflection of the mind ruling over the natural realm. The whole stance of language must be reversed in order to bring about a new poetic.

The denotational core of words must be rescued from neglect; logical classification and the principles of syntax must be suppressed and a new, unruly seizure of phenomena put in their place. Only then could it be said that the poem was grounded once more in actual experience; its words would be elements of specific experience, and its form would result from the poet's intuitive grasp of their relations. Olson's own poetry is the primary instance of this new poetic: his poems strike us with an unfamiliar and sometimes disturbing discordance of sound and verbal texture, the result of a determined effort to bring into them a mass of language and event absent from what we usually expect in lyrical discourse. His style, whether he is writing prose or poetry, is characterized by a density of specific terms and a sodden weight of data. But the illuminations he can sometimes provoke from these jagged aggregates of words have a startling effect upon the reader.

Olson came to his convictions during a period of cultural trauma. In the same year that Hiroshima and Nagasaki were devastated by atomic bombs, scenes of the Nazi death camps had been filmed, and the lurid images of mass graves and the piled remains of cremated Jews would enter obliquely into Olson's earliest poems. Although he did not address himself to these events directly in anything he wrote during this time, we must assume that irrational violence and hatred affected him deeply and contributed to his growing sense that Western thought had drifted into an illusory world where language no longer inspired moral conduct.

At the same time that these events were defining the new age of the mid-century, Olson was writing and revising his book on Melville, *Call Me Ishmael*, which he published finally in 1947 after deleting almost three hundred pages from the original version. In that book, he articulated his own belief that since the middle of the last century scientists and philosophers had begun to redefine the behavior of nature in ways that revealed an entirely new sense of reality, characterized chiefly by its kinetic state and its atomic particularity. Laid against this new sense of the actual was the older Western conception of a fixed, hierarchical model of reality, which Western language continued to impose on cognition through its grammar and syntactical laws.

As he observed to Cid Corman, "writers are terribly behindhand, in not discovering, as Cavalcanti discovered the physics of light in his time, the important bearing on their own work of the relativism of space-time concept."[6] He recognized in Melville's fiction, particularly in his masterwork *Moby-Dick*, a perception of that new, changeful sense of things, and *Call Me Ishmael* is partly an early manifesto of his acceptance of this view.

By 1947, in other words, Olson had concluded that Western modes of thought continued to depend upon a version of reality no longer tenable in the twentieth century. What was Western thought holding on to?

Olson would probably have said its institutions and its base of power, which depended on its own system of order, which in turn the new concept of reality threatened to sweep away. The decade of the fifties, the era of Senator Joe McCarthy and the ousting of dissident individuals from positions of responsibility, was a time of tremendous fermentation and innovation in the arts. As a new American esthetic was being formulated, social control was becoming all the more obvious in American life. A radical dichotomy, in Olson's view, was beginning to unfold at mid-century between the government's monistic social philosophy and the contrary doctrine preached by avant garde artists. It was a breach in Western metaphysics, "a time," he wrote in 1946, "when forces large as centuries battle," a decisive event in the dialectical rhythms of cultural history.[7]

A conviction of this magnitude and moment would require a lifetime of careful articulation and argument, and even then only some fragmentary view might come clear. Olson was impatient to argue his position with whatever lay close at hand, and the result was that he alienated much of his potential audience by the very flimsiness of his arguments, the slipshod scholarship and hasty generalization that characterize some of his most polemical writings. He wrote well and with passion, but his arguments sometimes depended upon a very personal reading of his sources, and his evidence was frequently vague indeed. But despite the clumsiness, the blind leaps of speculation, the inaccuracies that crept into his statistics and dates, he threw into the face of the experts and specialists a quality of stubborn courage which is invigorating, even when he makes us howl with disbelief. As Jonathan Williams, the poet and his one-time student at Black Mountain College, recalled about Olson's scholarly vauntings, "If you wanted to nail him, you know, he'd puff on his cigarette and his eyes would get round and he'd laugh it off and say, 'Si! Si!' "[8] He *is* outrageous in his writing, but at the same time that he exploits and manipulates the evidence of his most seriously held points, he has expressed himself exactly—which is a significantly different kind of error from merely being wrong.

But our premise requires further elaboration to explain Olson's theoretical position. He was not inspired to formulate a new cult of savagery in American poetry, however much he believed that the real vitalities of this art lay in the recesses of the psyche. He was a stern critic of the organizing powers of civilization, and he dealt with these as though they covered over the individual's access to his own primordial energies. He appreciated the psychological theories of Carl Jung, with their assertions of ancient archetypal experience. But Olson was not a new American version of Jean Jacques Rousseau, interested merely in the *primitif* for its own sake. Rather, he had a high regard for certain of the acquisitions of civilized man: language and the technologies of agriculture and building, the means by which human beings have come to insure their survival amid the adversities of the natural environment. He drew a sharp line between these improvements of the human condition and the distinctions civilization had created among its members, limitations of caste and privilege imposed on personal freedom and experience. He admired, then, the first stages of civilization having to do with survival itself, when the integrity of the community was still intact. But Plato's expulsion of the poet from his utopian republic was the culminating gesture of the move toward factionalism among early civilizations, and Olson treated capitalism as another manifestation of the same dispersive will, the drive in present civilization to seize and control existence.

Olson was not always in rebellion against his own culture—he came to that disposition by a slow and indirect route. Although a biography of Olson has yet to be written, George Butterick has appended a "Chronology" to his dissertation on *The Maximus Poems*, which provides a useful guide to Olson's whereabouts from year to year and to important events that shaped his mind.[9]

Charles Olson was born December 27, 1910, in Worcester, Massachusetts, and grew up there the son of a letter carrier. In a photograph taken when he was fifteen, he is shown standing between his parents; he is a tall, awkward-looking young man with horn-rimmed glasses, hair parted in the middle, an ill-fitting double-breasted suit hanging from his wide shoulders.[10] He looks scholarly and self-conscious as he poses for the camera. His mother, who is a much beloved but tormenting memory in his poems, stands with her head barely reaching to her son's shoulders. At full maturity Olson stood somewhere between six feet seven and six feet nine inches—no one seems to be quite sure exactly how tall he was.[11]

In 1928, while a senior at Classical High School in Worcester, he won third prize in the National Oratorical Contest, a free ten-week trip to Europe. Later that year, he entered Wesleyan University. During the summer of 1929, Olson attended the Gloucester School of the Little Theater, where he performed in several plays and took dance lessons from Constance Taylor, who taught a series of exercises in posture which he later recalled in "Maximus, to Gloucester" and "Letter 14" of *The Maximus Poems*.[12] After graduating Phi Beta Kappa from Wesleyan in 1932, he returned to Gloucester that summer and performed with the Moorland Players. He reentered Wesleyan for graduate study the following semester and, having sufficiently distinguished himself as a student, received an Olin Fellowship, enabling him to take additional graduate courses at Yale University.

He earned a master's degree at Wesleyan in 1933, having written a thesis on Melville entitled "The Growth of Herman Melville, Prose Writer and Poetic Thinker." In the following year he remained at Wesleyan and did further research on Melville's library, with impressive results. Through contacts he made with relatives of Melville, he was able to recover a number of volumes of the original library, including Melville's copy of Shakespeare, which he later used in writing a paper entitled "Lear and Moby-Dick" while a student at Harvard under F. O. Matthiessen. It was published in *Twice A Year* in 1938 with the help of Edward Dahlberg, whom he had also met at Harvard.

For two years, 1934 to 1936, he was an instructor at Clark University in Worcester, and in the fall of 1936 he entered Harvard as one of the first doctoral candidates in the newly organized American studies program. These were significant years for Olson. He met and became friends with Dahlberg, who later helped him rewrite *Call Me Ishmael*, and he came into contact with a number of distinguished scientists and historians whose methods and techniques of research impressed him greatly. His life-long interest in the history of the American West began with courses he had taken at Harvard, particularly Frederick Merk's course "The Westward Movement." He was also in the Harvard-sponsored "Sciences of Man" program, which introduced him to other technical disciplines, such as geography and archeology, and showed him the applicability of scientific methods to research in the humanities, a possibility Olson took very seriously thereafter. Years later, while rector of Black Mountain College, he organized a similar program, which he called the "Institute of the New Sciences of Man."[13]

Olson finished his course work toward the Ph.D. degree in the spring of 1939 but left without submitting a dissertation. He had won a Guggenheim Fellowship to continue research on Melville and spent the summer and fall with his mother in Gloucester writing a preliminary draft of the book on Melville, which Dahlberg had advised him not to publish.[14] In the winter of 1940, Olson went to live in New York, where he met the artist Corrado Cagli, whose drawings later accompanied his first book of poems, *Y & X* (1948). And by February of 1941, he had begun a short-lived political career as publicity director for the American Civil Liberties Union.

His political career is a curious period in Olson's life, and few writers have commented about it. Judging from his connection with the American Civil Liberties Union, he was an earnest liberal who believed that many of the social abuses of the thirties could be ameliorated by enlightened legislation and government policy. His next political post was with the Foreign Language Information Service of the Common Council for American Unity. His chief concern of these years was the protection of rights of foreign nationals and racial minorities. In September of 1942, he went to Washington to work in the Office of War Information, where he advanced to Assistant Chief of the Foreign Language Section, from which post he later resigned in protest against the policies of the OWI Director, George W. Healey. The incident was reported in the *New York Times*, where Olson and his associate Constantine Poulos, who had also resigned, were quoted as saying that they had been prevented from "functioning to offset Axis propaganda aimed at creating dissension among America's 35,000,000 citizens of foreign ancestry."[15] Several months later, in an essay entitled "People v. The Fascist, U. S. (1944)" in the Socialist monthly *Survey Graphic*, he aired his frustrations with Healey at the same time he addressed the rather delicate issue of prosecution of libel cases involving minorities. Olson was fully aware that up to then such cases had become entangled with questions of constitutional freedoms, especially freedom of speech, and that whole classes and civic groups might constitute the plaintiff. In spite of these difficulties, he argued very forcefully the need for additional legal protections of minorities in the form of civil and class action suits:

> . . . a law awakened to the demands of the people can prove one
> arm in the struggle [against oppression]. That is why the civil
> law, where the people can bring their own suits, is important.
> That is why libel law which goes beyond individual and liberal
> concepts of "liberty" must be made available to a people joined
> together, as we are, in the groupings which modern technological
> society makes inevitable. To frame such a law is a challenge on
> the doorstep of the believers in civil liberty. A people locked in
> combat with the fascists must fight on all fronts.[16]

Before his resignation, he had collaborated with the artist Ben Shahn, who was also with the OWI, on a government pamphlet entitled *Spanish Speaking Americans in the War* (1943).

The essay for *Survey Graphic* gives us a view of Olson as a tough-minded young political idealist, one of the bright Ivy League liberals who had been attracted to government service in the name of social reform. In fact, President Roosevelt appears to have been aware of Olson's work for the OWI, for after his resignation he was invited to be the Director of the Foreign Nationalities Division of the Democratic National Committee and to support Roosevelt's reelection effort in the Democratic National Committee. But at some point during this service Olson became disenchanted with politics and quite possibly with the very workings of federal government itself. He left for Key West, Florida, in the winter of 1944–45 and, while there, refused offers of an assistant postmaster generalship and a "high Treasury Department post," thus ending a promising political career barely five years after it had begun.[17]

His first thirty-five years were thus marked by early academic distinctions, honors, and awards that would have been gratifying to any young man born of lower working-class parentage, whose summers were spent at hard labor in order to pay his expenses at college. The publication of an article while a graduate student at Harvard, two Olin Fellowships to Yale, the first of two Guggenheim Fellowships (another would come in 1948), a close friendship with a distinguished writer (Dahlberg), and then the rapid advancement of a political career—all contributed to his confidence and perhaps subdued his critical nature until the middle of his life. The winter in Key West, although only a few poems are the record of it, is a mysterious period of transition in his thinking, for during that time he underwent a radical change of attitude toward American social life, indeed toward the very conditions in which he had advanced so rapidly.

When Olson returned from Key West to live briefly in Virginia, he wrote a short essay for *Partisan Review*, "This is Yeats Speaking," addressed to Ezra Pound, who had been returned to the United States after his long detention in Pisa, Italy. Pound had not been alone among intellectuals in Europe in finding reason to espouse fascist social philosophy; Eliot had also been sympathetic to certain aspects of authoritarianism. The political tension, the unrest among the working populations of European capitals, a looming sense of moral decadence, the phenomena of strikes, and the surges of revolutionary activity made fascism seem to many a direct and powerful means of stemming the fragmentation of European society. But Pound's attacks upon what he felt was a conspiracy of Jewish financiers in Europe amounted to defamation of a minority. In part, Olson's task was to come to terms with a libelous author who had supported fascism in Italy, the very evil which Olson had attempted to prosecute vigorously while in the government and against which his *Survey Graphic* article had lashed out with fury and frustration.

But after his withdrawal from government service Olson had become interested in an entirely different kind of conflict, which Pound also seems to have embodied at that moment. In the Yeats essay he limits his condemnation of Pound's anti-Semitism to a compressed paragraph:

> He was false—out of phase—when he subordinated his critical intelligence to the objects of authority in others. If the Positive Man do that, all the cruelty and narrowness of his intellect are displayed in service of preposterous purpose after purpose till there is nothing left but the fixed idea and some hysterical hatred.[18]

But the new subject that had Olson's attention was of far greater interest to him than anything he had turned his mind to before: the sense that Pound, Eliot (to a lesser extent), and Yeats, through whom Olson was speaking, had contributed new techniques and forms of art as part of a profound shift of consciousness in the West:

> O writers, readers, fighters, fearers, for another reason, that you have allowed this [Pound's arrest] to happen without a trial of your own. It is the passivity of you young men before Pound's work as a whole, not [the Rome Radio] scripts alone, you who have taken from him, Joyce, Eliot and myself the advances we made for you. There is a court you leave silent—history present, the issue the larger concerns of authority than a state, Heraclitus and Marx called, perhaps some consideration of descents and metamorphoses, form and the elimination of intellect.[19]

He closed his essay with a declaration, as if spoken by Yeats for his time yet expressing his own sense of where the new writers of his day should be headed: "You are the antithetical men, and your time is forward, the conflict is more declared, it is for you to hold the mirror up to authority, behind our respect for which lay a disrespect for democracy as we were acquainted with it."[20]

"A disrespect for democracy" was a phrase written out of a fundamental turning of his mind, composed perhaps only weeks after he had severed his connections with Washington politics. An incredible change of attitude! But we can almost see the change begin to occur back in 1944, for in his *Survey Graphic* piece several sentences come to mind that do not fit with all the others; they have a new, discordant ring to them: "The purest sons of capitalism, we tend to take libel seriously when it strikes at profits. We take it less seriously when honor, race, morals, creed is attacked."[21] Groups, then, have little or no protection in a democracy; only the individual does, according to his argument here. It is the beginning of a new critical attitude toward democratic capitalism that would in the years ahead turn into a program of new, postmodern art forms and a conviction of the necessity for radical social reform "as America accommodates herself to the twentieth century."[22]

The change that had occurred in Olson's thinking was radical: if he had originally believed that government policy could protect the rights of cultural and racial minorities in America from fascist-inspired dissension, he now believed that the government itself and the corporate economic system were responsible for undermining the formation of group identity in America, that they dissolved communal life in a deliberate leveling of the population into competitive individuals.

He wrote defiantly against this tendency in *Call Me Ishmael* and devoted much of his life to a long poem about a township on the coast of Massachusetts, Gloucester, where the dream of a communal life for its citizens began and died. By this abrupt change, he had become a "postliberal," as Donald Byrd has suggested.[23] Olson no longer believed there was any real value in extending the power of government to improve the social condition, but he did not abandon his conviction that such change had to come about. His hopes now rested in the power of educators and artists to cause those changes by which America could once again become a nation of cooperatives and communities.

In January 1946, Olson began visiting Pound and discussing with him some of the ideas about poetry that he would later advocate in his essay "Projective Verse," of which I will have a great deal to say in the ensuing chapters. But this friendship would endure only until the spring of 1948, when Pound's anti-Semitism reasserted itself in an offensive interrogation about Olson's possible Jewish ancestry. No doubt Pound had grown suspicious of Olson's work for Jewish causes in the OWI. But Pound's attitude was so distasteful to the younger man that he left and carried with him a lasting indignation. Olson's meetings with Pound at St. Elizabeths were intensely painful and frustrating to him; he was disappointed at every turn with the older poet, whom he found blinded by prejudice and hatred.[24] Olson's early concerns over national unity remained with him a while longer, as in 1946, when he participated in the first meetings that established the United Nations in New York, after which he returned to Washington and continued his meetings with Pound.

Olson did not become a force in the avant garde all at once; the radical shift of thought that had taken place over the winter of 1945–46 had to be digested slowly. His contacts with Pound and the final successful revisions of *Call Me Ishmael* were an important beginning, but the poems he had written in Key West two years before and those few short, highly polished lyrics of recent months were not in any sense bold or particularly original, although they did express the gravity and depth of his beliefs. And he placed these poems in the most established and respectable journals, *Harper's Bazaar*, *Atlantic Monthly*, *Harper's*, perhaps to prove that he was a good poet, perhaps purely out of naiveté, for such journals were inimical to the very things he was just beginning to reach for in his own mind. At any rate, he later ceased to publish his work in such magazines. In 1948, he received his second Guggenheim Fellowship for a study of a now familiar interest, the interaction of racial groups during the settling of the American West, to be called "Red, White & Black," but he never finished it.[25] Finally, in 1948, an *annus mirabilis* for Olson's brand new career, Caresse Crosby, the Washington editor and publisher of the Black Sun Press, who had previously brought out some of D. H. Lawrence's work, printed a brief pamphlet of his poems, *Y & X*. And in the fall, Josef Albers, rector of the highly innovative Black Mountain College, which had become famous for the brilliance and fame of its poorly paid faculty, asked Olson to give a series of lectures, after which he replaced Edward Dahlberg as visiting lecturer for the next year.

In February of 1949, he finished one of his best poems, "The Kingfishers," which constituted a successful breakthrough to a new technique of versification. He could now with confidence begin to write his own manifesto for poetry, "Projective Verse," to come a year later. In the summer of 1949, Olson directed a theater program for Black Mountain College and then returned to Washington to attend full-time to his writing and to establishing journals that would become the official organs of the new writing in America, the writing that would become a clear declaration of a shift in Western consciousness.

Once the essay "Projective Verse" came out in October 1950, in *Poetry New York*, he began to contact individuals who might be thinking of launching new literary reviews, and when Cid Corman, the Boston poet who had a radio show, "This Is Poetry," got ready to publish a magazine of his own, Olson immediately began a six-year correspondence telling him exactly how it should be organized and keeping up a steady spate of commentary, advice, belligerency, and praise.[26]

Since I deal with this issue in detail in later chapters, it is well to pass over this part of Olson's biography here, except to point out one of the important themes that dominated his correspondence with Corman: he was clearly attempting to have Corman so arrange the works in *Origin* that the reader would immediately perceive that the new artists of the moment, while very diverse in imagination and sensibilities, were gathered into these pages as a group, a community of minds, all aware of the new conditions of reality. In other words, Olson was still actively concerned with the whole question of the life of groups, communities, their identity and nature, amid the sprawling populations of American democracy. *Origin* would demonstrate, among other things, the fellowship of art; among America's minorities, artists were a lively, raucous, irreverent group, whose luxuries of mind and attitude needed to be given voice.

In February of 1951, shortly after the death of his mother, Olson left Washington to spend six months in Lerma on the shores of the Yucatan peninsula. Lerma was an intense experience for him. He wrote frequently to Corman and Creeley, and in these letters first conceived several important literary projects, particularly his essay "Human Universe." He now had the opportunity to study first-hand the artifacts of a non-Western civilization, and his discoveries about Mayan culture would ultimately find their way into his later essays. At the moment, however, one conclusion was already evident to him: Mayan art, which had sprung from sources beyond Greco-Roman influence, expressed a more intense human attention to experience than did Western art. And as Creeley later remarked, "The alternative to a generalizing humanism was locked, quite literally, in the people immediately around him, and the conception, that there had been and *could* be a civilization anterior to that which he had come from, was no longer conjecture, it was fact."[27]

Meanwhile the students at Black Mountain College had invited Olson to return to teach for the remainder of the summer, and he proceeded to North Carolina once more. The faculty, however, was divided over his appointment to a permanent position, so that when he arrived he faced considerable discord among his colleagues. But by the beginning of the fall semester, his advocates prevailed and he began to teach in the regular sessions from then on.[28]

During his rectorship, from 1951 till the closing of the college in 1956, Olson enjoyed some of his most productive writing years. Although it was a time of considerable instability for him emotionally, he was nonetheless inspired by the vitality of the college's life. A community was ready-made for his influence and shaping, including a student body of many potentially good poets to instruct. Further, Robert Creeley would join him in 1954 and start a journal on the campus. Other poets came to visit or teach, including Robert Duncan, and the various visiting painters and composers were also involved in articulating through their own media a new sense of reality. It is not surprising that Olson was deeply invigorated by the experience in North Carolina, despite the heartaches and disappointments of the college's demise. Martin Duberman summed up Olson's influence there as follows:

> By late 1952, Olson had converted Black Mountain into the "arts center" Albers had argued for during the 1948–1949 upheaval. But with a difference: much more emphasis on the literary than the visual arts, and an even more disheveled physical plant; a place distinctive, in other words, not in endowment, numbers, comfort or public acclaim, but in quality of experience, a frontier society, sometimes raucous and raw, isolated and self-conscious, bold in its refusal to assume any reality it hadn't tested—and therefore bold in inventing forms, both in life style and art, to contain the experiential facts that supplanted tradition's agreed-upon definitions.[29]

During Olson's years at Black Mountain he was also at work on a number of essays that together constitute a systematic, if fragmentary, articulation of a philosophy of experience he referred to as "Objectism," a phenomenological view of nature that attempted to clarify the new reality envisioned by the non-Euclidean geometers of the mid-nineteenth century and that has undergone various sophisticated revisions in twentieth-century physics and mathematics. Olson turned to the writings of the English philosopher Alfred North Whitehead and discovered other ways of talking about the processes of matter, especially Whitehead's thoroughly reasoned hypothesis that the dialectical behavior of matter tended to suggest an inherent will toward formal unity. This offered Olson the closest possible parallel to what he felt was occurring at the level of the individual poem, a poet fashioning a near randomness of sounds and signs into the formal unity of an art work.

Olson was responsible for tending to the sale of the property of the college after it had closed its doors in October 1956. He remained in North Carolina off and on for another year, and in July 1957 he returned to the summer home of his childhood, Gloucester. As far back as

1947, Olson had conceived the possibility of writing a long poem, modeled after the sequential poems of William Carlos Williams and Ezra Pound, based on his experience and understanding of the town of Gloucester—it was to be a thorough expression of the meaning of this town to the poet, an exhaustive concentration of his faculties upon its past and present, its geography, industry, economic history, original settlement and difficulties, his own childhood memories of it—everything, that is, that could possibly be projected from the conscious mind of its observer, the persona Maximus. The return to Gloucester completed a larger cycle in the poet's life: from childhood and his venturing into politics to his discovery of a new poetic and its establishment in the journals of the avant garde and in the classrooms of an experimental college and then back to Gloucester again, with those riches of experience to draw into the increasing length of the *Maximus* sequence.

These years of research into Gloucester's past were fruitful but have a background of continual financial hardship. Olson had by then established a considerable following and was invited occasionally to lecture and give poetry readings on the college circuit. By 1960, a number of his important works had been published in sufficient issues to bring him to the attention of a broader spectrum of the reading public. Donald Allen's *The New American Poetry: 1945–1960* opens with Olson's poems and reprints the "Projective Verse" essay of 1950. *The Distances*, the first selection of Olson's poems to be printed by a major press (Grove), also came out in 1960. And most importantly, *The Maximus Poems*, containing the first three books of his sequence, appeared, handsomely bound in paper covers which reproduce sections of a navigational map of Gloucester harbor.

During the next three years of his residence in Gloucester, he completed work on *Maximus Poems IV, V, VI*, the second section of the *Maximus* sequence. This work departs widely from the earlier volume both in content, which is decidedly more mythological in its references, and in articulation. He was involved in a far more sophisticated use of that part of his poetic he called "field composition," which seeks an arrangement of poetic content in other than conventional syntactical relationships. His interest in the full use of conscious response in poetry even led, in 1961, to a few collaborative experiments with Timothy Leary in using consciousness-altering drugs.

Olson was also a prominent figure at the Poetry Conference held in Vancouver, British Columbia, in 1963. That year, he left Gloucester to join the faculty of the State University of New York at Buffalo, where he taught American poetry and mythology. Some of the students he had taught at Black Mountain College rejoined him in Buffalo, and new student poets emerged from his classrooms there. In 1965, his reputation was enhanced by the publication of *Human Universe and Other Essays*, again edited by Donald Allen, an influential collection arranged according to the facets of Olson's theories. He also attended the 1965 Poetry Conference at the University of California at Berkeley, and he received the prestigious Oscar Blumenthal–Charles Leviton Prize, awarded by *Poetry* magazine. But he abruptly returned to Gloucester from Buffalo in the fall of the year and in 1966 left for London.

Olson stayed in England for a period of five months and did research on new poems for the *Maximus* sequence, particularly on the early history of the Dorchester fishermen. In 1967 a selection of his essays and poems appeared, edited by Creeley, and in 1968 the second volume of the *Maximus* poems came out. In 1969 he was invited to join the English department at the University of Connecticut as a visiting professor, but by then he was ill with cancer and able to conduct only five sessions of a seminar before leaving to enter a succession of hospitals until his death.

His last ten years he lived at a reckless, energetic pace. His work was receiving public recognition and attracted a wide circle of writers, students, and fanatic admirers, many of whom placed considerable demands upon his time and energy. From 1964 on, his work on the *Maximus* poems and his other activities taxed him increasingly. The large, seemingly inexhaustible energies of the man began to wane slowly under these burdens. He pushed against his limitations; a lonely and sensitive man, he was intent to enjoy the way of life his public recognition had created. After suffering a short illness, he died on January 10, 1970, in New York Hospital. An obituary in the *New York Times* the following day noted the passing of one of America's most influential postwar poets.[30] His papers and books were purchased by the University of Connecticut and now constitute an important archive for research in postmodernist poetry.

I shall proceed now from this premise: the essential Olson lies somewhere in a momentous rejection of a culture, a civilization, the values and philosophy of which have gradually diminished the unruly vitality of human awareness. In place of the communal relationships humans originally enjoyed have come disciplined populations of resentful, competitive individuals, each remote from his own real desires and indifferent to the natural world he lives in. Everything Olson wrote—the essays, the poems, the rambling harangues—speak to this one concern: how to restore to human beings their own primal energies.

Indeed, the very seamlessness of his work posed one of the significant difficulties of proceeding with this study: how to divide his writing into subject categories in order to discover the relationships among certain works. The plan of the following chapters involves a certain amount of arbitrary sorting, but there are clear advantages to this procedure.

In chapter 2, for example, I have grouped together most of Olson's prose to delineate the various facets of his theory of experience, the philosophy of objectism that he reasoned over much of his life. Tracing its development, we are thrust into a bizarre series of adventures as we follow Olson's nervous tracks into the remote past, the dim regions of scientific speculation, the theories of continental shift, the labyrinth of ideas he worked up into a system. We view the process by which Olson struggled to tear his own mind out of the fabric of Western conceptions to gain a new view of the world.

Chapter 3 is a systematic analysis of Olson's poetic ideas, where he got them, and to what extent he synthesized the poetic principles of Ezra Pound and William Carlos Williams. This is a crucial subject since so much of the criticism against Olson turns on the suggestion that he merely imitated his masters and did little on his own. I refute this view and offer an alternative interpretation of the nature of his borrowings, if that is in fact the proper word for them. No other poet of his time had put to such serious use the gains made in the imagist tradition as did Olson; he gathered up what he felt had been the best innovations of the recent past in order to continue to revolutionize American poetry. In the second part of chapter 3 we follow the unfolding arguments of his short poems; many of these have been dealt with individually in published criticism, but an overall view of his canon is here attempted for the first time. The survey of his poems has two intentions: first, to show the connection his poetry has to his larger concerns as a thinker; and, second, to reveal the thematic unity that exists in the span of his work.

Chapter 4 is a reader's guide to Olson's chief work, the *Maximus* sequence. The poem is a relentless heresy against our poetic tradition; it departs widely from the orthodoxies of American verse. The aim of the commentary is to convey a feel for the three volumes of the work, to show its form and methods, and, finally, to reveal its deepest intentions. The work is strange; it tries the patience of any reader who enters it. But throughout its difficult unfoldings, we take an odyssey into modern consciousness, in which Olson reveals, under the rubble of disbelief and confusion, the lingering remains of ideals human beings have cherished throughout time. The aim of this noble and eccentric masterpiece is to re-create Eden from these undying aspirations.

In chapter 5, I have engaged finally the difficult problem of measuring and testing his influence on certain other poets, those whom Allen grouped together in his anthology and called the "Black Mountain Poets." Many writers have objected to this category and suggested that it is not a legitimate description of so many diverse styles and attitudes. But the conviction stated here is that there are indeed valid grounds for such a grouping, for each of the poets analyzed has not only stated explicitly his indebtedness to Olson's ideas but has shown clearly in his work that he understood and agreed with Olson's own urgent sense that the necessary direction for poetry is toward the self and the exploration of the hidden recesses of consciousness.

2. Toward a New Reality

The assumption is that everything's been turned about, and yet that
that is true is not as known as anyone of us might think it is;
indeed, I don't know that any one of us is caught up and going
at the speed or at the depth of both the knowledge of reality we
now possess, and thus the speed and depth of the reality itself,
especially as that reality is busy inside anyone of us. Except as
none of us will ever be satisfied, we are quite making it, except for
that I am persuaded that at this point of the 20th century it
might be possible for man to cease to be estranged, as Heraclitus
said he was in 500 B.C., from that with which he is most
familiar. . . . man lost something just about 500 B.C. and only
got it back just about 1905 A.D.
                                    —*The Special View of History*

At a poetry conference held in Vancouver in 1963, Robert Creeley and
Allen Ginsberg faced an audience and discussed the nature of their
work. With typical candor, Creeley tried to clarify what his work was attempting but then admitted, "I can not tell you what I think a poem is."[1]
The difficulty he felt here was that the poetic art itself had undergone
such radical redefinition over the last fifteen years or so that there was
no easy way in which to describe the new poetry in terms of the theories
which had emerged during that period.

But he went on to explain that a larger shift had occurred which had
swept old techniques of poetry before it. "All the terms of consciousness
are, at the moment, undergoing tremendous terms of change. . . . There
is an alteration of a very deep order going on in the whole thrust or
push of the consciousness," which broadens out, in his view, to the point
that "the very premise on which consciousness operates is undergoing
modifications that none of us, I think, are at the moment capable of defining." To this he added, "The terms of reality . . . are changing. . . . I
think that the change which is occurring now is more significant than the
Second World War by far, because it's the residue of that war in reference to the atom bomb and, equally, the shift in all terms of human relationship that have been habitualized since, oh God, thousands of years."

And before turning away from this subject he concluded that the recent changes which had occurred in Western art go "back to correct, not to correct, but to reorganize premises that have existed for thousands of years, concepts of person . . . ," and so the brief monologue trailed off.[2]

Creeley was at this moment expressing a view close to Olson's, and we can find this same millennial thinking in many of the poets of the Black Mountain movement.[3] Certainly the shock of the sudden emergence of nuclear warfare at the close of World War II was sufficient to make these poets feel as though one age had come to an end and that another, of strange and terrifying moment, had just begun. Yeats had expressed in several of his late poems similar fears that a profound shift in consciousness was about to dawn, particularly in "The Second Coming." Pound had thought many times that he participated in a revolution of great complexity, in which all levels of life, social, economic, political, judicial, esthetic, would be transformed. Millennial thinking itself is not new to the poetry of the post-Enlightenment period. It is most evident in the early poems of Blake as a simple intuition of imminent violence, of contraries arrayed against each other; and as Blake's poetry matures, the intuition becomes a vision of an all-inclusive cosmic metamorphosis, the reintegration of the heavens to form the original, unsundered body of Albion, the cosmic organism. Nearly all the romantics expressed the conviction that they stood between two ages of civilization, watching, on the one hand, the total collapse of medieval principles and institutions and, on the other, the rise of new forms of thought. Romantic poetry, with its loosely structured poetic principles, its essayistic format, seems ready to record these changes; the low intensity of the poetic line is a deliberate cushion against the shocks of change that each of these poets was in readiness to observe. Shelley's long, flowing youthful essay on cosmic transformation, *Queen Mab* (1813), articulates with an almost jaunty air the convulsions that are yet to rock Earth and overwhelm her. Keats is dreamy in his own visions of the great dialectical shift, as his questing persona finds the old regime of gods dying on their couches in "The Fall of Hyperion" (1819). Byron's Don Juan willingly inherits a world given over to a final feast on the immense but unwholesome riches of the past. Throughout the Victorian period this theme is still perceptible, although its intensity gradually diminishes. But it is as though the brooding sense that great changes await the whole shaky edifice of human understanding was a response to the convulsion or transformation that had already occurred—if "convulsion" or "transformation" does not exaggerate the significance of the changes England had already undergone in the first years of the nineteenth century, from an ancient, agricultural way of life to a frantic, novel existence as the first nation to develop an industrial economy.

There was somehow a sense that a world had truly come to an end when the German philosopher Hegel concluded *The Phenomenology of Mind*, which is a summary, as George Lichtheim notes, of all that philosophy had been able to assume about the world as the human mind had come to know it: "With perhaps a conscious touch of symbolism he finished the Preface to the *Phenomenology* on October 13, 1806: the day before Napoleon would finish off the ghost of the Holy Roman Empire at the battle of Jena. Like Goethe, Hegel concluded that the event was irreversible: the Middle Ages were over."[4] Like a second Aristotle, Hegel had looked behind him to organize the thought that had accumulated since that Greek philosopher had summarized knowledge in his time.

Behind Creeley's quiet ruminations about the momentous changes he felt occurring lie two centuries of foreboding and exultant anticipation. He expresses his own astonishment at these shifts with a remarkably casual tone: "I think that any of us here is in a position to be responsive to this feeling that's so immense, so definite, and so insistent. Not because we can *do* anything with it. It simply is, it's a big change, it's a deep change in consciousness, and I'm curious to see what's going to happen—which is a mild way of putting it."[5]

In the years immediately following the end of World War II, a number of writers, philosophers, and sociologists sensed themselves thrust into the beginning of this profound new terrain Creeley describes. The many studies that came of their bewilderment deal with such topics as the new commercial crassness in American society, the phenomenon of alienation, and the revival of Spenglerian prophecies of doom.[6]

Three of the many books written in this period of the late 1940s and early 1950s are more searching in their considerations than most such commentaries of the period, and each has a firm theoretical grasp of the changes taking place in American social life. Taken together, they are the minor classics of mid-century thought. Their views are wide-ranging: from the dark and bitter despair of Max Horkheimer's *Eclipse of Reason* (1947) to Paul Goodman's cheerfully militant program for self-preservation in *Gestalt Therapy* (1951) and to the sweeping prophecy of doom for one age and triumph for another in Olson's *Call Me Ishmael*.

Each scrutinizes the condition of American society, and although none of the authors knew or was influenced by the others, all three drew many of the same conclusions; all three books illuminate a similar thesis through different, complementary perspectives. But, more importantly, these works constitute a guide to the thinking of many of the poets who experimented with the techniques of poetry in an attempt to register the dangerous or invigorating shifts they perceived occurring about them.

Max Horkheimer was a member of the Frankfurt School of Social Research (Das Institut für Sozialforschung), which began at the University of Frankfurt in 1923. In his view, modern Western societies had grown irrational out of neglect of the conditions of reality under which they had to exist. The essential issue of *Eclipse of Reason* is that reason is no longer an "organ for perceiving the true nature of reality" but has been transformed into an instrument for self-preservation. Originally, "a diametrically opposed view of reason was prevalent. This view asserted the existence of reason as a force not only in the individual mind but also in the objective world—in relations among human beings and between social classes, . . . in nature and its manifestations."[7]

The effect of the subjectivization of reason has been to dissociate human aspirations and potentialities from the idea of objective truth. The mind ceases to reflect or to understand the actuality it seeks to dominate. "In reality, the emancipation of the intellect from the instinctual life did not change the fact that its richness and strength still depend on its concrete content, and it must atrophy and shrink when its connections with this are cut" (p. 54 f.).

The autonomy of nature, human and nonhuman, is made to surrender to the domination of the subject (self), by which process, however, the subject falls prey to domination itself. Having repressed all those qualities which are natural and spontaneous in the self, all that remains is an "abstract ego emptied of all substance except its attempt to transform everything in heaven and earth into means for its preservation" (p. 97). Both human beings and nature are then stripped of their intrinsic meaning.

In the final chapter of *Eclipse of Reason*, entitled "The Concept of Philosophy," Horkheimer articulates the less explicit tenets of Olson's esthetic thought, as well as the critical stance of the American avant garde as a whole, in his prognosis that a transformation of society cannot occur until the present suppression of nature, human and nonhuman, had ended. He argues that "subjective reason is that attitude of consciousness that adjusts itself without reservation to the alienation between subject and object," rendering human existence an alien presence in a universe devoid of spirit (p. 173).

> If one were to speak of a disease affecting reason, this disease
> should be understood not as having stricken reason at some
> historical moment, but as being inseparable from the nature of
> reason in civilization as we have known it so far. . . . The true
> critique of reason will necessarily uncover the deepest layers of
> civilization and explore its earliest history. From the time when
> reason became the instrument for domination of human and
> extra-human nature by man—that is to say, from its very begin-
> nings—it has been frustrated in its own intention of discovering
> the truth. This is due to the very fact that it made nature a
> mere object, and that it failed to discover the trace of itself in
> such objectivization, in the concepts of matter and things not
> less than in those of gods and spirit. (p. 176)

In other words, "When Plato or Aristotle arranged concepts according
to their logical priority, they did not so much derive them from the
secret affinities of things as unwittingly from power relations" (p. 181).
The fall of the individual in the present time is a process that began
with the "Hellenistic concentration on pure inwardness," which allowed
society to transform itself from a community into a "jungle of power
interests destructive of all material conditions prerequisite for the se-
curity of the inner principle" (p. 184).

Horkheimer's image of the etiolated individual, a creature cut off from
his instinctual life and from the group, is the condition which Paul
Goodman's theoretical formulations in *Gestalt Therapy* seek to transcend; it is almost as if this text were intended as an intellectual and
emotional survival kit for the world Horkheimer surveys. (Indeed, Ralph
Hefferline's "Mobilizing the Self," which comprises Part I of the book,
is devoted to exercises designed for reopening the self to areas of the
body, to subtle feelings, arousal, instinctual pressures, which have been
walled off from the diminished sensibility of the average adult.) Goodman is in many ways—as a writer, as an evangelist of a new mode of
consciousness, as a controversial figure at Black Mountain College—
Olson's counterpart in educational theory and social thought, although
there is no evidence that the two ever met. Kenneth Rexroth once observed of him:

> One of the persons who endured through all the changes was
> Paul Goodman, who taught at Black Mountain a part of the year
> for many years. Goodman emerged from the war years a pacifist,
> and a communitarian anarchist. He was also one of the very few
> American intellectuals at all connected with the Establishment

who was part of the main stream of international modernism—in life attitude, in philosophy, in literary style. Had Goodman written in French he would have been world famous by the time he was thirty. He was a social philosopher, a political analyst, a devoted pedagogue, a poet and dramatist, and a novelist and short-story writer. Twenty-five years after the war the Old Left was still complaining that the New Left was without theory, strategy, tactics, or objectives, and this charge was largely true, except for Paul Goodman, who had continued as the only comprehensive and systematic philosopher in the United States of the libertarian revolt and the secession into an alternative society which was to be the dominant tendency of the second post-war world.[8]

His contribution to *Gestalt Therapy*, "Theory of the Self," begins by establishing a context for its argument in the theories and social criticism of Freud and Marx. Goodman is clearly among those whom Paul A. Robinson has described as the "Freudian left," philosophers whose vision of experience partly depends upon the assumption that neurotic and psychotic behaviors have their origins in certain institutionalized deprivations that are intended to discipline the individual but have the delayed and lethal effect of alienating him.[9]

In terms of its psychology, Goodman's theory implies a blanket rejection of behaviorism, an attack begun when the first German Gestaltists emigrated to the United States following the Nazi purges of the universities. It is a curious coincidence that both Max Horkheimer and Max Wertheimer, the first theorist of Gestalt psychology, were driven from Frankfurt at about the same time. The German Gestalt psychologists brought with them a body of specific research into perception that they then pursued in the few American universities that hired them.[10] Goodman synthesized their research, rewrote the unfinished manuscript of Frederick Perls, who had pioneered in group therapy techniques using Gestalt theory, and developed an elegantly reasoned program for the revitalization of identity.

Among the points he pursues in this discussion, Goodman urges a view that perception is a complex process involving memory, emotion, and bodily sensation as well as intellection, and when any of these sources of input is repressed there is a proportional diminution of excitement, and the self begins to atrophy. A definition of self emerges from his discussion of the nature of repression, for repression has to do with the organism of the individual, which is a complex of needs, reflexes, instinct, satisfactions, and irritations, in which rides the mercurial self, an everchanging network of the sensations of the organism.

> The self is the system of contacts in the organism/environment field; and these contacts are the structured experience of the actual present situation . . . the existing field passing into the next moment is rich with potential novelty, and contact is the actualization. Invention is original; it is the organism growing, assimilating new matter and drawing on new sources of energy. The self does not know beforehand what it will invent, for knowledge is the form of what has already occurred. . . . The complex system of contacts necessary for adjustment in the difficult field, we call "self."[11]

It is Goodman's thesis, then, that through the full participation of the organism with the field of its environment, the self is created, a conception that is at the heart of Olson's poetic theory and of his philosophy of experience, objectism. The significance of Goodman's essay for modern poetics has not been fully appreciated by critics of postwar poetry. His definition of the self as a synthesis of organismic activity articulates a basic assumption of the poets writing in the imagist tradition.

Olson began writing portions of *Call Me Ishmael* as early as 1932, when he was at work on his master's thesis, which he finished a year later. By 1939 he had reworked this thesis into a book-length study but abandoned it and started an entirely new version in 1945, which he finished in five months.[12] By January 1946 he had submitted the manuscript to several publishers but was turned down; he then gave it to Pound to read when he began visiting him at St. Elizabeths. Pound was impressed with the book, even though his attitude toward Olson was never more than condescending. Pound sent it to Eliot, then an editor at Faber and Faber, with the recommendation that it relieved one of having to read Melville's novel! Eliot returned the manuscript with the comment that it was "too American," to which Pound responded, "Eliot is now paralyzed from the neck up: he must be to turn back a book like yours."[13]

The final version published in 1947 is only 119 pages in length, but within this brief space Olson compressed a complicated, tightly reasoned examination into the meaning and significance of Melville's novel. The study is really an evolution of Olson's ideas about the work, the result of fourteen years of intermittent scrutiny, and the argument reads as though each step of his complex thought had been trimmed to essentials and then stitched very deliberately into sequence. The prose never flows, it leaps from one moment of close concentration to the next; our attention is always focused on a series of details as a thesis is fashioned that explains and integrates them. At no time are we allowed to relax with a broad overview of the whole novel, nor are we given clear signs of where the next step will lead us. The effect is that of being led quickly through the stages of a revelation that Olson suspends until the last sentence.

Three years later, in the "Projective Verse" essay, he acknowledged that Edward Dahlberg had taught him how to use this unusual mode of exposition. The principle, he wrote there, "can be boiled down to one statement (first pounded into my head by Edward Dahlberg): ONE PERCEPTION MUST IMMEDIATELY AND DIRECTLY LEAD TO A FURTHER PERCEPTION."[14] Olson applied this principle in Call Me Ishmael and then made it an essential part of his theory of projective verse. The intention of the book, then, was not to provide a scholarly exposition of a well-defined thesis but to reenact and keep the prose present to the process by which individual perceptions led to his conception of what Moby-Dick signifies. As we shall see in the next chapter, the method employed in writing Call Me Ishmael would become the dominant mode of his poems.

Although much of Olson's book is directly concerned with making an intense analysis of a classic American novel, it is evident throughout that he intended to rival the other seminal studies of the era: Dahlberg's Can These Bones Live; D. H. Lawrence's Studies in Classic American Literature; and William Carlos Williams' In the American Grain, all of which seek an ultimate definition of American experience. Olson is earnestly engaged with the making of Moby-Dick, and he is careful to present the source materials that Melville drew on: the disaster of the Essex, his notes and research about the event, his close reading of Shakespeare, and the technical innovations this provided him in characterizing Ahab. Olson also explores the intellectual and emotional changes which came over Melville after the novel was completed. These are the facts and arguments he had originally begun with, but as the work underwent revision, the emphasis of the study changed. The novel is not the primary focus of Call Me Ishmael; rather, America is. And the novel is closely examined as a document that illuminates the American condition in the mid-nineteenth century.

Olson's argument is subdivided into five distinct parts, each covering a phase of his subject. But the actual advance of his thesis is subtler and occurs in the slow shifting of perspective through which he regards and judges the novel's central character, Ahab. Olson begins Part One with the declaration, "I take SPACE to be the central fact to man born in

America, from Folsom cave to now."[15] He then asserts that it was Melville's discovery, expressed in his novel, that the deepest passion of the Americans was to conquer the vastness of their land, to compel this space to yield to their will. In the brief section entitled "What lies under," Olson quickly assembles the evidence to prove that the first real manifestation of this willfulness in the American spirit came with the whaling expeditions. The enormous investment in equipment, the size of the fleets, the strict hierarchy of personnel, the discipline and organization of the management constitute for Olson the signs of the first major industry in American history. "I'm putting a stress Melville didn't on whaling as *industry*," he admitted, but it is necessary if we are to appreciate the point he is leading to: Ahab is the embodiment of subjective reason, a creature cut off from all other access to himself but this one obsession to control, to turn everything in his grasp into a resource.

The very nature of industry requires the ordering and control of a multitude of things, human beings no less than other resources, according to an ideal of efficient operation:

> Whaling started, like so many American industries, as a
> collective, communal affair. See any history of Sag Harbor or
> Nantucket. And as late as 1850 there were still skippers to
> remember the days when they knew the fathers of every man in
> their crew. But it was already a sweated industry by the time
> Melville was a hand on a lay (1841–43). (p. 21)

The paradox that Olson perceives in *Moby-Dick* is that the emergence of industry posed an ideology polar to that of democracy. The crew of the *Pequod* fulfilled the democratic ideal in that the members were from different nations, of diverse races and creeds, and lived and worked together on the ship in the semblance of a community. But the industrial order in which they were cast was aristocratic; its hierarchy was composed of investors, a management, and their equipment, which included workers. The American democratic ideal, according to Olson, was subverted by the economic structure it had nourished: "So if you want to know why Melville nailed us in *Moby-Dick*, consider whaling" (p. 23). In his summary of this section Olson writes,

> Melville didn't put it all on the surface of *Moby-Dick*. You'll
> find the frontier all right, and Andrew Jackson regarded as
> heavyweight champion (READ end of first KNIGHTS AND SQUIRES
> chapter for the finest rhetoric of democracy). And the technic of
> an industry analyzed, scrupulously described. But no economics.
> Jefferson and John Adams observed that in their young days

very few men had thought about "government," there were very few writers on "government." Yes, the year *Moby-Dick* was being finished Marx was writing letters to the N. Y. *Daily Tribune*. But Melville . . . . . . (p. 24)

In Part Two of the book, Olson sifts through the evidence of Shakespeare's influence on Melville with two purposes: the one immediate, to show how Melville adapted the form of dramatic tragedy to the pacing and structure of his novel; the other, broader and more speculative, to show that Shakespeare's exploration of villainy and betrayal constitutes a psychology of evil from which Melville drew for his creation of Ahab. With this larger premise, Olson is really extending his argument that Ahab embodies the irrational propensities of subjective reason; only here he attempts to discover the nature of Ahab's aloofness, a solitude that is the consequence of regarding all but himself as a chaos to be ordered for use.

Olson begins to probe into the character of Ahab by means of certain polarities he sees between Ahab and Pip and between Ahab's egotistical delusions and the contemplative, open-minded dispositions of Bulkington and Ishmael. Ahab's madness is profound, corrosive, and evil; it turns all his energy away from God, toward Satan. Ahab can only "bless" his harpoon in the name of the devil since the purpose it is intended for is satanic: "Ego non baptizo te in nomine patris, sed in nomine diaboli." Having discovered the rough notes for this speech in Melville's copy of Shakespeare, Olson observes of Ahab:

> He invokes his own evil world. He himself uses black magic to achieve his vengeful ends. With the very words "in nomine diaboli" he believes he utters a Spell and performs a Rite of such magic.
>
> The Ahab-world is closer to *Macbeth* than to *Lear*. In it the supernatural is accepted. Fedallah appears as freely as the Weird Sisters. Before Ahab's first entrance he has reached that identification with evil to which Macbeth out of fear evolves within the play itself. . . . They both endure the torture of isolation from humanity. The correspondence of these two evil worlds is precise. In either the divine has little place. Melville intended certain exclusions, and Christ and the Holy Ghost were two of them. (pp. 53–54)

If Ahab's mind is torn by madness that is evil and "undefinable," as Melville noted, its manifestations are at least understandable: Ahab is driven to gain power over the most resistant force he has yet confronted, an enormous white whale. Olson is urgent on this point—the whale is the "SPACE" which he says it is the character of the American to wish to subdue. In other words, Ahab's delusions are the uncontrollable extremes of this willfulness toward the enormity of the North American continent. Industry has cast Ahab in the only role in which he can allow his madness to extend itself to its limits. The whaling industry is already a significant manifestation of this American will as its fleets roam over the major oceans. Ahab is the most vigorous agent of this will to possess, to lay claim to, to use, and although it is madness to go beyond the goal of bringing in the largest kills, his confrontation with Moby Dick follows the logic of this will—the desire for conquest leads inexorably toward more and more difficult, unsubduable whales, until Moby Dick becomes the measure of total conquest, exhaustion of that will. That is why Olson insists that the white whale is more than a sea creature: it is the symbol of all that the will of the American yearns for. It embodies the totality of nature, including man's own instinctual life, which the American has pitted himself against. And the tragedy of this madness is that democracy is made the instrument of a self-destructive delusion. The workers, the men of the crew, are pressed into the service of this insane pursuit; they are loathed by Ahab, worked beyond their capacity, only to perish in the inevitable failure of the challenge.

Pip's nature is in direct contrast to Ahab's; he is the creature without will at all. He is the fool made wise when he is plunged into the ocean's depths and discovers truths that overwhelm him:

> . . . Pip is mad, possessed of an insanity which is "heaven's sense." When the little Negro almost drowned, his soul went down to wondrous depths and there he "saw God's foot upon the treadle of the loom, and spoke it." Through that accident Pip, of all the crew, becomes "prelusive of the eternal time" and thus achieves the converse Ahab has denied himself by his blasphemy. (p. 56)

This madness, although benevolent, renders Pip nearly incomprehensible, as out of touch with the crew as Ahab is. It is perhaps for that very reason that these two live together away from the crew. Olson remarks of this friendship that it humanizes Ahab. Well after he has turned his harpoon against the crew and so cut himself off permanently from any contact with them, beyond that of his power to order them about, he takes the sharp-tongued Pip for his only companion: the two are seen to complement each other. Each has a madness which is absolute and incommunicable.

Olson contrasts Ahab and Pip with two other members of the *Pequod*, Bulkington and Ishmael, whom Olson views as the true "moral" heroes of the novel. Their dispositions toward nature and humankind approximate an ideal stance that Olson only tentatively sketches in *Call Me Ishmael*, but it is clear that the fully opened minds they turn to experience remained for Olson models of the opened consciousness he argued for in many of his subsequent essays. Whereas Pip is an instance of the madness that is "heaven's sense," another way of divine converse is achieved by Bulkington and Ishmael:

> "Right reason" is the other way to God. It is the way of man's sanity, the pure forging of his intelligence in the smithy of life. To understand what use Melville made of it in *Moby-Dick* two characters, both inactive to the plot, have to be brought forth. (p. 57)

These are the antithetical men lying in wait under their oppressor Ahab until such unforeseen time as they will be liberated. Olson sees in these two the other form that will can take as it reaches toward the American "SPACE." The principal difference between them and Ahab is that they enter it with humility and devotion, and their relation to it is not through conquest but through contact: they form a union with this space by allowing it to enter into them to the extent of their capacity to perceive it. Bulkington, whose very name answers directly to this argument, is bulk, a "coffer-dam," a vessel of natural phenomena. "Bulkington is Man who, by 'deep, earnest thinking' puts out to sea, scorning the land, convinced that 'in landlessness alone resides the highest truth, shoreless, indefinite as God' " (p. 57).

Ishmael, the lone survivor of the *Pequod*'s tragic end, is the only fully opened man, and it is his all-embracing consciousness that we peer into for the story of Ahab:

> Like the Catskill eagle Ishmael is able to dive down into the blackest gorges and soar out to the light again.
> He is passive and detached, the observer, and thus his separate and dramatic existence is not so easily felt. . . . When he alone survived the wreck of the *Pequod*, he remained, after the shroud of the sea rolled on, to tell more than Ahab's wicked story. Ahab's self-created world, in essence privative, a thing of blasphemies and black magic, has its offset. Ahab has to dominate over a world where the humanities may also flower and man (the crew) by Pip's or Bulkington's way reach God. . . . It

was Ishmael who learned the secrets of Ahab's blasphemies from
the prophet of the fog, Elijah. He recognized Pip's God-sight,
and moaned for him. He cries forth the glory of the crew's
humanity. Ishmael tells *their* story and *their* tragedy as well
as Ahab's. . . . (p. 57 f.)

Ishmael is the redeemer of the novel; his survival marks the end of an
age, even a civilization, for Olson views Ahab as the last of the heroes:
"END of individual responsible only to himself. Ahab is full stop" (p.
119). Ishmael begins a new age of "Pacific Man," marking a great shift
in history away from individualism. Ishmael is the first Westerner of
the new consciousness, a creature so open to the world that his ego is
dissolved in the breadth of his attention.

This is the first perspective through which Olson judges Ahab: he is
the human turned villain, his virtues and affections all perverted by a
monstrous, devouring ego that blinds him to all but his lust to subdue.
His character is a distillation of the Greco-Roman inheritance, the inevitable outcome of a culture that apotheosized the human, encouraged
individuality, nourished the vanity of the human mind through abstract
philosophy and generalizing language, and looked upon nature with
disdain.

But in Part Three of *Call Me Ishmael*, Olson suspends his discussion
of this first perspective and introduces a second which pursues an entirely different judgment of Ahab, one that seeks an explanation of his mo-
tives. To this end, we are asked to see Ahab as primordial and mythic.
He is likened to Kronos, who achieved his paternity by the castration of
his father, Uranus. In this mythological context, Olson argues that Ahab
embodies the human soul's ageless vengefulness as he looks to the powers
of nature and seeks to achieve his manhood by challenging them.

Melville, Olson observes, "agonized over paternity. He suffered as a
son. He had lost the source. He demanded to know the father" (p. 82).
Enceladus, the giant who had failed to overthrow the old regime of
gods to gain his own paternity, was "a constant image in Melville," Olson writes. "The fable of *Moby-Dick* is vengeance," then, and he argues
that Ahab, who, Melville says, "piled upon the whale's white hump the
sum of all the general rage and hate felt by his whole race from Adam
down," is representative of all humankind (p. 83). He is "enceladic,"
one who fails to achieve his desired majority. Through his exploration
of this mythological dimension of Ahab's character, Melville had uncovered what is for Olson one of the oldest and most profound passions
of the human mind, its rivalry with the elements themselves: "There is

a way to disclose paternity, declare yourself the rival of earth, air, fire and water" (p. 85).

This is a necessary part of Olson's argument. Ahab's primordial passions are beyond blame. His rivalry with the whale has its ultimate source in his race's emergence from total unconsciousness, the powers of which he turned against to create his own identity. It is merely a fact of being human.

In the concluding section, entitled "Noah," Olson tries to merge both perspectives into an inclusive reading that will embrace not only the book but the American experience that the book illuminates. Olson does not repudiate the rivalry between humans and what he calls "space," the phenomenal totality that constitutes nature. If a judgment can be made of Ahab, it can only be directed at what the Greeks made of the human being, for they had considered the unconscious life only in its destructive aspect, when in fact its other and equal value is creative. The ego is both imperiled and sustained by the same force of nature, and to exclude one or the other philosophically was a fatal distortion of reality. The truth is that the ego lives in the ferment of both, and dies or is blinded when that symbiosis of conscious and unconscious realms is denied. Thus, the grotesquely large ego of Ahab is the result of seeing nature only as the enemy and not as the creative principle as well. He seeks to conquer a force that includes himself. Ahab blindly strives for conquest, but life is only possible in the rhythm of struggle and reconciliation. The passion to rule over nature is the human fact that will not change; but Ahab's ego, his individualism, the industry that raised him to power, prevents him from seeking the uncertain harmony in which humanity might prosper and live. Instead, he turns against his fellow mortals and the whole of nature. He betrays his friends and is like the tragic villains of Shakespeare's plays who also turn their murderous hatred toward their own kind. The ancient, unalterable rivalry against overwhelming powers, in other words, has, through the delusions of egotism and solitude, become perverted into fratricide.

At this stage of our discussion of *Call Me Ishmael*, it is appropriate to mention that although these arguments show Olson's unique boldness of speculation, he was not the first to insist on such readings of the character of Ahab. After Olson, at Dahlberg's suggestion, had abandoned his first book-length study of Melville in 1939, F. O. Matthiessen published his comprehensive study of American transcendentalist literature, *American Renaissance*, in 1941.[16] It was in one of Matthiessen's seminars at Harvard that Olson had written his paper "Lear and Moby-Dick." In Matthiessen's discussion of Melville, which runs to more than 130 pages, he mentions Olson's article four times and pays him tribute for having written an imaginative and vigorous study of Shakespeare's influences on Melville. But the professor chides his student, as he does others in this broad study, for having been hasty and sometimes plainly inaccurate in his hypotheses. Matthiessen's own discussion of Melville and Shakespeare, however, bears clear evidence of his debt to Olson for many of the insights he brings to his discussion of the tragic form and methods of *Moby-Dick*.

But Matthiessen's discussion also ranges into the same speculative theses that Olson would take up some six years later. It is very unlikely that Olson would not have read his professor's text on a subject he had been so long at work on himself, especially when his essay had been mentioned favorably in it several times. It seems most likely that Matthiessen's book helped Olson broaden his own considerations of Melville beyond the close focus he began with. For one thing, Matthiessen approaches *Moby-Dick* from a Marxist perspective. Like Olson, he too regards the crew as Melville's portrayal of a subverted ideal, democratic humanity thrust down into a miserable labor force, over which the egocentric Ahab rules without pity:

> Melville's hopes for American democracy, his dread of its lack of humane warmth, his apprehension of the actual privations and defeats of the common man, and his depth of compassion for courageous struggle unite in giving fervor to the declaration of his purpose in writing *Moby-Dick*. (p. 444)

But Matthiessen also recognizes Melville's attraction to Ahab's fatal solipsism:

> Notwithstanding the depth of his feeling for 'the kingly commons,' Melville knew the strength of the contrast between the great individual and the inert mass. He expressed it in Ahab's power to coerce all the rest within the sphere of 'the Leyden jar of his own magnetic life.' Melville himself was caught and fascinated by his hero. (p. 445)

He further elaborates on the bond with Satan that partly explains the force of Ahab's will, the energy it draws on, which Olson also discusses. But even more striking, Matthiessen probes the depths of Ahab's character and perceives Melville's intimation of an ageless, primitive motive in Ahab's revenge:

> Ahab's savagery, not unlike that of a Hebrew prophet, has

rejected the warmly material pantheism of the Greeks. . . . Melville had enacted the same fundamental pattern [of certain modern artists] by 'sinking to the most primitive and forgotten, returning to the origin and bringing something back, seeking the beginning and the end.' . . . [Melville] wanted nothing less than the whole of life. He symbolized its vast and terrifying forces when he likened Ahab's 'darker, deeper' part to those hidden antiquities beneath the Hotel de Cluny, where man's "root of grandeur, his whole awful essence sits in bearded state." The flavor of that image is even more Biblical than Greek. It takes man beyond history to the source of his elemental energies.
(p. 466)

It was inevitable that Olson should find useful ideas in Matthiessen's broad, sweeping survey of Melville, even though the purposes of the two studies are so different from each other. Matthiessen wanted to show the extent to which Melville shared the Transcendental doctrines of his literary contemporaries, and Olson wanted to test his theory that Melville had created a new and important myth in Western literature. But it is indisputable that Olson's commentary frequently echoes Matthiessen's, from passing literary allusions and particular quotations from Melville's letters to the rhetorical emphasis given certain points. It seems most reasonable to conclude about this cross-fertilization of ideas that in the six years he had to think over Matthiessen's arguments, Olson internalized them till they became indistinguishable from his own ideas.[17] This is part of the style of Olson's thought in any instance: he so fully absorbed the texts that influenced him that he wrote in a mosaic mode, closely mingling his own thought with the paraphrase or near quotation of what he had read.

After Eliot had turned down *Call Me Ishmael* as being "too little, and too American a book,"[18] it was again rejected by Harcourt, Brace by one of its readers, F. O. Matthiessen! It is easy to see why: Matthiessen's own critical procedures are paced and methodical, and even where he is speculative, he remains close to his text and is primarily interested in illuminating the literary work as an artistic form. But as Ann Charters has argued in her book *Olson/Melville: A Study in Affinity*, Olson writes in the tradition of Emerson and Dahlberg; he attacks his subject as a "philosopher-poet."[19] My own emphasis is similar: Matthiessen rejected the book for the very reason that it was not directly about its subject but was using the novel at hand as a pretext for some larger, more ambitious, and only partly articulated aim. Olson is not concerned in his

study to illuminate all of the content of *Moby-Dick*, and he takes liberties with the actual text when he needs to make more of a point or carry
it further than Melville did—because Melville's work is only a means of
making his own visionary pronouncements.

He is the poet who finds this particular novel with its subject and
treatment expressly suitable as a basis from which to project all of his
own views about the American condition. Over the years he had worked
with the novel, his perceptions of it had evolved to the point where
what he insisted *Moby-Dick* revealed was what he himself believed truly
characterized American experience. The power of Olson's book lies not in
what he is able to reveal about Melville but in its expression of a manifesto from an important theoretical poet of the mid-twentieth century.

To this end, Olson articulated a typology of consciousness in Melville's
characters and formulated the conditions of a profound shift in American history from one kind of awareness, the enclosed ego-oriented consciousness of Ahab, which is solely interested in power and is neglectful
of all other experience, to the open consciousness of Ishmael. The two
forms are antithetical at many levels: the drive to power is a narrowing
of energies toward the one aim of domination; the open consciousness
seeks converse with nature instead of the power which ends in exclusion;
the open consciousness seeks inclusion in nature to satisfy its hunger for
contact with phenomena. Both are forms of the human will, but it is perhaps more exact to say that they are the dialectical extremes of will:
Ahab is the mind closed in its knowledge; Ishmael seeks to increase his.
Later Olson will call the closed mind the one seeking or having power;
the other mind, open to experience, is a mind of achievement. But Olson's own desire to see the shape of experience makes him akin to Ahab;
in the *Maximus* sequence, especially, he is determined he shall make understanding of his subject final: he seeks the limits of knowledge of
that township. And there is a dogmatic streak that runs throughout his
writing: he will make broad, impossible generalizations to further an
argument. At the same time, however, he is conscious of the necessity to
remain open, to keep the door to the world ajar, and the real course of
the long poem he wrote would seem to emphasize the open, speculative
intelligence, rather than the closed and certain one that Ahab represents.[20]
And Olson states his own alliance with the open consciousness throughout the study, as well as in the title itself, which takes Melville's opening sentence personally: call *me* Ishmael. And when we place this book
in the context of the other two, *Eclipse of Reason* and *Gestalt Therapy*,
its celebration of a wider, more sensitive awareness can be seen as part

of a larger concern of writers on the political left who sensed the exhaustion of one intellectual tradition, which they attacked for its abuses, and the imminence of another, envisioned by each according to his own ideals.

Conceptually, *Call Me Ishmael* stands in the center of these other two seminal texts of mid-century thought, for in Olson's typology of consciousness Ahab has come to stand for all those tendencies that Max Horkheimer bitterly comments on in *Eclipse of Reason*. And his conception of Ishmael as the figure of awareness takes up many of the same points that Goodman makes in discussing the vital self in *Gestalt Therapy*. As Olson's thought matures in subsequent elaborations of his views, this original typology is never abandoned; rather, the two characters and their polar attitudes come to represent for him the tendencies that define the two ages he envisions colliding and struggling in the dialectic of history. In his later essays, Olson is chiefly engaged in pointing out the detrimental effects of the will of Ahab in various spheres of human activity and introduces in each case the necessary antithesis, the attitude of Ishmael. It is the principal rhythm of most of his arguments: the mind of Ahab, with its perverse vanity and cerebral aloofness, is the foil for his doctrine of total awareness based on Ishmael's character.

But Olson's investigations of myth and language in *Call Me Ishmael* occur in a larger context than that of social criticism at mid-century. For several decades European thought had been fomenting a revolution of its own that sought to displace the mechanistic tenets of twentieth-century rationalism through a renewed emphasis upon the organismic character of human awareness. Structuralism and phenomenology are the more distinguished facets of this broad movement and their fundamental arguments closely agree with many of the issues Olson raised and attempted to resolve in *Call Me Ishmael* and his later essays.

Structuralism has had an impact on American literary criticism only within the last decade, but its European roots extend into the last century and incorporate some of the principles of early Marxist literary criticism. But Marxist criticism has tended to concentrate on the ideological content of the art work, whereas structuralist criticism regards the whole work, from language to final form, as the lucid metonym of the social structure in which it was fashioned. Its articulation of experience, its ordering of events, its valuation of life partially illuminate the reality which a society structures for itself. Human consciousness is a deep form, in other words, which any instance of human life manifests. Every behavior is considered to be a language with a grammar that is the key to this underlying deep form.

As Geoffrey Hartman has made clear in his essay "Structuralism: The Anglo-American Adventure," structuralism has broken down "the naïve dichotomy of mechanical versus organic . . . , and the word *organicism* is seen to stand for the fact that the whole is greater than its parts, and that the whole is a system."[21] Like a plant, a work of art, or a machine, the social reality expressed through all its behaviors is itself both organismic (since it arises from living organisms and is a reflection of their lives) and systematic (for all parts bear evidence of relatedness that stops at the boundary of an inside quantity and an outside realm).

At the heart of structuralist method lies the implicit assumption that consciousness is sensuous, organic, and (in some way only partly understood) systematic. Hartman may exaggerate the extent to which structuralism attempts to exploit technology, but the point is valid if we understand him to mean that it interprets cultural life as a system divisible into many parts.

Claude Lévi-Strauss devised a taxonomy of ritual and myth in primitive cultural systems, complete with major forms and their numerous deviations. At this extreme, structuralism has attempted to understand consciousness as a realm not unlike the ecological system of nature, where thought is seen to evolve according to universal laws and to take form from the interplay between the organism and the physical environment.

Olson came close to this aspect of structuralism when he studied Mayan culture and early primitive societies, particularly the Sumerians. He argued that such cultures revealed a vital bond between man and nature rarely expressed in Western civilization. The content of consciousness revealed in the art of such cultures seemed especially faithful to the phenomena of nature; in Mayan art, Olson argued, the human was depicted in the embrace of nature. The structure of Mayan art, in other words, revealed a healthier system of relations, where the human still regarded himself as a participant entity and not as an alien of special powers. But Olson was not interested in devising a taxonomic system from the remains of Mayan or Sumerian art; he cited these other cultures as part of a larger purpose, to show the distorted sense of relation between human and world that he found in Western art.

But the parallel with structuralist critique goes a step further when we recognize the depth of Olson's interest in Jung, whom we might think of as a structuralist of the unconscious. Olson's research into myth, which seems to dominate his interests in later years, is really from a structuralist viewpoint. Myth revealed the history of consciousness and its evolving order. Jane Harrison, an early structuralist whom Olson read with great interest, explored Greek myths from an evolutionary perspective, as did Robert Graves to a lesser extent, and the ideas of both writers found their way into Olson's *Maximus* sequence.

Call Me Ishmael is germinally a structuralist critique. When Olson isolates the mythic framework of the novel, he is linking the work to the continuum of mythological thought throughout history. Even more to the point, Olson's discussion of Melville's peculiar prose style implicitly assumes that language illuminates the structure of social awareness. What is found in language is metonymic to the whole condition of society. In other words, Melville's prose reflects some deeper upsurgings of the psyche of society which to Olson signaled a change in the direction of Western thinking. He links Melville's prose structurally with the new theses of non-Euclidean geometers to prove that the perception of reality was undergoing profound transformation throughout the West in the middle of the last century.

Olson's thought continues to parallel structuralist theory in his writings after *Call Me Ishmael*; indeed, it is one of the more illuminating perspectives in which to regard the body of his theoretical work. His criticism of contemporary art, which we shall turn to presently, is aggressively partisan in its structural analysis. Olson vigorously discriminated between a structural mode of art that shows man absorbed with his alienation in nature and a new structure showing man reestablishing his place in the world as he takes up his experience and tries to understand it anew. It was partly the task of his essays to explore the differences between these two structural modes of art, but his inquiries are erratic, and he rarely pursues his argument beyond the evidence of a few loosely defined linguistic characteristics. Conventional grammar and syntax belied the analytic, alien stance of the old structural mode; this orderly representation of reality, composed of carefully selected details from the real, unruly welter of nature, was another sort of evidence. The new structure was characterized by risk and adventure, a recklessness with the mystery of existence; grammar is wrenched apart to fit the order of lived experience. He thought Creeley best exemplified the new mode of prose fiction; he enjoyed the way in which Creeley seemed to suppress any control over form in order to register perception exactly as it happened to him. The new structure was not organic, but organismic. Its violation of systematic discourse was at the root of its differences; the new structure abandoned the hierarchies of reason for the hierarchies resulting from direct perception. Even the projective poetic he had fashioned by 1950 and defined as "composition by field" seems to agree closely with the structuralist concept of literature as fields of meaning. As Hartman observed, "It is hard to think of a more important development for modern criticism than this change [in structuralist interpretation] from particle to field theory."[22]

Phenomenology also has a long history of fermentation in Europe, and its roots extend to Kantian and Hegelian epistemology. But what we take to be modern phenomenology begins with Edmund Husserl and his ablest interpreters, Martin Heidegger and Maurice Merleau-Ponty. Only within the last decade has phenomenology become a serious philosophical concern of American philosophers, and as James Edie remarked in his "Introduction" to *Phenomenology in America*, even these philosophers hesitate to identify themselves directly with this movement.[23] Olson's knowledge of phenomenology appears rather limited and cursory; only two books in his library specifically relate to it, Heidegger's *What is Philosophy?* and Merleau-Ponty's *Phenomenology of Perception*.[24]

It may be confusing to talk of a slow absorption of phenomenological thought in America after the sudden and intense vogue of existentialism and phenomenology in the early years of the last decade. Existentialism and its correlative branch of thought, phenomenology, were cult reading for many youths attending college in the late 1950s and early 1960s. That vogue spent itself in succeeding years, and a more practical discussion of some of its premises has taken its place in philosophical circles. But it is easy to see why phenomenology attracted a broad spectrum of the young; it offers a vital, even jaunty approach to the study of human nature and perception. In the work of Heidegger and Merleau-Ponty especially, ambiguity is given positive value once more; "Being," the term used to capture the essence of the human being, would have us forget the duality of body and soul that rationalism has devised and offers instead a sense of the human being as a single entity with body and soul inseparably woven together.

There is a wonderful exuberance in Heidegger's criticism as well, a joie de vivre that was particularly attractive in the rebellious atmosphere of the last decade. As Marjorie Grene commented in her brief study *Martin Heidegger*, "By his own account Heidegger is first and last and always not an existentialist at all, but an ontologist: one who would restore Being to its rightful place in our thought, to the power it lost, according to him, in the time of Plato."[25] He had planned "to achieve a 'destruction' of traditional ontology by going back through Kant, Descartes and Aristotle to an earlier spring of ontological insight . . . ; an urge to return to the purer vision of pre-Socratic philosophy has been a persistent theme in Heidegger's thought."[26] His criticism of "traditional ontology" rests on a premise Olson pursued in his own writings: the wholeness of Being was fragmented in Greek philosophy, and only rationality was cultivated; the other faculties, including the irrational, were devalued and ignored.

As Grene states, "Mind—the human spirit, which should be the shepherd of Being—is itself debased; and it is this aspect of the situation which Heidegger stresses. . . . First, mind is misunderstood as 'intelligence,' the faculty of logic. So conceived, it comes to be considered purely practical, a sort of intellectual gadget for making more gadgets."[27] William Luijpen makes the connection between Heidegger and Olson even more apparent when he remarks that "in Heidegger phenomenology develops into a philosophy of man as openness."[28]

Cartesian dualism obscured the role of the body in perception, according to Merleau-Ponty. Phenomenology is a philosophy that seeks to reinstate the primacy of the organism in the act of perceiving. Body is the frame in which the mind acts; body is the perceptor of the world, and mind is merely the terminus of such perception, the organ in which categories are invented and language is fashioned. "His philosophy," Alden Fisher writes, "is precisely to enlarge reason, to make reason adequate to and inclusive of the non-rational and the irrational. Philosophy's attention to the contingent, the vague, the dark underside of things is for Merleau-Ponty only a way to be more faithful to the task of reason itself, the task of unrestricted reflection."[29]

Phenomenology generally emphasizes a return to "direct perception" of experience, a return, in Husserl's phrase, "to the things themselves." Such a return requires a larger sense of what occurs in the act of perceiving any datum, because impinging upon the categories of mind are all the surfaces of the body, including the unconscious, and each of them has its role in determining the human meaning of an event. This return to "the things themselves" reminds us not only of the credo of imagism at the beginning of this century but of Williams' famous dictum, "No ideas but in things." And Olson's poetic is rooted in the law that the poem is a construct of objects taken as they are found in nature and simply captured by a language that is obedient to the poet's powers of close attention. Phenomenology has its own internal system of predicates and emphases that do not fully agree with Olson's poetic, but each agrees in essence on the same necessity: man must reintegrate himself in the present time, and reintegration lies chiefly in recovering the consciousness of the body's participation in thinking. In 1951, a year after Olson had written "Projective Verse," in which he formed a poetic that includes the body in composition, Merleau-Ponty observed that "our century has wiped out the dividing line between 'body' and 'mind,' and sees human life as through and through mental and corporeal. . . . For many thinkers at the close of the nineteenth century, the body was a bit of matter, a network of mechanisms. The twentieth century has restored and deepened the notion of flesh, that is, of animate body."[30]

But it needs to be said again that Olson was not directly influenced by the literature of either of these major movements of European thought. However closely his arguments may agree with these larger philosophical issues, he came by them on his own. It should strike us, however, that a poet at mid-century developed theories about his art that have a considerable sophistication and depth. His typology of consciousness in *Call Me Ishmael*, where he distinguishes the modes of thought represented in Ahab and Ishmael, sweeps us into the currents of modern philosophical discourse. When he seizes upon Ishmael as the model of open consciousness, he provides a fairly complete model of the integrated human that modern thought has generally postulated.

In the years immediately following the publication of *Call Me Ishmael*, the essential antithesis between Ahab and Ishmael is fresh in Olson's mind. In his essay "Projective Verse," we can see a preliminary use of this polarity in terms of rival poetic modes. The will of Ahab is just under the surface of what Olson refers to as "closed" forms of verse, traditional modes of composition in which the poet consciously molds his expression to the demands of formal convention. His will is eminent in this act as he suppresses vitality for the sake of design. The open mode is that of Ishmael, which Olson offers to poets as the necessary alternative—where the poet's consciousness is brought over to the poem whole and unmediated.

In the second part of this essay Olson refers for the first time to a doctrine of experience he calls "objectism," and it too is directed at dissolving Ahab's duality of ego and world that the older modes of composition espouse. Objectism, he announces, "is the getting rid of the lyrical interference of the individual as ego" by the simple insistence that man is not the center of phenomena but is merely an object among all other objects of nature.[31]

"The Gate and the Center," an essay that Olson published in the first issue of Cid Corman's journal *Origin* in 1951, is an attempt to define the rhythms of human history in terms of these polar attitudes. And we can begin a survey of his theoretical writing from this essay because he so explicitly attempts to set up some coordinates in which to view history as a structure continuously being transformed through a dialectical process. It is a spirited piece of writing, full of scholarly bluff, unmindful that some of the sources he puts in service of his arguments were quite discredited at the time. An earlier version of the essay featured so much of L. A. Waddell's specious historical theorizing that Cid Corman chafed at printing it.[32] The later revisions played down references to Waddell but retained certain of his historical dates, which Olson deploys here as the boundary markers of historical process. This is an apt metaphor, for his concept of history is spatial; it emphasizes movement, migration, the shapes civilizations assume over a period of millennia.

Olson's discussion moves rapidly to a basic assumption that the most fundamental pattern of historical progression is dialectical. In the broadest possible sense, history is the exertion of two contrary forms of will. He means will as a ruling passion, a force that seizes all levels of thought and controls it for millennia. There are the "WILL TO CO-HERE" and its antithesis, the will to disperse. Using Waddell's chronology, Olson describes human history as having begun in the seizure of this "First Will," the passion to cohere:

> What Waddell gives me is this chronology: that, from 3378 BC (date man's 1st city, name and face of creator also known) in unbroken series first at Uruk, then from the seaport Lagash out into colonies in the Indus Valley and, circa 2500, the Nile, until date 1200 BC or thereabouts, civilization had ONE CENTER, Sumer, in all directions, that this one people held such exact and superior force that all peoples around them were sustained by it, nourished, increased, advanced, that a city was a coherence which, for the first time since the ice, gave man the chance to join knowledge to culture and, with this weapon, shape dignities of economics and value sufficient to make daily life itself a dignity and a sufficiency. (HU, p. 19)

The year 1200 B.C. is a terminus of this first will, after which "a bowl went smash." The shape of a coherent civilization had, however, been deteriorating for some centuries, as a contrary will began to make itself manifest:

> What has been these last 700 years, is the inevitable consequence of a contrary will to that of Sumer, a will which overcame the old will approximately 2500 BC and succeeded in making itself boss approximately 1200 BC. It is the long reach of this second will of man which we have known, the dead of which we are the witnesses. (HU, p. 20)

The will to disperse has a complex meaning for Olson. It accounts for much of the dynamic of the Greco-Roman tradition; it is the motivating force of human migration itself, the movement of peoples from the original Eastern center westward, in which he views America as the first continent of discovery. We can locate part of the argument he uses in *Call Me Ishmael* in this broad historical context: the whaling industry itself was part of the final encircling of the globe that completes migratory history. The western edge of America is the Pacific Ocean, which laps against the Asian continent, where human migration had begun. But, more importantly, the will to disperse spawned Greek abstract philosophy and began the whole process by which man desired to separate himself from his surroundings. The dispersive will created Ahab as hero:

> And the only answer of man to the rash of multiples which that
> wish to disperse causeth to break out . . . was one thing only,
> the only thing man had to put against it: the egocentric concept,
> a man himself as, and only contemporary to himself, the PROOF
> of anything, himself responsible only to himself by the exhibition
> of his energy, AHAB, end. (HU, pp. 20–21)

But the will to cohere is again ascendant. Olson discerns its manifestation in the restless movements of history over the last several centuries: "If I am right . . . , once again, and only a second time, is the FIRST WILL back in business" (HU, p. 21). And we can now understand the significance Ishmael's survival had for him; he embodies the new will of cohesion. Melville's "myth" in *Moby-Dick* depicts the great shift of will, told in the epic terms of the death of one kind of hero and the birth of its contrary.

In the final excited paragraphs of the essay, Olson seeks a new definition of hero to fit the conditions of the emerging will to cohere. In other words, heroism in the old sense of the term meant distinction, being a creature separate from the community and celebrated for prowess, with capacities that he alone possessed. But the new hero must be differently measured:

> Quickly, therefore, the EXCEPTIONAL man, the "hero," loses
> his description as "genius"—his "birth" is mere instrumentation
> for application to the energy he did not create—and becomes,
> instead, IMAGE of possibilities implicit in the energy, given the
> METHODOLOGY of its use by men from the man who is
> capable precisely of this, and only this kind of intent and
> attention. (HU, p. 22)

He is, in other words, Ishmaelian man, holding in his consciousness a vast amount of experience that is continually altering his existence; he is one with the phenomena he confronts.

In the essays, pamphlets, notes, and commentaries that Olson wrote following this prolegomenon to his theory, we can discern two points of interest around which many of these individual pieces naturally seem to group. One part of his attention was concerned with the philosophical bearings of artists and how they might be shifted to the new condition of reality in the present age. A second category of writings is chiefly concerned with elaborating more of the details of what he came to view as an esthetic methodology for rendering the new conception of reality. There is even, perhaps, a third group of essays, mostly in his late period, which we can best describe as approaching an almost mystical intuition of the character or essence of reality, which he labored to articulate. He came close to identifying what he felt might be the spirit that moved in nature. We do not have the kind of scrupulously written essays that represent earlier stages of his thought; what remains of this period are the transcripts of lectures he delivered from notes, or the sketches of possible longer works, as in *The Special View of History*. The lectures have an implicit order, but his extemporary articulation of his theses is digressive, rambling, full of false starts and amazing perceptions left untreated.

It seems the best procedure to discuss each of these groups of essays in turn, rather than to attempt to follow the evolution of his thought from essay to essay, which is in many ways indeed a crooked path. Olson wrote these prose pieces the way a sketch artist draws: he was aware of the whole design of his thinking, but his attention was concentrated on isolated areas of this larger conception, and it is not until we have looked at the range of his work that we can perceive how it comes together and forms a concerted thesis about humanity's new relationship to experience.

Olson's literary criticism is an effort to establish a new canon of taste for contemporary literature. He takes up the more salient virtues and abuses of contemporary literary practice as pretexts to call attention to those manifestations of the Ahabian will, the literature of egocentricity, and of new flutterings of Ishmaelian art, any work suggesting some larger reckoning of experience. "The Escaped Cock: Notes on Lawrence & the Real," which appeared in the second issue of *Origin* (Summer 1951), picks up on the theme we have so far been pursuing in its interpretation of D. H. Lawrence's novella *The Man Who Died*.

Lawrence was an important writer for Olson, who cited him frequently as among those who form the tradition of the new esthetic. It was Lawrence who had first suggested to him the rhythm of civilizations, their rise and fall during periods of thaw between ice ages, in his stimulating preface to the essay *Fantasia of the Unconscious*. Olson considered himself a student of the present thaw and traced the origins of his own civilization back to the Pleistocene age.[33] Olson believed that Lawrence's fiction was boldly expressive of the condition of modern consciousness— especially in his presentation of characters who suffered from the atrophy of once powerful instincts that now only confused and tormented them.

Here, in his review, Olson sees Lawrence stating the terms of a shift in consciousness through the death and rebirth of the Christ-like protagonist. Olson insists that the death is that of the aggressor, the ego-centered individual who has exerted his will sexually and satisfied it. Once he does, he wills himself to death and returns an Ishmael:

> It is not so easy to put the simplification this time except that it is a direct question, the question the Man Who Died asks himself, on his return: is anything worth more than the most precise sharpening of the instrument, a human, to the hearing of—the hearing of *all* there is *in*—the bronze clang of a cock's crow?
> (HU, p. 124)

The reborn man of this novel is in possession of "THE WHOLE SENSES," and on this point Olson excitedly turns the evidence into an esthetic imperative:

> There is one requirement, only one requirement, anywhere . . .— the clue: open, stay OPEN, hear it, anything, really HEAR it. And you are IN.
> You are all, all of you, so glib about what is human, so god-damn glib. Take a look. Just open your eyes, as he did, the Man who died:
> 1: the day of my interference is done
> 2: compulsion, no good; the recoil kills the advance
> 3: nothing is so marvellous as to be done alone in the phenomenal world which is raging and yet apart (HU, p. 125)

We shall note later that Olson's thought becomes deeply absorbed with the possibilities of the third point, especially in the last stages of his life: the phenomenal world, the dimension of simple, kinetic matter, becomes an Eden which the human soul yearns for against the mind's refusals to liberate it; his conception of space and matter is comparable to the verdant paradise of pastoral literature (a genre of art which, curiously enough, he found abhorrent because the distinctions it assumed between sylvan and urban life were arbitrary and pretentious, part of the whole classifying mentality of Renaissance Europe). The rebirth of the man who died, in Lawrence's novel, enacts such a liberation of the soul; Olson emphasized the calm and elegant relief of the reborn man. The furious sexual impulsiveness is behind him. In such later pieces as "Proprioception" and the lecture *Poetry and Truth* Olson comments tentatively on the possibility of seeing body and spirit as distinguishable components of the human integrity, an idea first suggested by this early speculative essay.

But "Human Universe" is Olson's classic indictment of egocentric literature. With the conviction of a new Copernicus, he inveighs against the egocentricity of recent writers; his declaration is fundamental: man shall continue to distort reality and not have access to it so long as he imagines himself to be the controlling center of even his own phenomenal field. The essay is an assault upon that very solipsism in what passes for the latest new writing. It began as a series of angry comments first aired in a letter to Cid Corman, after having read some of the short fiction in James Laughlin's annual *New Directions in Prose and Poetry 12*.[34] There was nothing "new" in the direction of this fiction, as far as Olson was concerned, and to find it under such a rubric was an affront to his literary conscience. A short time after his letter to Corman, Olson developed his commentary into the carefully worded essay which appeared in *Origin* in the winter of 1951. Olson posed his argument in the characteristic terms of a polarity: the foil in this case is contemporary writers of fiction, who manifest the Ahabian mind in the subjectivity of their expression. The Ishmaelian counterpart is the Mayan Indians of the Yucatan Peninsula, whom he was living among at the time. He felt that modern fiction writers used language as though it were "an absolute, instead of (as even man is) an instrument" (HU, p. 4).

When language is permitted to assume its own laws for ordering and presenting experiential content, the range of expression permitted to the artist is radically diminished. Olson traced the source of this condition to Greek abstract philosophy, which fostered the discursive methods of logical formulation and classification. For Olson these are the most rudimentary means of arranging and sorting experience. But "the harmony of the universe, and I include man, is not logical, or better, is postlogical, as is the order of any created thing" (HU, p. 4). Instead, the majority of modern writers "can only make a form . . . by selecting from the full content some face of it, or plane, some part." As a result, "It comes out a demonstration, a separating out, an act of classification, and so, a stopping, and for all that I know, it [reality] is not there, it has turned false" (HU, p. 5).

From Greek philosophy to the present, language has become a universe of its own, which permits experience to be expressed only as it obeys its purely made-up conditions:

> What it comes to is ourselves, that we do not find ways to hew to experience as it is, in our definition and expression of it, in other words, find ways to stay in the human universe, and not be led to partition reality at any point, in any way. For this is just what we do do, this is the real issue of what has been, and the process, as it now asserts itself, can be exposed. . . .
>
> There must be a means of expression for this, a way which is not divisive as all the tag ends and upendings of the Greek way are. There must be a way which bears *in* instead of away, which meets head on what goes on each split second, a way which does not—in order to define—prevent, deter, distract, and so cease the act of, discovering. (HU, pp. 5–6)

Beyond language lies "direct perception," but the modern writer does not penetrate to this actuality; instead he "sets up a series of reference points" in which individual objects are merely described in terms of other objects. In such writing, "each thing is not so much like or different from another thing (these likenesses and differences are apparent) but that such an analysis only accomplishes a *description*, does not come to grips with what really matters: that a thing, any thing, impinges on us by a more important fact, its self-existence, without reference to any other thing" (HU, p. 6).

The alternative to this tyranny of linguistic laws is a new esthetic that regards the human being, both organism and intellect, as an instrument for discovering the nature of reality. Our "systemic particulars" record the subtle impingements of phenomena, and it should be possible for us to translate these sensations and discoveries into a medium of signs and sounds free of any but the most flexible laws of usage. The subtle language of organismic response requires an order of words that most closely approximates our particular discoveries of the phenomenal world.

The rapidity with which man takes in information from the external world has been measured by scientists, who have described the skin of the fingertips as photo-electric cells, but Olson insists that the whole organism is involved in the reception of stimuli, that every part of the human system is interpreting at the speed of light what it receives. And he goes further to suggest that all the content of consciousness is the result, the froth, of what the organism has absorbed from its manifold contacts with phenomena: "[man's] dreams, for example, his thoughts (to speak as the predecessors spoke), his desires, sins, hopes, fears, faiths, loves" are not to be "separated from the external pick-ups" (HU, p. 10).

> The process of image . . . cannot be understood by separation
> from the stuff it works on. . . .
>   In other words, the proposition here is that man at his peril
> breaks the full circuit of object, image, action at any point. The
> meeting edge of man and the world is also his cutting edge. If man
> is active, it is exactly here where experience comes in that it is
> delivered back, and if he stays fresh at the coming in he will be
> fresh at his going out. If he does not, all that he does inside his
> house is stale, more and more stale as he is less and less acute
> at the door. And his door is where he is responsible to more
> than himself. (HU, pp. 10–11)

The less acute he is, in other words, the more he becomes the demonic,
irresponsible egotist, an Ahab, whose "league with evil closes the door
to truth," as he wrote in *Call Me Ishmael*. Only an Ishmael is "responsible to more than himself"; he consumes his ego through his attention
to what lies beneath and beyond it.

Such are the Mayans, Olson concludes, although the contemporary
Mayan Indian has only a vestige of the full vitality of his former civilization. With all the skills and clever technology of the Mayan age now
forgotten, the modern Mayan retains only "love and flesh." He does not
pull back from the touch of the stranger, as the modern American does,
but allows intimacy and contact as "the natural law of flesh" (HU, p.
6). At the peak of Mayan culture

> men were able to stay so interested in the expression and gesture
> of all creatures, including at least three planets in addition to
> the human face, eyes and hands, that they invented a system of
> written record, now called hieroglyphs, which, on its very face,
> is verse, the signs were so clearly and densely chosen that, cut
> in stone, they retain the power of the objects of which they are
> the images. (HU, p. 7)

Olson wrote Creeley from Yucatan that

> a Sumer poem or Maya glyph is more pertinent to our purposes
> than anything else, because each of these people & their workers
> had forms which unfolded directly from content (sd content
> itself a disposition toward reality which understood man as only
> force in field of force containing multiple other expressions[35]

Any grievances Olson had about the fictional content of *New Direc-*

tions 12 were handsomely redressed the following year, 1951, in *New Directions 13*, which presented five of Robert Creeley's short stories with an "Introduction" by Olson (misspelled Olsen).[36] In this short commentary, Olson gives us a highly compressed summary of his ideas on fiction, using Creeley's five stories as examples of an alternate narrative method. His comments center on a distinction between "fiction" and "RE-ENACTMENT." The word "fiction" suggests to Olson the gamut of contrivances commonly used in narrative writing, the exaggerations of reality through complex plots, or, worse, the self-adoration of narrators who assume "themselves to be more interesting" than the events they tell (HU, p. 128). Either way, we have the elements of the older ego-consciousness at work. Against this kind of fiction, Olson notes two methods of reenactment: one is documentary in the sense that the writer's "ego or person is NOT of the story whatsoever" and only the events or characters are treated; in the other the narrator is totally preoccupied with how to express the movement of his own consciousness. The latter is Creeley's method. Both methods "drive for the same end, so to re-enact experience that a story has what an object or person has: energy and instant." They "keep original force in at the same time that that force is given illumination" (HU, p. 127).

In verse, Olson said, one needed to get rid of the "lyrical interference of the individual as ego," and in prose, one needed to be rid of the egotistic limits of the fictive mode. His approach to dramatic literature is virtually the same.[37] In a highly speculative essay entitled "Notes on Language and Theater," Olson asserts that in pre-Aeschylean drama the actor faced the audience alone, in his own person, and recited lines as he made rhythmic movements with his body. Aeschylus

> added a second actor, and had dialogue, and . . . added masks
> (and had that hollow thing, mechanical projection). It was a
> double change he effected: words as gab and masks to magnify
> sensation. And the result? The birth of that exaggerated individual
> called hero, and of that exaggerated narrative called tragedy.
> (HU, p. 73)

But he is quick to suggest here, as he does for other modes, the alternative that drama must take if it is to regain its dynamic:

> The theater, as we call theater, will soon be once more *rhabdian*,
> plots gone, gab gone, all the rest of the baggage of means,
> stripped down, these "recitations" now going on in public hall
> a sign, but Dylan Thomas more, the hunger of people merely

to hang their ears out and hear, not any longer the jigging of
their eyes, all that "luxury," Schubert seats etc. (HU, p. 75)

Olson defined "*the rhabdians*" earlier in the essay as "single actors with
a stick beating out verse and acting out narrative situations in said verse"
(HU, p. 73).

Olson wrote such an experimental play of his own, *Apollonius of
Tyana*, which was published in *Origin* 6 (Summer 1952) but never performed (HU, pp. 24–45). It is subtitled "A Dance, with Some Words,
for Two Actors." As a play it suggests a modern Western version of
Japanese Nō drama, for it is largely concerned with the proper psychological training of the protagonist, and the notes direct the actor to move
with stately, slow rhythms about the stage, as each step of his coming to
consciousness requires some new spatial relationship to the other actor,
Tyana, who is described as "The voice" and is the spirit of "place."
Apollonius is first made visible to us in the close embrace of Tyana; he
slowly separates himself, undergoes the stages of awakening, and when
fully cognizant and tutored in how to respond, returns to Tyana, and
the play ends. The protagonist is literally unfolded from the content of
his location in phenomena, undertakes a small odyssey through the world
of the stage, and returns with enlightened humility to his origins. It is
less a play than a meditation in the dramatic mode, but it succeeds in
presenting Olson's image of the artist that lies beneath the essays we
have been examining.

We turn now to the second group of essays, in which Olson attempts
to define the characteristics of the phenomenal field to which he has insisted the artist must open himself. For Olson, the shift of consciousness
involves not only an increase of sensory alertness and the suppression of
egocentricity but also a fundamental recognition that the objects of perception can no longer be ordered according to any scheme of humanistic
values. Objects exist in a network of wholly different laws from those of
human society. The more any individual willingly confronts this reality
to learn what "secrets objects share," the more he may discern that such
laws do in fact govern his own existence in more basic ways than do
human norms and edicts. When that person shifts his attention from
traditionally humanistic concerns to what lies around him as nature, he
may discover that human conduct is often ignorant or in violation of
natural laws that would enhance his existence and make life more meaningful. The destruction of the environment we depend upon, the irrational course of modern technological societies, the immense energy and
resources devoted to modern warfare are dimensions of an inward-look-

ing age that has lost the capacity to look to nature to increase its wisdom.

In one of his longest letters to Cid Corman, written on June 13, 1952, Olson tells how he spent an evening "exposing the nature of these States" to a young couple of the "protest class."[38] An ideology based on "the Right and the Left" is no longer tenable, since "each comes, by the final act of itself, more to resemble the other" and neither side is in any real sense the rational alternative. If change is to come from any sector, allowing that politics is a closed intellectual system of only seemingly opposed ideologies, it will have to come from those artists who have found the only exit from an illusory society, the phenomenal totality:

> It is not my kick, as a post-modern and so a post-Darwinian, yet I grapple again and again with these terms, to see. What the session [with the couple] did, though, was to reemphasize for me the conviction that the only morality is art, and that this has been becomes now so crucial that one can be sure that art as a principle is once more back in business as the only essential "revolution"—that only as men are bred to think of expression as the only social act worth any interchange with another human being is there anything ahead but more of same. . . . [39]

It is not sufficient, however, that an artist merely turn toward nature, or even recognize that its reality is of a different order, but he must understand his own organism and its unique intake of the world, which is the only means he has for contacting the environment. In this same letter he remarks that "there is a stage where man is free of dream. And that that stage is where he is utterly clear, limpid, in this sense that he has so possessed his own 'form,' so knows the structure of himself (in the face of all other forms) that he works from that alone."[40] He must, in other words, be free of even these vestiges of the ego, the dream as wish-fulfillment, if he is to achieve anything.

These initial remarks prepare the way for a discussion of what Olson calls his "methodology," which is not a new departure in his thought, necessarily, but a more rigorous and systematic formulation of the view that the art work must be made from the artist's unmediated, direct perception of reality. The methodology is the connecting link between the artist and the totality of nature. The artist who "so knows the structure of himself" understands, in other words, the properties of his own "field" of phenomena, which are the evershifting limits of his consciousness. This is a crucial condition if we are to understand what the methodology purports to offer.

The artist is at any given moment a field of awareness which is forever being intersected by the field of phenomena lying around him. No part of that larger field is ever experienced as an individual, discrete entity; each comes to him in the situation of its own field of relations. Awareness, then, is a continually alerting condition of consciousness as it is penetrated by parts of the larger field one is contained within. And the methodology is an attempt to make an esthetic based on this theory of cognition.

"Methodology keeps forcing itself into my mouth as the word to cover the necessities that the execution of form involves." Olson uses this term to make clear his insistence that "we do get down to principles of procedure . . . and that we do see ourselves or any given thing as materials to be arranged." He would secure for the artist exactly those clear procedural steps for making forms out of phenomena that now lie in the hands of that symbol of concerted willfulness, the modern corporation; "the act of the present (on the part of a man of art) is to capture, from the enemy, the very forces which make them the leadership."[41]

Corporations have succeeded in their own vast designs through internal organization, which involves the "principle of *efficiency*, the characteristic of the machine," and "quantity," or the view they have come to take of the world as a coherent unity, a complex interrelationship of resources, distribution, markets, and consumers. The artist must learn a similar efficiency in his own work, and he must come to see objects as belonging to a vast coherent system of relations. To have that sense of quantity, Olson tells Corman, is to see reality as it now "rests on a series of altogether new intellectual premises, more, total premises and behaviours which the world TOTALITY (understand me, not as a descriptive phrase, but as a recognition of the dominant kinetic which informs the reality we are a part of) does indicate."[42]

One of the central new premises is that the totality is coherent. "To cohere means to stick together! To hold fast, as parts of the same mass! And coherence is defined as connection or congruity arising from some common *principle* or idea."[43] The emergence of the theory of congruent space constitutes for Olson one of the decisive signs of the shift in Western consciousness toward a coherent world view.

Olson had studied non-Euclidean geometry with the mathematician Hans Rademacher while at Black Mountain College, and the fact that three theoretical mathematicians—John Bolyai, Nikolai Lobatschewsky, and George Riemann—arrived at an almost identical theory of spatial congruency without knowledge of each other's work seemed proof enough that a kind of intellectual spirit had manifested itself in the 1840s. Olson did not exaggerate the importance of the new theoretical geometry of space; indeed, it has been compared to the Copernican revolution in astronomy. But with characteristic bluff he simplified the complex speculation and unanswered problems of this difficult branch of mathematics to fit his own theory of intellectual history.

In a review he wrote in 1958, "Equal, That Is, to the Real Itself," we can see a familiar argument surface when he evaluates Riemann's contribution to the theory: Riemann "distinguished two kinds of manifold, the discrete (which would be the old system, and it includes discourse, language as it had been since Socrates) and, what he took to be more true, the continuous." The same intellectual spirit that moved these geometers in Europe also moved Melville, who knew nothing of these events but who nonetheless made "the first art of space to arise from the redefinition of the real" (HU, p. 117). Melville was the first artist, in other words, to view the world as a sensuous reality, the first to join art to the coherence that the theoretical mathematicians had discovered. For Olson, then, Melville pointed the direction that art has to take if it is to survive the decline of the "old system." In the 1958 review, Olson argues that Melville broke through the new reality by allowing language to become "a point-by-point mapping power of such flexibility" that the shapeliness of totality, with all its figures in continuous motion, reassembles itself in the formal constructs of his prose:

> The new world of atomism offered a metrical means as well as a topos different from the discrete. Congruence, which there, in mathematicians' hands, lifted everything forward after Lobatschewsky (via Cayley especially, another contemporary of Melville, and Felix Klein) makes much sense, as no other meter does, to account for Melville's prose. Congruence was spatial intuition to Kant, and if I am right that Melville did possess its powers, he had them by his birth, from his time of the world, locally America. (HU, p. 120)

Melville penetrated to the real when he mastered the terms of physicality: "object and motion, those factors of a thing which declare what we call its physicality," are the means Melville employs to express the precise consciousness we have of dimension, of "literal space." In the chapter of *Moby-Dick* entitled "The Tail," Olson argues, no other writer has so forcefully captured dimensionality as an "event which comes into consciousness" when we are in the presence of an immense thing. His ability was to "go *inside* a thing, and from its motion and his to show and to know, not its essence alone . . . but its *dimension*." The chapter "The Tail" achieves this effect of dimensionality of the whale's tail fins through a congruence of words that seemingly "map" the contours of the tail itself. Olson argues that language could map objects if it were made to obey the laws of physical congruence rather than the conventions of discourse. How this is so is difficult to imagine, but he claimed nonetheless that Melville "was essentially incapable of either allegory or symbol for the best congruent reason: mirror and model are each figures in Euclidean space, and they are *not* congruent. They require a discontinuous jump" (HU, p. 121).

In an earlier review of Melville scholarship entitled "Materials and Weights of Herman Melville," Olson remarks that "given the stance he took toward object moving in space," his conception of characterization went beyond the methods of traditional fiction: "With such a sense of totality and yet with senses crisp enough to keep him usually safe from generalization, he had to go beyond the familiar causatives of environment, psychology and event" in creating his characters (HU, p. 114). Olson points out that Melville "likens character, in this case Hamlet's, to a Drummond light raying out from itself on all other things by movement from its sources on all sides" (HU, p. 114). In other words, Olson is suggesting that Melville's fictional characters are portrayed as "fields of force" in their own locations in the field of totality, and he settles upon this image of the Drummond light to illustrate his point.

But he goes back to an earlier complaint, first made in *Call Me Ishmael*, that Melville was only able to characterize the anti-hero Ahab, who rejects the possibility of large awareness as he exerts all his energy in a single mad pursuit. When Melville tries to go beyond Ahab to present the hero, he can only create Billy Budd, the "Christian Hero (it is an oxymoron: a Christian can only be a saint)" (HU, p. 115). The saint attends only to a transcendent world, not to the phenomena of actuality. And for Olson the true hero whom Melville only begins to reveal in his brief portrayal of Bulkington, and little more so in Ishmael, is a measure of the immense capacities of the human being to absorb and understand the surrounding totality. Such a figure is what Olson intends the artist should be to his readers, the "hero" who by the record of his written forms becomes the measure of human capacity. "In creating the anti-hero Ahab and in trying to go beyond him, Melville put himself squarely up against the hero, and thus at the heart of narrative and verse now" (HU, p. 115).

Olson captures the insistent theme of these essays when he writes in *The Special View of History* that a person's existence "occurs in a universe which is the context of his events—he has no intersections [sic] points without the common field of reality in which he is placed, disposed, acts willy-nilly his own precious forwardness, direction, and value. What Socrates did was to isolate the value and thus raise and isolate the man-time from space-time." And the solution he continually points to is that "any new humanism, in resetting man in his field, actually is doing no more than giving him back his 'time.' "[44]

The hero Melville failed to realize in his fiction is that creature who recognizes this condition of life and seizes the opportunities it presents. *The Special View of History*, the collected notes and drafts of a series of lectures he delivered at Black Mountain College in 1956, is Olson's attempt to define the hero and to show how he takes advantage of the conditions in which he exists. The title of these lectures refers to the re-definition of history he feels is necessary if we are to understand the hero he is describing. History is what a person happens to be doing in his life: it is the sum of his various acts. "History is what he does. Too long it has—by discourse too—been only what he has done, thus a bore, for we live now and have all the problems, and what do we care for those who have done previously?" Olson puts this another way when he argues that anyone's individual life is an oblique line drawn across the graphlike patterns of the space-time continuum, whose existence consists of "man-points of intersections composing a man-line which are his acts and experiences," and are his history (SV, pp. 26–27).

We are on familiar ground again, though, when Olson turns to indi-viduals who have distinguished themselves for the extent and signifi-cance of their acts. He discerns two types of mind among this group: the one is Ahabian, whom he now calls the "Man of Power"; the other is the Ishmaelian hero, the "Man of Achievement." These designations are taken from a letter by John Keats, an excerpt from which serves as an epigraph to this series of lectures and reads in part, "Several things dovetailed in my mind, & at once it struck me, what quality went to form a Man of Achievement especially in literature & which Shakespeare possessed so enormously—I mean *Negative Capability*, that is when man is capable of being in uncertainties, Mysteries, doubts, without any irri-table reaching after fact and reason."[45]

In the lecture entitled "The Metrical," the "Man of Power" is seen reaching after fact or reason:

> Without going beyond [Keats'] thought one can spell this out
> by recognizing that he is exposing two different [i.e., alien]
> methodologies; reaching after fact is the experimental method
> and reaching after reason is logic. And I need not, I should

imagine, emphasize that, in these two methodologies, you will recognize the whole previous history of Western man from the 5th Century in logic and the whole history of man since the 17th century [sic] in physics. (SV, p. 41)

Throughout his career Olson was intent upon stating that his own ideology was new and independent of any established doctrine. His criticism of American society and of capitalist economic theory, his rejection of the corporate monopoly structure, suggested that he was sympathetic to Marxist theory, and for that reason perhaps, he frequently disavowed any such tendency in his thought. His attitude toward Hegel may seem contradictory, unless we recognize that he perceived two Hegels in this thought: the first was the historic Hegel who wrote a long and complex apology for the Prussian state and who is more or less taken as the fashioner of a vast, closed system of thought; the other Hegel was philosopher of the dialectic, the theory of which Olson found entirely compatible with his own ideas and, indeed, took over at strategic points as a means of explaining his sense of the kinetic and formative processes of reality. In his review "Equal, That Is, to the Real Itself" he thrusts Keats and Hegel together as the warring opposites of contemporary ideology: "Keats, without setting out to, had put across the century the inch of steel to wreck Hegel, if anything could" (HU, p. 117). But in the conclusion of his lecture "The Metrical," Hegel is reinterpreted and his dialectic now provides a context in which to define the "Man of Achievement."

Olson slowly came to realize that Hegelian dialectic breaks through to the actual processes of reality. He quotes Hegel's own definition at one point: "Wherever there is movement, wherever there is life, wherever anything is carried into effect in the actual world, there Dialectic is at work" (SV, p. 42). To this extent, at least, dialectic is in agreement with Olson's theoretical concerns.

Olson then summarizes the "moments" of dialectical reason, but his comments are too condensed to explain fully how he finds them of use. It might be helpful to digress for the moment and define these "terms" or "moments." Dialectical reason is the means by which the "subject" (individual) achieves its consciousness. According to Hegel, thought moves among contradictions that are implicit in the content of its contemplations. This is roughly parallel to the phenomenal welter in which Olson casts the individual. In Hegel's view, dialectical reason consists of three perceptible stages, which he calls "moments."

The first of these is Being, in which thought perceives a nucleus of relationships in the content of its musings, which it then abstracts and fixes in its understanding. Olson calls this merely the "Abstract side." The understanding is simply this act of abstracting from the totality of forming and dissolving relationships some single determination of particulars. But Being manifests itself in such a way as to propose its own negation as well, and it is only by a "sort of violence" that this negation is concealed from consciousness. Being leads to the second "moment," which is Nothingness, or the "negation of the determinate thing." The negation is a recognition of the abstractness of this determination; thought now plunged into the intuitive unconscious perceives that a part of a process has been momentarily isolated and is insufficient by itself. The third term "results once any determination has been enriched by its negation and transcended; it is produced rigorously whenever two terms are in contradiction, yet it is a new moment of Being and of thought."[46] In other words, each time Being is manifest in thought, the totality reasserts its primacy over the intellect's limited awareness and the mind is thrown back into the depth of pure potentiality again, only to return to consciousness anew with its understanding made larger.

Being is forever asserting particulate knowledge, which is gradually augmented and enriched through its cycles of immersion into Nothingness. Such is the progress of the mind toward greater self-consciousness. But Hegel's own historical works are not dialectical in the sense he proposes since his theories led to a sanctification of the Prussian state as the final manifestation of the spirit of history. As Olson remarks in his lecture, Hegel "takes what is condition as result, instead of leaving it, as Keats does, *penetralium*" (SV, p. 43). Instead of remaining poised between certainty and new knowledge, Hegel arrived at a state of absolute knowledge, and, as Olson comments, his mind had simply found a way of remaining in its state of Being, which is the "slip of the whole holding to POWER." The Man of Power thus "falls to the status of Understanding—what Hegel defines as '*nothing allowed to remain vague or indefinite*'" (SV, p. 44). He rejects any but his own rigid view of things and is determined to force all else to submit to it. An Ahab.

The Man of Achievement is the contrary alternative. Instead of consolidating his own state of understanding, he fulfills Keats' description of negative capability; he willingly remains at that stage of his thought where he resides in the uncertain vastnesses of totality and takes thought on that which he can perceive. This is what Olson assumes that the third term of the dialectic implies: "to *take* thought, or to *make* it thought, not merely to let it lie either in understanding (the finite seen as such) or in the dialectical (the observed seen to be flux. . . ." (SV, p. 44). The third term completes "a sentence," he argues, since the third term is the completed thought one can make after the "nouns" of understanding are once more set in motion and relation by the "verb" of the dialectical unconscious. The decision to remain in the state of Being or to go forward and to take thought are willful directions of the mind. "One," the drive to power, "is the self as ego and sublime. The other is the self as center and circumference," center because it is one sentient entity in a vastness of things, and circumference, because all that vastness is potentially what that mind could come to understand and make a part of itself (SV, p. 45). The new hero is therefore to be seen as cognitively progressive, and the old hero as cognitively stationary.

Prior to writing these important lectures, Olson had been closely studying the cosmological theory of the British philosopher Alfred North Whitehead.[47] The breadth and comprehension of Whitehead's metaphysical thesis in *Process and Reality* suggested to Olson another manifestation of the new will to cohere. Whitehead proposed to explain through his philosophy of organism how all the evolving forms of the totality are tending toward some final harmonious order which, he argued, will be the material embodiment of God. The staggering dimensions of the thesis declare to Olson "man's own powers of imposing form on content." It is "another way of seeing how much the present presses toward a concept of order which is different from that one which the attention to Kosmos involved man in, succeeding phases, from the 6th century B.C. to the 20th A.D." (SV, p. 47). The movement toward harmony is not directed from any outside force acting upon the chaos; it is occurring through the success of its own accidental combinations. What Olson never really comments on is that Whitehead fashioned a cosmology from the terms of Hegelian dialectic. Whereas Hegel concentrated upon the actions and evolution of thought, Whitehead located the same processes in the whole of nature and the universe. He made the universe, in other words, the mind of totality, or the mind of God. God's own mind comes to greater self-consciousness through all the successful accidents of organic evolution in the universe.

It is not this thesis by itself that stimulates Olson; rather it is the very grandeur of the act of Whitehead as he "takes thought" on his own perceptions. His speculation is that the bewildering prehensive activities of all levels of matter do have a goal, and he speculates boldly on what that goal might be. Part of Whitehead's argument has to do with the precise formative event in nature; to explain how it is that some entities receive formation and others deny it, he ascribes to any entity or formal group stages of "feeling." Olson finds this explanation the most compelling feature of Whitehead's book. Whitehead has ascribed to any atom or planet the precise behavior of the human being himself, and Olson seizes upon this connection in his lectures:

> I return now to the three stages of feeling. The first is that in which the multiples of anything crowd in on the individual; the second is that most individual stage when he or she seeks to impose his or her own order of order on the multiples; and the third is the stage called satisfaction, in which the true order is seen to be the confrontation of two interchanging forces which can be called God and the World. (SV, p. 50)

We can see how close these three stages are to Hegel's three terms of dialectic. The first stage of feeling is comparable to Hegel's first term, Being dissolving into negation; the second stage is like the second term; and so on. And Olson reaches much the same conclusion about the third stage of feeling, "satisfaction," as he does about "speculation," the transcendent third term of the dialectic:

> I spell it out. In the first stage of feeling, the chaos of physical enjoyment is both the reality and the process, but as process (in other words, as in motion) already Spirit (which is pneuma and means breath—wind, air) is operative. In the second stage, when the individual impresses his or her sense of order on the multiples, already Desire or Eros has begun to leaven the matter; already the vision of form (Kosmos, order harmony the world) is operative. And in the last stage, satisfaction, when both the enjoyment and the desire are one (the desire for form is the creative force, or what has been usually called God), the process of feeling becomes the reality and man is "satisfied". . . . And at that point any man or woman recedes as God does from his creation. And for a good reason: that he or she or Him must then go on to another creation. The very motive powers, enjoyment and desire, require it. (SV, p. 51 f.)

Throughout the lectures on Whitehead's cosmology, which Olson entitled "The Topological," the stress of his commentary is clearly on the becomingness of things in the totality, the human mind included. In Olson, and in Whitehead himself, we get the strongest impression that space is a voluptuous, fertile paradise of growing things, a surrealistic garden of formal delights; humanity is merely another of the polyplike forms rising to harmony with all else. The hero for Olson is anyone who can open his eyes and see what an Eden of totality he has been given; where he thrives in this heavenly earth, others toil and destroy, blind to all the beauty they stand within. That is the vision; but as we shall see in the next chapter, the forces of the old dispersive will still outnumber and overwhelm the first missionaries of divine coherence. Many of Olson's best poems depict the long, unending struggle between a fragmenting civilization and the heroic individuals who live and act in a freshly conceived reality.

When in 1955 Ed Dorn, a student at Black Mountain College, asked Olson to suggest a reading list for him, Olson responded by writing *A Bibliography on America for Ed Dorn*, which renders America itself a sufficient totality for the "hero" to be thrust into, to lose himself among its particulars and to come eventually to take thought about his discoveries. He gives Ed Dorn a wide-ranging and scholarly list of readings, with the emphasis upon trusted writers who have been precise in their observations and who make broad and sweeping interpretations of the phenomena which they have investigated. The bibliography is really the notes for the making of an American Ishmael, the "hero" as poet. In a diagram made of two intersecting lines, Olson surrounds "E. Dorn" with the whole impinging universe: "MILLENNIA," the field of events from 12,000 B.C. to A.D. 1955, in which Dorn's personal existence is located; "PROCESS," the whole prehensive activity of things as Whitehead described them, in which any of his acts takes place; "QUANTITY," the recognition of a whole earth of things, multiple and continuous; and "PERSON," or "THE INDIVIDUAL," the unique field of thought and memory that receives the events of the larger field and is the screen on which any perception is finally projected. As he tells Dorn in closing, "Best thing to do is *to dig one thing or place or man* until you yourself know more abt that than is possible to any other man. It doesn't matter whether it's Barbed Wire or Pemmican or Paterson or Iowa. But *exhaust* it. Saturate it. Beat it. And then U KNOW everything else very fast: one saturation job (it might take 14 years). And you're in, forever."[48] Dorn will be "in," he will have gained access, we must suppose, to that paradise of reality Olson has conceived in these essays.

In the final years of his life, Olson became more and more convinced of his conception of space as a visionary realm. It is a surprising turn for a man who, in spite of the speculative cast of his thought, did insist on the plain, precise truth of experience and cautioned against the appeals of a transcendent order of things. This was the undoing of Melville, he thought, who had gone from exposing the anti-hero to adoration of the transcendent man, Christ. But in the two late lecture series *Causal Mythology* and *Poetry and Truth* we have Olson speaking boldly about the spiritual implications of his conception of reality. We have described this stage of his thinking as mystical, and to an extent this seems the proper word. His lifelong concern had been the reintegration of man into the orders of nature. "Objectism," the word he used frequently to describe the set of ideas we have been examining, is intended to define the human being without the usual humanist distinctions, as an object, like any other. But after all of these carefully reasoned elaborations of his theory of experience and of how a person might engage himself in actuality, there is a note of despair in the late lectures and notes. It is as if he had realized that humans would not be human unless they were at least partly alien to the harmony of the cosmos. The image he had had of Ed Dorn, in the *Bibliography*, as having to bore in against the crustlike edge of reality—"And you're in, forever"—is not quite the image he had in the 1960s.

In "Proprioception," a set of work-sheets, mere jottings and notes, made between 1959 and 1962, Olson covers much of the ground of his earlier essays, except that at one point in the outline he equates the self with "SOUL, the intermediary, the intervening thing, the interruptor, the resistor. . . . The 'soul' then is equally 'physical.' Is the self."[49] The whole body of the human organism, as remarked before, is the sensory system that feeds into consciousness. The body can originate its own experience merely by moving, which engages all the interoceptors of the viscera and muscular system. The definition of self he proposes here comes closest to Paul Goodman's theory of the self in *Gestalt Therapy*, for he remarks that all the sensations of the body are, in sum, the mercurial configurations that we call "self." The organism's selection and rejection from the totality we might liken to the movement of one density (the sensible organism) through another (the phenomenal totality), and the turbulence such movement causes, Olson would say, is what constitutes selfhood. And when a person turns this self outward into language, projects that self, he is discriminating between that part of his organism which has become a subject and that which remains untransformed, or potential object. The soul is forever rising, in other words, out of the organismic content. But since the soul is physical, its existence depends upon the potential, which it negates or makes actual. The soul, or self, is like the flames that arise from kindling: the flame exists so long as there is kindling to consume. The soul and the organism are mutually inclusive qualities of humanness. And that is why humans can never be totally assimilated into the harmonies of the cosmos. If the whole organism were fully transformed into awareness, it would, like the flame, extinguish itself in the exhaustion of all its potential. It would cease to resist.

In the lectures he delivered at Beloit College in 1968, entitled *Poetry and Truth*, Olson pushes his thought a step further. The soul does long to become this liberated energy and would accept the oblivion which this paradise demands, but the mind, that organ of man which has a contrary longing, to achieve power, refuses. In this exotic argument, the perfect heaven of space and its processes awaits the soul, and the mind stands vigil at the gate:

> That, as a creature of, as creatures of organism [Whitehead's philosophy of processes], the original difficulty is that of the soul having its chance to realize its separateness from the body; but that only the mind can free it from its fetters to the body. . . . you arrive at a point where the mind refuses the soul any further progress, will *not* let the soul into the heaven of itself. And at that gate—which sounds absolutely like theology and parable at this point . . . you suddenly have nothing but matter. . . . I just wish at this moment to fiercely see if truth can be said to be itself, and if possible, against I think all history except our own as a people, to be so articulate, or to have failed in being so, as to say that matter is the fourth scalar—the world which prevents, but once felt, enables your being to have its heaven.[50]

In these final remarks, Olson came to the limits of his theorizing. The human being, that finite creature, travels in the infinite realms of matter, his true paradise. He longs to transcend his limits, to join the rhythms of matter, but to do so he must give up his vanity, that pleasure he derives from being a unique, a separate thing. Like any other heaven of theology, space also demands that one leave his corporeal self behind and come into the realms of God:

> In the end, when all the estrangement is over, when the familiar is known, who isn't up against the face of God like a wall or a mirror where the shadow or the cut-out shape or the light is the reflection or the light or the figure of himself in species? (SV, p. 26)

One is or becomes a part of God, in other words, when he submits fully to that which lies around him. These are the furthest reaches of Olson's objectist doctrine, the final point of convergence of all the various strains of his thought about experience and the conditions of human existence. In the next chapter, we will descend rather rapidly from the thin atmosphere of these musings, as we consider first the poetic that springs from the rudiments of objectism and the poetry, which attempts to articulate the exact behavior of the self's awareness.

3. Projectivism and the Short Poems

. . . man at his peril breaks the full circuit of object, image, action at any point. The meeting edge of man and the world is also his cutting edge. If man is active, it is exactly here where experience comes in that it is delivered back, and if he stays fresh at the coming in he will be fresh at his going out.

—"Human Universe"

the *principle* . . . : FORM IS NEVER MORE THAN AN EXTENSION OF CONTENT.

the *process* . . . : ONE PERCEPTION MUST IMMEDIATELY AND DIRECTLY LEAD TO A FURTHER PERCEPTION.

—"Projective Verse"

The Poetic

The aims of the previous chapter were to define what Olson meant by the term "objectism" and to trace the many permutations of his thought as a philosophy of experience emerged from his sense of that term. In his initial use of "objectism" in the essay "Projective Verse," Olson envisaged a condition of existence in which the boundaries between subject and object would be dissolved. His philosophy urged the individual to see himself primarily as an object amid all other objects that constitute the world; not to do so, he thought, was a perilous venture into irrationality. His zeal to denounce the present age, where subjective boundaries seemed uppermost, was that of a missionary preaching to a heathen civilization a new doctrine of the cosmos.

While Olson was formulating and refining his objectist position, he produced poetry which sought to express the quality of alert consciousness that he thought possible through objectism. At the heart of both Olson's poetic and his poetry lies an essential paradox which gives his work its peculiar tension: he wants to perceive the unity of experience by means other than abstraction and logical deduction. His alternative is an elaborate form of induction, in which each step of the inductive process moves against a dense thicket of that moment's feeling and thought.

The intellect's powers of discernment are here humbled before the sheer disarray of the body's whole knowledge of things. Perceptions emerge from the reluctant intellect as they are wrested from the disorder that overwhelms it.

Olson's various statements on poetics and his poems pursue the possibilities of an esthetic *praxis* for objectism. As a doctrine of alertness or as a program for the recapturing of lost sensibilities, objectism lacks clear and defined tenets from which a practical methodology can easily be deduced. Olson's published writings rarely deal directly with the problems of composing poetry and when they do, his commentary, as in the essay "Projective Verse," hints rather than fully states the outlines of a new poetic.

And it is only in the most general sense that the poetry he composed subsequent to this famous essay conforms to its main ideas. The body of Olson's poetry varies so widely in method and intent that it suggests no fixed conception of how a poem should be made. But his writing on poetics and much of his poetry are explicitly concerned with how the individual can increase his awareness of himself as an entity in a world of things, and to that extent it is programmatic of an objectist doctrine.

Critics of Olson's work have too often relied upon the "Projective Verse" essay as a definitive statement of his aims as a poet. Following its publication in *Poetry New York* in 1950, the essay had an immediate impact upon other poets, and much that has been written about Olson since then has been taken from comments in the essay, especially on the use of a typewriter for recording the composition of a poem. But the essay seems to take away from poetry more that it gives, for its most explicit points condemn the conventions of artifice; offered in return are rhythm, sound, and perception—the irreducible properties, he argued, that constitute the poetic act.

The essay was really a polemic against the status quo in poetry at that time: the projective stance is what remains to the poet when the restraints of convention are removed from his craft. The conditions for a new poetry were stated with scant detail, suggesting that this document was really a point of departure for the poet, not a conclusive, rigorously argued set of doctrines for verse. Olson's own poetry clearly shows that he was not bound by any new set of conventions but was exploring the poetic medium he felt he had liberated.

But if some critics have overstated the significance this essay had for Olson, it is not justifiable to dismiss it as merely a polemic exercise, either. Olson had completed *Call Me Ishmael* three years before, and, as Donald Byrd has suggested, the essay "represents his first significant, public attempt to solve the methodical problems which *Call Me Ishmael* had raised."[1] The Ishmael envisioned at the close of that book is post-individual man, a survivor of the will to disperse, and it was the character and language of this new figure that Olson had yet to formulate.

Olson's thinking at this moment was profoundly influenced by four literary figures with whom he felt great affinity: Robert Creeley, Edward Dahlberg, William Carlos Williams, and especially Ezra Pound. The "Projective Verse" essay may even be thought of as an effort to find the right synthesis of the ideas of these four men, as well as his own, in order to fashion a new and valid poetic.

For several months prior to the appearance of "Projective Verse," Olson had been carrying on a correspondence with Creeley on the nature of poetry. One of the fruits of their letters is the principle that form is never more than an extension of content, a concept only touched upon in the essay but of considerable importance to Olson later, especially in the second triad of the *Maximus* poems, where form arises partly from the accidental juxtapositions of consciousness as much as from more direct manipulation of materials. Creeley has certainly allowed this law to operate in his own work, especially in the more open-ended, fragmentary poems of *A Day Book*.

Olson refers to this principle in the essay only to suggest that traditional forms are imposed by conventions which preserve the separations of self and world: the poet is asked to change the shape of his feelings to conform to certain uniform expectations of poetic response. Hence, by the act of freeing the words of the poem to assume their own particular configuration, semantic and typographical, the poet is discovering his own uniqueness.

From Edward Dahlberg's severe editorial condensation of the original draft of *Call Me Ishmael* Olson learned, he says, how Creeley's "principle can be made so to shape the energies that the form is accomplished. And I think it can be boiled down to one statement (first pounded into my head by Edward Dahlberg): ONE PERCEPTION MUST IMMEDIATELY AND DIRECTLY LEAD TO A FURTHER PERCEPTION."[2] Again, Olson only touches here upon a significant aspect of his actual practice as a poet, for it was in the severe discipline of this kind of progression, from one clarifying assertion to the next, that he achieved the peculiar abrupt momentum that characterizes his best short poems. Dahlberg's influences on Olson are complex; the two writers had formed a close relationship that was reluctantly ended in the 1950s following a misunderstanding over a review Olson was never able to write for Dahlberg.

But it is clear that Dahlberg's communitarian ideals are one of the important formative influences in Olson's own ideology of the *polis*, or the return to communal living. Letters from Dahlberg to Olson that survive in the University of Texas archives strongly suggest the teaching role Dahlberg played at the time and Olson's seeming readiness to become the pupil of any man he thought had attained some mastery of his art.[3] Clearly Dahlberg's help in paring down a voluminous and shapeless critical study, warmed over in part from a master's thesis, to a lean and scintillating theoretical statement impressed Olson greatly. Just as the prose he was to write thereafter is of a severely abbreviated nature, the areas of his poems where the argument is carried forward have a dizzying quality about them, as they race ahead of the reader's speed of comprehension, widening, molding, extending the attention by quick, jerky steps in perception. Of all the practices Olson resorted to in making his poetic, this is by far the subtlest and most compelling and the one that defines the most striking modality of his finest poems.

The influences Williams and Pound had on Olson's essay are at once more pervasive and more diffuse; their ideas on poetry are inextricable from the tenor and attitude of Olson's remarks. Although Olson was harshly critical of the deficiencies he found in these poets and had several times urged Cid Corman to keep "masters" out of *Origin*, his work is a direct extension of their own.[4]

It is difficult to sort out the ideas of these two men as they came down to Olson. M. L. Rosenthal, in his introduction to *The William Carlos Williams Reader* (pp. xx–xxi), comments that

> Pound exerted a tremendous influence [on Williams] from the start, though in part this influence generated a movement in poetry directly opposed to his own conceptions. The first thing Williams's preface to the *Selected Essays* tells us, for instance, is how he came to know Pound. And if we glance, however idly, through the pages of that collection of essays and reviews, we can hardly help noting the many reminders of Pound and his passions.
>   . . . In both writers, too, an attack on the main direction of American society goes together with a radical rejection of modern economic practices and a call for a violent breakthrough of human creativity. Williams's insertion of a Social-Credit propaganda leaflet in the poem *Paterson* and his portrait of Poe striving desperately to originate a truly American poetry amid the corruption and imitativeness of the national drift are two obvious examples among many of this identity or at least overlap of attitudes. Certainly Williams and Pound are at one in a driving conviction,

evangelical in nature, that man's best possibilities, brutally subverted and driven underground, must be brought to the surface
through a freeing of pagan impulses—a "revelation" which is
also a moral and cultural revolution. . . .

But when Olson discusses the kinetic properties of the poem, the basis
of this idea is from Williams, even though Pound had dealt with this
subject in some detail in editing Fenollosa's book *The Chinese Written
Character as a Medium for Poetry.* The idea of a kinetic prosody, involving aspects of relativity theory, occupied Williams more and more
toward the end of his life, at a time when Olson and those of his circle
were consciously identifying themselves with his general approach to
poetry. Olson refers to projective poetry as a "COMPOSITION BY
FIELD" and describes the kinetic properties of the poem as a transfer
of energy from "where the poet got it," the world around him, his own
organism, "by way of the poem itself to, all the way over to, the reader."[5]

Field composition, he writes, is a method by which the poet ventures
into the act of making a poem by allowing the content to suggest its
own formal destiny: "He can go by no track other than the one the
poem under hand declares, for itself." In a brief note on prosody, "A
Foot is to Kick With," published in 1956, Olson stresses the formative
will of the materials in his comical image of the poet who is rushed
headlong by the poem as it is being written:

> You wave the first word. And the whole thing follows. But—You
> follow it. With a dog at your heels, a crocodile about to eat you
> at the end, and you with your pack on your back trying to catch
> a butterfly.[6]

In 1948, two years before the appearance of "Projective Verse," Williams gave his well-known talk "The Poem as a Field of Action" at the
University of Washington, in which he expressed his sense of a new
prosody about to transform contemporary poetics. This feeling, he says,
"is similar to what must have been the early feelings of Einstein toward
the laws of Isaac Newton in physics. Thus from being fixed, our pro-
sodic values should rightly be seen as only relatively true."[7]

Williams' concept of the "variable foot" and his later poetry, especially in *Paterson,* which emphasized the restless movements of the poet's
consciousness, derive in part from a long familiarity with the writings
of the scientist-philosopher Alfred North Whitehead. Mike Weaver has
observed in *William Carlos Williams: The American Background* (p.
54) that among the poets included in *An "Objectivists" Anthology,*
which Louis Zukofsky edited in 1932, "only Williams had a first-hand

knowledge of Whitehead's" terminology. Williams was introduced to Whitehead's theories through John Riordan, an engineer interested in literature, who actively sought out principles common to art and science. He encouraged Williams to read scientific literature, but Williams was apparently uncomfortable among the grandly abstract designs of Whitehead's thinking; he read only what Riordan suggested to him and evidently did not go on to Whitehead's *Process and Reality*, as did Olson. Williams took from Whitehead what he thought was practical for poetry, amounting to a theory of perception which recognized the unavoidable distortions of linear thinking and called for cognizance of the object through multiple perspectives.

Whitehead had made him aware of the dynamic quality of reality and of the need to approach it from various vantage points if the object were to be precisely, vividly rendered. As Weaver observed, Whitehead's chief contribution to cognition in modern thought is that he introduced the organic properties of the observer who attempted to measure his world. Indeed, it might be said of art in the twentieth century that it has chiefly tried to explore the nature of the organic consciousness which nineteenth-century thought bequeathed to it.

In probing what was organic in the thinking process, Williams came to emphasize the physical influences on consciousness to the extent that in Book II of *Paterson* the walking observer in the park takes his thought from the rhythm of his paces; the coordination of the musculature engages the thinking mind as well. Weaver (p. 206) cites a number of relevant passages from Beckett Howorth's "Dynamic Posture," an article on walking as a "way of life," from which Williams quotes in one passage of Book II. The newly defined organic processes of thought constitute for Williams what he calls elsewhere in Book II the "new mind," from which he expects great advances in poetic technique:

> Without invention nothing is well spaced,
> unless the mind change, unless
> the stars are new measured, according
> to their relative positions, the
> line will not change, the necessity
> will not matriculate: unless there is
> a new mind there cannot be a new
> line, the old will go on
> repeating itself with recurring
> deadliness. . . . (p. 50)

The excitement of this passage, which appeared in 1948, carries over to his argument in "The Poem as a Field of Action," which urged an identical demand. Two years later, Olson would begin "The Kingfishers" with a similar exclamation: "What does not change / is the will to change," hailing, among other things, the rise of Mao and the transformation of Chinese society from a static hierarchy to the flux of a new social system.

Williams' poetic conceived of the minimum of artifice; the technical simplicity of his earlier lyrics and even the more ambitious first books of *Paterson* gave other poets little to learn in the way of a new grammar for poetry, except for the notational style of his early lyrics. In spite of his reluctance to discuss philosophy, it is essentially Williams' philosophical orientation to experience, brought over to his poetry and articulated in his critical prose, that constitutes his primary influence on others. It is that general aspect of Williams' thinking that pervades Olson's essay—the emphasis on the real, the reifying powers of language, the integrity of individual particles within the embracing form of the whole poem.

Pound's preoccupation, on the other hand, is very nearly the reverse of Williams'; he rarely addressed the philosophical question of the nature of art without speaking through another authority, as in his edition of the Ernest Fenollosa manuscript, but he was confident and voluminous in his remarks on the technical implications of a poetic of direct perception. His preference for Confucianism, with its emphasis on practicality, over Taoism, an austerely conceptual branch of Chinese thought, also reveals his pragmatic mind even in these remote reaches.

When Olson began seeing Pound at St. Elizabeths Hospital in the late 1940s, it was to learn technique from the master. Pound left no record of his conversations, and Olson's scant memoirs of this period seem almost entirely to be taken up with Pound's outrageous attitudes, especially his anti-Semitism. It would seem from the various journal entries he made at the time that Olson did not find Pound personally helpful as a teacher of poetry. Olson's knowledge of Pound in 1950 derives chiefly from his reading of published works and not from his personal acquaintance with Pound several years before.

Much of what Olson knew of Pound goes back to the boisterous, halcyon days of the late teens and early 1920s, when Pound held international court and reigned sole arbiter of what was new in poetry. *Guide to Kulchur* (1938) is partly a summation of his thought in that breezy period of his life. It is speculation, of course, but it is possible that, in his visits to St. Elizabeths, Olson found it difficult to coax out of Pound ideas and concepts of poetry he had not seriously discussed since turning his attention in the early 1930s to economic theories.

The 1930s were years in which Pound began repeating himself in his criticism, depending on earlier writings to give substance to such otherwise breezy books as *The ABC of Reading* (1934), a doctrinaire manual on reading and writing that reupholsters the more concise "How to Read" of 1928. But as Hugh Kenner has shown in "Part Three" of *The Pound Era*, it was in the 1930s that Pound put an end to self-conscious poetic technique and took up a new subject: the economic dilemma of monopoly capitalism. If Pound's critical acumen seems blunted in these years prior to the war, his poetry appeared to gain in intensity of speech and control of theme. *The Fifth Decad of Cantos XLII–LI* (1937) introduced the abuses of usury; there followed *Cantos LII–LXXI* (1940), in which the roots of civilization and its general decay through usury are traced; then came *The Pisan Cantos LXXIV–LXXXIV* (1948), culminating with memories and desires of a solitary captive figure lamenting the fall of man from grace: "As a lone ant from a broken anthill / from the wreckage of Europe, ego scriptor" (Canto LXXVI).

The Pisan Cantos are among Pound's most personal and revealing poems; the self that contemplates the guard towers and endures the wind and rain of the Pisan autumn is the compelling force of this whole section. For a poet in search of craft, Olson found a master who had finally made poetic rules and principles part of his nature.

At the time and under the circumstances of having just finished *The Pisan Cantos*, Pound was in a position to offer the "self" he had so masterfully portrayed: a creature of thought who was more lifelike and interesting, more imposing in his ideology and passions, than the lonely, more modestly proportioned creature who broods in *Paterson*. This Poundian self appears to be what Olson finally accepted as a lesson in poetry; practically everything he wrote afterward, in spite of the misunderstanding that grew between the two poets, groped toward the creation of a self equal to the master's.[8]

In *The Pisan Cantos*, the most noticeable feature of the persona is his consciousness, which expands and contracts in a slow and stately rhythm, appropriate to the thought itself. At first the persona is aware of the packing crate on which he composes his lines, an immediacy which his thought overflows until mind and world appear to be without boundaries; at that point we are shunted into a new contraction, a sudden awareness of the billowing tent flaps as the sun sets, from which the mind then overflows its bounds and unites once more with the world at large.[9]

This figure at the center of *The Pisan Cantos* was a direct link with and, more crucially, a modern instance of what Olson had just been exploring in *Call Me Ishmael*: the open self, postindividual man. The line of thought from Melville to Pound was direct, or so it seemed to Olson, who sought to draw the line further through himself. The fact that Pound liked *Call Me Ishmael* and aided in getting it published must have further confirmed Olson's sense of a connection between himself and Pound.

Melville's Ishmael also transcended his own subjectivity as he reached out in thought to understand that which confronted and surrounded him; his vision at the end of the novel, according to Olson, is of a world of relatedness. Pound's Pisan self also reaches out beyond the guard towers, and although the dream of relatedness endures, he speaks through suffering and a sense of immediate defeat: "Les larmes que j'ai creées [sic] m'inondent / Tard, très tard je t'ai connue, la Tristesse" (Canto LXXX). The similarities are implicit, for both Ishmael and the Pisan captive look outward through the wreckage of a civilization. Ishmael swims among the battered remains of the *Pequod*, that microcosm of a capitalist society, while Pound's persona regards the rubble of capitalist Europe following the Second World War:

> [Only shadows enter my tent
>   as men pass between me and the sunset,]
> beyond the eastern barbed wire
>   a sow with nine boneen
> matronly as any duchess at Claridge's (Canto LXXX)

The first part of Olson's "Projective Verse" essay is really a composite of all available means for freeing verse from tradition, in order to make the concept of the open self the cardinal principle of composition. The open self is what constitutes "open poetry." And because the poet's sensibilities form the substratum of this projected self in the poems, the means are chiefly those which aid in the direct transcription of the poet's mental processes and physiological responsiveness to thought.

The slow and elegant rhythms of *The Pisan Cantos* suggested how rhythm itself was integral to the poetic act, but Pound had not gone far enough when in 1912 he wrote, "As regarding rhythm: to compose in the sequence of the musical phrase, not in the sequence of a metronome."[10] Several years later, he added, "A man's rhythm must be interpretative, it will be, therefore, in the end, his own, uncounterfeiting, uncounterfeitable."[11] Olson wanted to stress more than a break with set metrical convention; instead of asking for the musical phrase, he argued that the breathing of a poet is the rhythm of the line, determining at once the pace of the words themselves and the length of the lines. The breath is the formal determinant of the poem; the configuration of the poem is a function of the poet's response to his own content:

> And the line comes (I swear it) from the breath, from the breathing of the man who writes at the moment that he writes, and thus is, it is here that, the daily work, the WORK, gets in, for only he, the man who writes, can declare, at every moment, the line its metric and its ending—where its breathing, shall come to, termination.[12]

If breath is the new principle that liberates poetry from set meters, the sounds of language free the poem from the strict conventions of syntax and logic. Olson's comments on sound and on composition by syllable derive from some remarks Pound made in "How to Read." In his anatomy of the three kinds of poetry, Pound defines *logopoeia* as " 'the dance of the intellect among words' "; instead of the poet's obeying the conventional arrangement of certain words and phrases, he freely experiments with their sound and semantic potential by throwing them into fresh and different contexts. By this means, Pound says, the poet communicates an esthetic experience specific to language alone.[13]

In "Projective Verse," Olson stresses this point to the extent that he sees all poetry as logopoetic. The primary event of the poetic act is the emergence of the syllable. The flow of syllables, the choice the poet makes of them, even as they violate the conventions of language, directly records the poet's unique mental processes, just as his breathing records the mood and passion of his thought:

> I am dogmatic, that the head shows in the syllable. The dance of the intellect is there, among them, prose or verse. Consider the best minds you know in this here business: where does the head show, is it not, precise, here, in the swift currents of the syllable? can't you tell a brain when you see what it does, just there? It is true, what the master says he picked up from Confusion: all the thots [sic] men are capable of can be entered on the back of a postage stamp. So, is it not the PLAY of a mind we are after, is not that that shows whether a mind is there at all?[14]

The master he refers to above is Pound, who did not take his comment from Confucius ("Confusion") but from T. E. Hulme.[15]

Olson's critics point out the many places where Pound has been an influence, as if this suggested a weakness on the part of the younger man.[16] His dependence may indeed have been slavish at times, but it is more accurate to say that Olson was among the first poets of the postwar period to reject Eliot and look to Pound for new directions. At first Olson followed Pound closely, even repeating Pound's peculiar neologisms and phrases and his tone and aggressive manner of putting things. His letters copy the Uncle Remus dialect that Pound so often used in his correspondence. All of this imitativeness is crude, but in spite of it Olson constructed a poetic that is a careful and intelligent synthesis of the best ideas of his immediate predecessors.

We can see this synthesizing process at work in the closing remarks of Part I of his essay, when he considers the use of the typewriter, still another instrument by which the boundaries of subject and object are transcended, since it is in the spacing and symbols of the typewriter that one has "the personal and instantaneous recorder of the poet's work."[17] The use of the typewriter as a technique in itself derives from tradition immediately prior to Olson:

> It is time we picked the fruits of the experiments of Cummings,
> Pound, Williams, each of whom has, after his way, already used
> the machine as a scoring to his composing, as a script to its
> vocalization. It is now only a matter of the recognition of the
> conventions of composition by field for us to bring into being an
> open verse as formal as the closed, with all its traditional
> advantages.[18]

The first part of the essay is closely organized around this central concern: to find the available means by which poetry might present the self's excursions into the world, as it immerses its subjectivity in all that impinges upon it from without.

To that end, Pound is by far the most useful source, but as we have seen, Olson's poetic welds together fragments of thought extending from Edward Dahlberg to Creeley, Cummings, and Williams.

It is a poetic of transference, in that the self, opening outward, re-enacts that opening process in the poem. For this reason, Part I necessarily leads to the larger question of what the self is opening toward. Part II sketches in briefly the doctrine of objectism, the "stance" toward reality in which the self is willingly drawn into the infinite diversity of things. The two parts directly complement each other.

But, more importantly, the elements that make up the essay, regardless of their source, create a poetic that is uniquely Olson's; his deliberate selectiveness from the tradition of twentieth-century poetry expresses his own conception of poetry as the reenactment of the total process by which an individual exercises understanding.

In *Ezra Pound: A Close Up* (p. 87), Michael Reck recalls, "About Olson Pound would only say irritatedly that he was concerned with abstractions, not with verse (probably referring to Olson's theoretical essays about poetry)." Pound may have been irritated at the way in which Olson stressed psychological and epistemological issues exclusively, but these were the working principles of his conception of poetry. Faithfully and comprehensively to reenact a moment of epiphany required mastery of physical and mental functions, as they responded to and participated in the perceptual event.

In a brief 1959 letter to Elaine Feinstein, Olson responded to some basic questions she had asked regarding further developments in his poetic. The letter, usually printed as a sequel to "Projective Verse," is the only other place in his prose where Olson expressly addressed himself to a new poetic, and in it he largely repeated his earlier ideas. But toward the close of the letter, he elaborated on points that have exclusively to do with the conditions in which the individual confronts his world and struggles to understand it. The world, he observed, is the Muse; and life, or what the subject holds as his share of experience, he calls the Psyche. They are represented in the letter in a mathematical relationship to each other:

$$\text{At the moment it comes out} \quad \frac{\text{the Muse ("world"}}{\text{the Psyche (the "life"}^{19}}$$

The "life" draws its data from the "world" in three conditions: the topos, or place, meaning the material actuality; typos, or the peculiar and unique constitution of the subject (his manner, style, personality, and so forth); and tropos, the real constant of the three, referring to the totality of what one can know of the particular actuality one is confronted with. Hence, experience or, more pertinently, the poem is achieved by the uniquely constituted subject facing the actual and taking in some approximation of the real fullness of data the actual contains. It is a simple epistemological scheme, and it adds nothing to the discipline in the way of innovative concepts; it merely confirms the fact that Olson took poetry to mean the enactment of learning, some luxuriously elaborate re-creation of excitement, as a man gropes his way to an ecstatic perception about himself or—which amounts to the same thing for Olson—about the world that surrounds that self.

If the poem could do that well, by making consciousness that highest of all pleasures, he felt that the reader would look for that understanding in himself and would renounce those social forces that repressed or denied this keenness of sensory and intellectual functions.

The Poetry

When George Butterick and Albert Glover collaborated on a comprehensive edition of Olson's short poems, entitled *Archaeologist of Morning*, they amassed 105 poems. Their task was essentially one of recovery, for the great majority of the poems had been placed in journals that had sprung up, like so many wild flowers, in answer to the various movements that lived and died in the ferment of the 1950s and 1960s. Most of these journals have long since disappeared; indeed, a good number of them existed for only a single issue and expired. But clearly Olson preferred these experimental, wide-open journals to more established publications, partly because they were on the social fringe and struggled against a common adversary, the alien culture of postwar America. It was inevitable and even necessary, perhaps, that they should live only briefly: they hailed a reality of change in a time when permanence and legitimacy meant connection with the Establishment.

Also, it is unlikely that many of the more traditional literary magazines would have published Olson's mature work, which seemed to violate simultaneously all the recognized conventions of poetic discourse. The appearance of an Olson poem is striking in itself: lines and words are scattered over the available space, arranged so loosely in places that they seem to have been randomly dropped onto the page. And this is precisely the intention: to arrange type in such a way as to work deliberately against the appearance of the conventional poem, with its column of type page-centered, and the strict order of capitalized words initiating each line. These conventions expressed a neatness and premeditation in keeping with a culture that had rejected the creative disarray of consciousness.

Every departure from convention in a typical Olson poem is part of a general desire to make the poem a sensitive transcript of the creative moment. The more the poem faithfully reflects what has occurred in the interior of the poet, even to the various influences on his thought that his organism, neural and muscular, might have at the time, the more the act of the poem succeeds in breaking down the barriers between subject and object.

The poet and his poem are one thing in that the poem is a fact of his total responsiveness, integral and unmodified; it is a precise projection onto paper, through the means of language and typography, of the poet's surfaces of awareness.[20]

Olson's poetry also departed from the laws of punctuation and standard American grammar, although not so rigorously or consistently as it did in line arrangement. Here, too, the intention is to punctuate only as the rhythm of the thought may require. His punctuation obeys the laws of the breath, and where the comma pause is of insufficient duration, there are other means for prolonging silence: by the slash, which calls for a slightly longer pause than does the comma, or by the simple means of separating words by uncommon space, which the eye must deliberately span. The pause can be made long or short by the length of separation between words and phrases and is thus a scoring device for the poet, who can indicate by the length of the space the degree of hesitation, indecision, or gripping emotion taking place in the speaker before he can go on with his thoughts. Although these seem to be merely empty spaces on the page, the poet can manipulate them as signals of response in his persona and even direct special emphasis to the words that abruptly end these varying pauses, simply because they issue at what might seem to be difficult junctures of the expression. Clearly, some of the more dramatic moments of Olson's poems occur just where a pause has suspended all argument until his persona can resume once more and even redirect his thought entirely.

The structure of Olson's English is not in open rebellion against all the basic laws of grammar, only the simple declarative sentence. The reader who first opens Olson is perplexed and annoyed by the way in which his lines imply statements and yet withhold their full sense. The obscurity is partly the result of the sentence structure itself, which surrounds subject, predicate, and object with dense verbal constellations that impede the basic elements from conveying an idea smoothly. The function of this impediment is to make the sentence a vehicle of consciousness, and not linear data.

Under careful scrutiny, the informing content of his sentence finally yields itself, but it comes to the reader embedded in a texture of neighboring thoughts. The sentence is rendered up with its parts intact, but with the tendrils of other thoughts and the rush of new associations clinging to it. As he remarked in the late poem "These Days,"

> whatever you have to say, leave
> the roots on, let them
> dangle

      And the dirt
            just to make clear
            where they came from[21]

In sentence structure as well, then, we can see a departure from convention in pursuit of an unmediated expression of the poet's consciousness. An example, found at random, comes from his sequence "West":

      . . . *There isn't* (after the small
      incitement of the scene those yards
      was it almost out from the Fort on
      Bozeman's gold road) *any longer,*
      thereafter, a connection to agricultural
      time. (AM, p. 198)

My italicized words make up the core sentence; the parenthetical material is a sudden interjection of correlative ideas. The sense of the
whole passage comes when the two are combined, showing that, with
the close of the Indian massacres, a Western agrarian culture ceased,
and the rush for gold began at Bozeman's Pass. In place of the rhythm
of sowing and harvesting came the grinding work schedules of a capitalist structure: "There isn't any longer, thereafter, a connection to agricultural time."

By itself, the sentence is linear and yields up only a small quantity of
information. The addition of the parenthetical material shows a pause
in which the mind rushes through a series of images before the general
assertion of the sentence cancels that momentary preoccupation.

If the progress of a simple sentence can be thought of as "vertical,"
with a beginning, middle, and end, then Olson's modified sentence
structure adds to this "vertical" movement many "lateral" excursions
without making an actual detour in direction. This "lateral" sentence
structuring also appears frequently in his prose.

But the most obvious characteristic of the projective poem is its unusual sprawling of words and strophes. Olson had already mentioned in
his "Projective Verse" essay the use to be made of Cummings' freer
typographical arrangements for the scoring of the poet's voice. Pauses
and rushes of thought could be indicated through the spacing of words
and lines over the page. But there is another and deeper intention at
work in the arrangement of words in many of Olson's best poems which
I will call semantic spacing. The drafts of many of his poems show that
he worked very carefully on the exact position of his words, often re-
ordering them in succeeding drafts before settling on a final form. The

positioning of strophes and lines in this fashion has little bearing on
vocal modulation or rhythm; rather, he was sorting his words according
to meaning and, quite possibly, according to the thinking process itself.
Creeley had noted much the same strategy in Olson's correspondence, as
he remarks in an interview:

> But you realize that it's all happening visually as well as intel-
> lectually or mentally. Olson, in his letters . . . you begin to realize
> Olson's spacing, the ordering of where things occur in his thought.
> He'll begin a letter like, "dear so and so," and then start with the
> information, and before he's, say, halfway through the page you've
> got these things jumping all around . . . the movement, is moving,
> trying to locate, like, let's put that there . . . no don't, now this
> goes here, oh but you can forget that . . . but you can't forget
> this too . . . you can't put them like that, because it's a lie, they
> don't exist that way, you've got to . . . He's trying in effect to give
> the *orders* of thought—in no pretentious sense—and a typewriter
> for him, for example, is something that has much defined his
> habits of writing, as he said himself in "Projective Verse."[22]

In other words, the shapes and clusters are the scoring of the poet's
thought. The ideas evolve and merge with other ideas through the "motion" of the scatterings and strophes of the language. We can look at
the projective poem and discern the process of the poet's preoccupations,
how each suddenly takes hold of the poet's attention, holds it for a moment, and then spends itself in the halting emergence of other ideas and
perceptions.

The projective poem has visual impact on the reader: one can glance
at the overall shape of the poem to be read and know with some accuracy whether the thinking is turbulent and difficult or meditative and
evenly paced. The method of "scoring" thought in Olson's poems and
those of other projectivists involves relatively few principles, but they
provide the poet with a dimension of expressiveness that is nearly limitless in its subtlety and nuance.

There are really two axes on the page to which the projective poem
is oriented. The first or horizontal axis, running from left margin to
right, marks the range of the poet's thought from objective utterance to
haziest reverie. The left side of the page is the point of origin of any
thought, and the language we find there is characterized by concrete-
ness, precision of observation, qualified judgment, factitude. It is the
language of the beginning of thought, when other processes of mind
are not involved in the ideation emerging. It is the articulation of im-

minent consciousness, when impingement is more attended to than the self that has been aroused to think. Language that darts or slowly moves toward the right margin becomes increasingly subjective and oriented to the interior processes of the self. In fact, this axis terminates in the recesses of awareness, where memory and dream, fantasy and inarticulate feeling merge and hover at the edge of speech.

The language that forms horizontally in this way shows us awareness as activity; the poet's thought is moving toward the ineffable. Premises dissolve along this axis and give way to a superlogical discourse; there is about this language a sense of the timeless; mind contemplates without having to shape conclusions from its uninhibited excursion into the self's recesses. The axis moves from the categorical faculty to that reservoir of sense where experience is a nameless entanglement. The line of poetry may be said to originate in the known and then to proceed into the self toward an unknowable substrate of life.

If the poem were to be written solely along this axis, there would be only an excursion into increasing disorder. No argument would form; no event would terminate; there would be only the preoccupation of the poet with the undirected activity of his consciousness. But neither Olson nor any other poet working in open forms has allowed the poem to develop along this axis for very long. The excursion into the self's interior is brief; the axis is continually being destroyed and reinstituted during the movement of the open poem.

The vertical axis is the complement of the horizontal. When the poet terminates the lateral flow of his line and moves to the next line, to begin again, a subtle transformation has occurred in the process of the poem: the horizontal axis has died into its dialectic complement, the vertical, along which plane the poem is continuously moving from start to end. Here the sense of time process is everywhere eminent; argument and event are the products of the vertical. Ideas begin and end as the poem moves down the page; they are suspended when the poem swells and pushes to the right.

For the most part, then, the poem occurs in the middle ranges of both axes; the poem is centered among all of its potential limits, centered in awareness, centered in time. But every poem is eccentric to a fixed center; it wobbles on this pivot. Its eccentric configuration is the pattern of the poet's awareness, his unique signature upon language.

Even the closed poem is a wobbling form. The sonnet, with its ribbon of rime words at the right edge, its unrimed capitals at the left, wobbles tightly around its own fixed center. It too is oriented to the axes I have described; the difference between the closed and the open poem may be

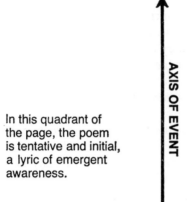

beginning

AXIS OF EVENT

In this quadrant of
the page, the poem
is tentative and initial,
a lyric of emergent
awareness.

The reach toward the
nameless and indefin-
able occurs as the
lines sweep toward
the right margin.

objectivity   **AXIS OF THOUGHT**   **subjectivity**

Here the poem passes
through the interven-
ing stages of idea and
argument in its prog-
ress toward fulfillment
in language. The left-
hand side of the page
continues to be domi-
nated by sensory ex-
perience, analysis,
etc.

In this quadrant the
poet may either leap
to final synthesis from
the revelations of his
aroused subjectivity or
halt at some impasse
and cease his inquiry.
Or, if he has resolved
his argument, he may
center his final words
on the axis of event.

end

seen most clearly in the light of these axes: the open poem reaches after the extremes of the poem's limits and fights the pivot it depends upon; the configuration of its speech is bolder, more wildly strewn around its center; the poet's awareness is allowed to register itself in language with fewer restraints, fewer demands for symmetry and compactness of form.

But the argument about poetic axes is speculative; it depends mainly upon the evidence of Olson's poems, for there is little or nothing to support it in his essays, letters, or notations. In 1966, he added a note to his *Selected Writings*, suggesting the idea of axes: "The lines which hook-over should be read as though they lay out right and flat to the horizon or Eternity" (p. 158). A curious notation, it means nothing unless we ascribe a particular significance to the direction of the line. He was also silent on the technique of spacing in the open poem, remarking only that the typewriter was convenient to the poet for vocal scoring. The frequent charge that the open poem was visually obscure, a chaos of verbal fragments, goes without answer from him. The premise of axes should, however, point out one way in which to regard the open poem as visually coherent, even visually expressive of its content.

Finally, we should note that the page itself, with these axes always active upon the surface, is forever the potential poem. A word placed anywhere can be seen to have a meaning merely by its location on the page. There is an almost limitless subtlety of connotation, then, in verbal location; Olson and other projective poets seized its use and experimented widely in its expressive possibilities. Lines and fragments are made to begin anywhere along the horizontal axis; other poems rush to termination by leaping down the page, leaving enormous gaps of unwritten space at the center. Olson experimented with placing two or three words at the center of the page, as if to test the power of the page to function as the rest of the poem. The page *is* the rest of the poem when we acknowledge these semantic axes.

Taken together, these various techniques of Olson's poetry constitute the means for an open form of verse. Olson so boldly exploited their potential that certain of their implicit limitations became vividly manifest.

These techniques of the poet take us below the level of artifice to that stratum of creativity where the workings of the mind are "unedited," unarranged. When that becomes the realm in which the art work is fashioned, where no intervening force is allowed to draw off the unessential and fragmentary, the work ceases to be distinguished by recognizable signs of craft and takes on some of the quality of drabness of ordinary reality.

The open poem is so faithful a transcription of mentality that it includes in its form the uninspired as well as the moments of dazzling clarity; the trivial takes its place alongside the crucial. Like a tapped telephone conversation, the poem passively reveals the minutiate of insignificant mental and emotional detail, often to a point of dullness. If the mind of the poet is not fixed intensely by a compelling idea, the scattering of energy leaves the poem limp and shapeless with trivial excess.

It is in how the open poem can fail that one begins to understand how it can also succeed, a line of speculation which Olson continually worked at and refined in the years following the publication of "Projective Verse." The open poem fails as the poet's responsiveness fails to be intense. The trivial and dull are those fragments of experience which have yet to be given their vital place in the order of experience; the poet of trivial utterance is one who has failed to perceive in the objects of his thought the compelling connections which they enjoy in secret, unknown to him.

If the poet is in the ecstasy of perception, in which his whole organism participates, and he does not compose the poem from all these various centers of feeling and thought, then the poem will project just this inertia of the spirit and fail as a work of art. Olson saw the poem as a social force, a way of arousing a torpid populace to seek their own freedom—by its thrilling display of the reaches of consciousness in just these moments of intense awareness.[23]

As Olson became convinced that the success of the open poem lay in its being a model of expanded consciousness, he gradually abandoned interest in those other features of his original poetic: the emphases of breath and ear on the generation of lines and syllables in the poem. In fact, in the second triad of the *Maximus*, these vestiges of artifice, the play of sound and the rhythms of line length, disappear altogether.

After "The Kingfishers," Olson's poetry slowly tends toward a poetic of pure perception. By the second triad of the *Maximus* poems, he is writing a kind of poetry held together mainly by his desire to find out connections among his ever-widening thoughts. Instead of pursuing strategies which would reenact in words the processes of consciousness, the poems now seek to note essential ideas in the leap to a larger vision of Gloucester and Dogtown. The language is no longer lyrical and luxurious with sound but often abrupt and specific; the words distill a thought and knit it to his other thoughts in the effort to synthesize the available historic data and other facts accumulated thus far. But this process of tying together the gists and piths of his knowledge is taken up intermittently. It is another of the means of knowing he pursues, but it is not raised to the status of an end in itself. Other poems simply repeat the facts as he finds them or are reprints of fragments and even whole documents he discovers in his research. In other words, Olson's poetic techniques have evolved to such an extent in this sequence that it may no longer be appropriate to call these various jottings poems. They are the prosaic bits and pieces of a longer work that is turning them into a poem. There was, of course, an effort to shape some of these poems of pure inquiry, especially in the *Maximus* poems, where a definite formal procedure is at work controlling the progress of the initial books.

Even as early as "The Kingfishers," however, Olson was employing certain devices in his poetry which are directly related to making the poem of self-discovery compelling and dramatic. The most important of these techniques is suspense, that traditional means of the fiction writer for sustaining curiosity. Olson casts the self of his best poems into the role of an inquirer faced with the disorganized evidence of human history: in most cases, the ruins of burial places, military forts, or battlefields. It is on such sites and with the array of his whole consciousness brought to bear that he moves about a landscape of objects slowly discovering their whole significance. The reader is drawn into the search for meaning in these barren scenes and is satisfied when the persona achieves a revelation of what the scene symbolizes.

But this suspense is enriched by the nature of the speaker's thought; we travel with him through his different inquiries into experience, and as we are borne forward we are given the seemingly unedited transcriptions of his passing thoughts, where even the most private knowledge comes to us tangled in his revelations and arguments. His thoughts may turn without warning to utterly private associations and recollections, data we cannot possibly unravel on our own. For many passages of the *Maximus* sequence, Butterick's dissertation notes that Olson had dreamed the incident in question, had overheard the comment while eating lunch, had thought he had read the item somewhere, and in some instances even Olson could not recall the sources for certain lines or situations of his poems. Even so, and admitting this fullness of thought can utterly fail to work at times, the frankly intimate expression of the speaker conveys to the poetry an uncanny sense of reality, where the reader is raptly enmeshed in the speaker's affairs and is made an active listener intently sorting what he needs to know from the drift of a rich and constant flow of discourse.

In *Call Me Ishmael*, Olson had already expressed his interest in the inquirer-figures he found in Melville. Both Bulkington, the quiet contemplator of the open sea, and Ishmael, who absorbed much detail of life aboard the *Pequod*, are judged superior among the crew. But Pound's persona in *The Pisan Cantos* serves more directly as the model for the various selves that act in Olson's poems. The solitary captive of the Pisan detention camp, reaching outward with the force of his own synthetic musings, becomes the paradigm of alienated man longing for transcendence.

Both poets create the estranged hero of the postromantic tradition.[24] And the Pisan persona is clearly Olson's starting point as a serious poet; his earliest poetry is an attempt to repeat the rhythmic contraction and expansion of attention that is so masterfully executed by Pound.

But his own development as a poet drove him further and further from imitation of Pound's style. Olson's largest objection to the Pisan figure is that he contemplates the world passively, forcing the facts of his experience to a common center, toward what Olson called "the beak of his ego."[25]

Olson's persona is deliberately active, in hot pursuit of explanation, a Herodotean figure whose methodology is that of " '*istorin*," "what you find out for yrself."[26] Olson's projected figure is that of cosmic detective, whose clues are the world itself and whose ultimate mystery is the nature of humankind. The difference between the two personae is one of stance: the Pisan self is enlightened and teaches its reader; Olson's figure teaches himself, and the reader listens in, as in the following extracts:

> Gee, what I call the upper road was the way
> leading by Joshua Elwell's to the wood-lots
> 1727
>
> and Cherry or the lower road was, 1725, the way that
> leads from the town to Smallmans now Dwelling house[27]
>
> I have had to learn the simplest things
> last. Which made for difficulties.
> Even at sea I was slow, to get the hand out, or to cross
> a wet deck.
>   The sea was not, finally, my trade.
> But even my trade, at it, I stood estranged
> from that which was most familiar. Was delayed,
> and not content with the man's argument
> that such postponement
> is now the nature of
> obedience,
>   that we are all late

in a slow time,
that we grow up many
And the single
is not easily
known[28]

Again, although Olson's persona is another village explainer, his learning is not encyclopedic and general but specialized and exhaustive in only certain categories. To a great extent, however, like Pound's persona, he knows of the world what he has taken from the printed word. This may be a limitation of all such personae of modern poetry, that they are heroes of the library who struggle with a world that has been filtered through the pages of printed texts. Olson's persona utters the fragments of scattered historical reading as he pieces together an idea or follows a line of theorizing toward a historical pattern.

Yet even the general goals of both personae are to some degree different. Pound's persona tries to fashion a coherent culture from his hoard of political fragments taken from history, in some of which we glimpse a fleeting moment of enlightened authority: the wisdom of a ruler, the cultivated mind of a powerful patron, the sophistication of a certain aristocracy. These images reflect the possibility of perfect rule, and the persona recollects them in the process of musing upon the condition of his own civilization. His own political ideal is not abstract; it is suggested by these various images of superior conduct by the powerful. The problem for Pound's persona is to gather such images into a form, to infer the right law from their evidence. The process of establishing a pattern of order from these many instances is endless and ultimately inconclusive, to judge from the course of *The Cantos*. At best, only a tentative and somewhat hazy political ideal emerges from these meditations, a social order based largely on preindustrial values, possibly even on a pastoral model in which the poet is esteemed by the ruler and where the perfection of one's craft is its own sufficient end. The persona seems to have dreamed of a society that agreed to pursue its own perfection and not barter away any of its achievements for the abstract reward of money.

Olson's persona does not look to history for salvageable elements with which to fashion a social ideal; the past is a realm of lived circumstance which has no other use than to reveal the exact nature of the present. History can enlarge one's consciousness of the moment now passing, simply by accounting for the form of events through past processes. His interest in mythology lies chiefly in its revelations of the pattern of history; myths are paradigms of recurring events. The social ideal which the persona considers is not so much an order but a condition of persons. The *polis* so frequently mentioned in the poetry is actually a state of existence of persons who have, like Ishmael, become so absorbed with the experience of their own lives in reality that they have forgotten their individual egos. Olson's persona seems to believe that, once beyond the stage of mere individuality, a person is able to perceive the spirit in reality. The *polis* is a collective of eyes and ears; it is a group of persons whose senses are still separate but whose spirits have come together through their participation with the mystery of the real. In a very "lateral" sentence from *The Special View of History* (p. 26), he describes this state of human and earthly integrity:

> In the end, when all the estrangement is over, when the familiar
> is known, who isn't up against the face of God like a wall or a
> mirror where the shadow or the cut-out shape or the light is the
> reflection or the light or the figure of himself in species?

In other words, at the end of the process by which humanity will have come to know the real and thereby gained its lost integrity as a society, the face of God will be a mirror in which the individual will see himself inseparably bound to all others.

Olson's poetry is variously collected in seven books, four of which contain his short poems and the other three his long sequence, the *Maximus* poems. These two groups of poems represent two different directions in his career.

The short works, which I will describe first, served Olson as a medium for expressing a consciousness of the moment. They range from the briefest jottings of five or six lines to poems of considerable development, running to three or four pages. Olson's typical short poem strives to exhaust a preoccupation of consciousness, either by a dense lyrical statement uttered with great directness and concision or by approaching the same issue from a number of perspectives. These poems are such sensitive records that they act as a running commentary on the growth and changes of his mind.

Olson's first collection of poems, *Y & X*, appeared in 1948, three years after he had quit his political career in Washington. The five short poems included in it are a declaration of fierce independence from political life: "Let those who want to, chase a king" (AM, p. 12). One poem, "Trinacria," is self-consciously literary in its allusions to Greek mythology, but its program of militant activism is clear:

Who fights behind a shield
Is separate, weak of the world

.   .   .   .

There is a sword. If not so armed
A man will hide within himself
The armed man too, but battle
Is an outside thing, the field
Its own reward, reality (AM, p. 11)

These early poems are technically conventional, except for some minor innovative details, and their tone is derivative, in spite of Creeley's high praise of their originality.[29] In "The Green Man," the stridency of voice echoes vaguely some of Yeats' sonorities:

Of bitter work, and of folly
cockatrice and cockolloly
furiously sing! (AM, p. 12)

But in the context of this present study, the poems are interesting for their very lack of experiment and originality: they are the work of a man who has not yet been influenced by Pound's poetry. In another way, the condition of these first poems is an indication of the state of American poetry in the late 1940s. *Partisan Review* issued writers a questionnaire entitled "The State of American Writing, 1948: Seven Questions," and the general response to its first query, "What, in your opinion, are the new literary tendencies or figures, if any, that have emerged in the forties?" was that there were few or none in the making. John Berryman's answer articulates the view of many of the writers questioned:

It has been a bad decade so far. If the twenties were Eliot's decade, and the thirties Auden's, this has been simply the decade of Survival. Wider military operations, their prolongation, their involvement of civilians, above all the preceding and accompanying genocide, distinguish wholly this war from the last. Everybody lost years, and many seem to have lost their nerve. There is a political, perhaps a moral, paralysis. The one movement of interest has been foreign, existentialism, and shows little artistic effect in America. The chief cultural phenomenon of the decade here has probably been the intellectuals' desertion of Marxism. What they have replaced it with, I cannot discover; nihilism is more articulate and impressive than in any other period of which I have knowledge.[30]

In spite of this gloomy picture, many new poets were just then publishing their books of poems. The late 1940s marked the appearance of Robert Lowell and W. S. Merwin. More established poets such as Theodore Roethke, Richard Eberhart, and Karl Shapiro also published work in this decade. T. S. Eliot concluded *The Four Quartets*, and Wallace Stevens and Robert Penn Warren both were prolific in the postwar period. But the impact of this body of work did not register until succeeding years, and for a poet anxious to know the latest innovations of his craft, it was a frustrating time. Among the poets that especially influenced Olson only Williams had published a significant new work: the first book of *Paterson* appeared in 1946, two years before Pound's *The Pisan Cantos*. But it is likely that Olson did not read it until 1950, when he discussed the poem fairly frequently in his correspondence.

In 1953, five years after *Y & X*, Olson established himself as a new force in American poetry with his book *In Cold Hell, In Thicket*. He had originally selected the poems that would go into the collection but in the rush of other business turned the materials over to Robert Creeley, who edited and then produced the book on his own Divers Press. It was published as the eighth issue of *Origin*. Creeley deleted three of the original twenty-six poems and changed the order of many others. The difference is subtle but noticeable: Creeley's edition is smoother and more emphatic in theme, whereas Olson's plan called for a rougher, more jagged progression in which the network of themes was left more implicit and difficult. In a letter to Corman, Olson had outlined *In Cold Hell*, dividing it into three parts and giving each a prefatory poem; Creeley preserved this plan with only slight change.[31]

For all the spontaneity and exuberance of his language, Olson was unsparing in his attention to the structure and format of his books. The partitions of this work are no exceptions: the poems are grouped by theme and subject with delicate precision. "Section I," beginning with "La Préface" (which also opened *Y & X*), is concerned with what I shall here call "the struggle," in which the poet disentangles himself from influences that misguide and suppress him. "Section II" is prefaced by "La Chute" (by "Move Over" in Creeley's edition), in which the poet challenges his listeners to return his wooden lute and drum and thus the sound and rhythm of verse; and the other poems answer by claiming an essential subject for poetry: life under pressure of feeling and discovery. The last section is preceded by "The Leader," a stark picture of the poet destroyed by those he torments with his song. He dies at their hands bravely. The other poems likewise take up the subject of the poet's responsibilities and his proper stance toward experience. Thus the three parts unfold Olson's emergence as a poet: the opposition he must struggle against to find his own voice; a subject worthy of poetry; and, finally, the methods and stances he must perfect to be original.

"Section I," then, headed by "La Préface," describes the conditions of a new reality of both horror and change following the Second World War. The poem was inspired by the drawings of a GI who was among the first to enter Buchenwald and free the remaining survivors.[32] There are allusions to the lurid evidence of Nazi death camps, as well as leaps back to the Altamira cave paintings, symbols of both the obstacles to human existence and man's prevailing will to endure.

In this opening section is one of Olson's finest poems, "The Kingfishers," already described in the previous chapter but worth our considering anew from technical and thematic standpoints. The persona, modeled on the Pisan figure, faces an Aztec burial site and reads in its fragmentary remains a complex interwoven pattern of changes, which in themselves complete only a part of an unstated and larger cycle of events. The choice of setting is unusual in modern poetry in that Olson has prepared a detailed landscape made up of his reading in Mexican history and archeology; he would not see such burial mounds himself until a year later. Like the Pisan figure, a persona weaves a narrative monologue from a wide range of sources. His attention is rhythmic and fuguelike as it engages one theme and abandons it, takes up another, then returns to the first, or proceeds to a third, each time developing the dominant preoccupation of the whole composition, the nature of reality: "What does not change / is the will to change" (AM, p. 44).

Part of what makes this poem so compelling is the ability of its precise language to reify the most fleeting noumenal impulse. Each of the themes that develop in the monologue is "experienced" by the speaker as a series of objects which he renders into language as vividly and accurately as he can. Relations among the different objects are stated through juxtapositions, alternating descriptions, or other means of clustering details, in the manner of a *montage* or *collage*, to preserve the equal status of each object in question. The speaker is a careful examiner whose statistical and other measuring propensities suggest the trained intellect of an archeologist cataloging his finds at a digging. The result is a sense that the speaker does in fact achieve the terms of the objectist dictum:

> In other words, the proposition here is that man at his peril breaks
> the full circuit of object, image, action at any point. The meeting
> edge of man and the world is also his cutting edge. If man is
> active, it is exactly here where experience comes in that it is
> delivered back, and if he stays fresh at the coming in he will be
> fresh at his going out. If he does not, all that he does inside his
> house is stale, more and more stale as he is less and less acute at
> the door.[33]

The precision of the language avoids the clichés of traditional lyricism. By the very stress on measurement, documentary evidence, and all
the other objectifying material found in Olson's poems, he provided his
richly psychological poetry with a rhetoric amounting to a new form of
poetic realism. And the technique is even used in reenacting dreams,
which also achieve the intensity of actual events.

Each of the three main sections of "The Kingfishers" builds on the
accumulation of detail which the previous section introduced. The first
section, made up of four parts, begins by mentioning indirectly that the
kingfisher is no longer traded as a commodity. The next part begins with
the speaker himself, who sustains three different subjects in his brief
monologue: "the E on the stone," the symbol that Plutarch had found
on the omphalos stone at the temple of Delphi; excerpts in French from
Mao Tse-tung's speech in 1948 to the Chinese Communist party, shortly
before Chiang Kai-shek was routed; and finally, quoted excerpts from
an entry in the *Encyclopaedia Britannica* (11th ed.) on the kingfisher.[34]

The E refers to a cultural order that has disappeared in the historical
process: reduced, possibly, to a mere character, but expressive of a civilization, a *polis* that had at one time achieved a high level of integrity
and etched its mark upon the center of its defined world, on a navel
stone. Mao's words depict a world fallen into corruption, the state of
cultural disintegration from which he now must rise, looking into the
rising sun as a complex symbol of renewal and illumination. The kingfisher, however, is a creature of constancy, and his flight into the setting
sun is a line drawn through the rise and fall of human civilizations,
from Mao's call to arms back into the reaches of the past, where the E
once had enormous meaning. The bird, in fact, becomes the central
metaphor of change itself; for its constancy is composed of the rhythms
of renewal and decay.

The careful description of the nesting practices of this species provides a metaphorical history of human civilizations, as they begin in the
ruins of prior cultures and thrive for a time, only to become the ma-

terials out of which a new age will form its "cup-shaped structure." The kingfisher has achieved permanence within change, has yielded perhaps to the strict conditions of the natural process in which stability is possible. Mao's words reflect the limited perspective of the conqueror, who is right in desiring to transcend decay, but whose methodology is rigid and subjective, and the order he finally establishes will endure only to the extent that it submits to the requirements of change in which it roots itself. The speaker of the poem hails the desire to rise above the filth and squalor of decaying cultures, but he looks beyond that ambition to the larger space, where human cultures have raged against reality and perished.

The last two parts of the first section are the speaker's commentary on this perishability of civilizations. The loot taken by Cortez in his conquest of Mexico is listed carefully as a preface to the last part, where various formulations of the nature of change are given as they occur to the speaker.

Section II reveals the site of all these musings, an Aztec burial ground, which the speaker now tours with a local guide, who explains to him some of the features of the burial rites. This scene clarifies for us the drift of the first section, for the subjects raised there were obviously provoked by this tour. Apparently unearthed by archeologists, the Indians sit pathetically in their narrow graves, their few belongings heaped around them. They are the food of lice. This scene of ravaged humanity embitters the speaker as he angrily contemplates the obstacles which any high civilization must confront in its weary struggle to exist. And if Mao sees light in the East, he argues, there is also light in the past, the West, an inextinguishable glory he sees in Aztec excellence: one cannot look only to the future for hope but must also look into the past, where the ideal was almost achieved. There is sustenance in both directions.

Section III resolves into one assertion the different themes that have so far been developed: the speaker discovers his kinship to these conquered Aztecs whom he finds in the burial site. He rejects the Greco-Roman heritage in favor of the Indian but goes further, too, in rejecting the status quo, which he has already described as a "pudor pejorocracy." His final comment absorbs all the various strains of his thought into one statement that accounts for his presence at this site:

> I pose you your question
>
> shall you uncover honey / where maggots are?
>
> I hunt among stones (AM, p. 49)

None of the other poems of this section of *In Cold Hell, In Thicket* rises to the rich subtlety of "The Kingfishers," which, with its multiple parts and indirect mode of assertion, is a model of the projectivist poetic executed successfully. The lines seem true to the breath, the breath true to the thought; lengths change as abruptly as ideas shift in the argument. Throughout the entire poem, the language is fresh and interesting to hear; the combination of sounds is crisp, at times as stately as classical oratory. The patterns of syllables rarely rely for their effect on simple novelty; words have a chiseled clarity about them as they accumulate in the phrasings of the poem:

> Or
> enter
> that other conqueror we more naturally recognize
> he so resembles ourselves
>
> But the E
> cut so rudely on the oldest stone
> sounded otherwise,
> was differently heard
>
> as, in another time, were treasures used: (AM, p. 45 f.)

And, again, in a difficult bridge of the argument, the sound dominates with its clarity and pointedness:

> . . . And what is the message? The message is
> a discrete or continuous sequence of measurable events distributed
>   in time
>
> is the birth of air, is
> the birth of water, is
> a state between
> the origin and
> the end, between
> birth and the beginning of
> another fetid nest
>
> is change, presents
> no more than itself
>
> And the too strong grasping of it,
> when it is pressed together and condensed,
> loses it
>
> This very thing you are (AM, p. 47)

The poem has incredible variety of spacings, clusterings, wide swatches of language, sudden changes where the wording staggers at an angle down the page:

Mao concluded:
                    nous devons
                              nous lever
                                        et agir! (AM, p. 45)

Lines begin along the horizontal axis at the flush-left margin, where the lines occur most frequently, and run as far to the right as the page will allow.

But the most interesting and least tangible quality of the poem is its resistance. The sound, the phrasing, the immense variety of shapes language assumes throughout the poem emerge from the resistance that is felt through every line of the work. With all of its resources the poem resists being abstract and communicates concretely what is nearly inexpressible as feeling: the anxiety of the speaker to find a culture in which change is understood, not fought or ignored to some tragic and brutal end.

"The Kingfishers" is a drama that enacts how the speaker comes to a conviction; the projective mode is completely suited to show the epistemological events that occur throughout this process. The lines, the strophes, the shapes, the weaving of themes and images, project onto paper much of the interior process of a difficult mental change; the poem functions as a map of intellection and emotion. It is reducible perhaps to two images, a bird and a burial mound; we can imagine its possibility in the imagist mode. But postimagism, as Olson formulated it, sought the roots of the image-making process as the thing to be projected onto the page. Hence "The Kingfishers" shows not the image but the forming of the image in the mind of the observer.

In other words, Olson is especially successful in a poem that poses a change of mind wherein process itself is the thing to be shown through all the resources of the projective mode. It is not the only subject on which he can successfully execute a poem, but it is where projective techniques are specifically necessary and effective in his writing. The other poems of this volume that appear to achieve the developed sense of process are the title poem, "In Cold Hell, In Thicket," where a similarly complex change of mind is enacted, and, to a lesser extent, "To Gerhardt."

But it should be emphasized that these are poems that seize upon profoundly dramatic moments and exhaust them in large formats. The projective technique is successful in mapping the process of less momentous experiences as well. In one way this canonical category shows us what

Olson did not render with success: the dramatic moment in which the mind is not discovering, but declaiming. Several of his poems ("A Po-Sy, A Po-Sy," in this volume; "Morning News," included in *Archaeologist of Morning*; "Letter for Melville 1951" and "I, Mencius," in *The Distances*) are for the most part uncontrolled poems, shrill in tone, repetitious, and carping. The anger, in other words, or the frustration, which is the substance of these poems, doesn't engage Olson fully; such poems make the projective mode seem almost meaningless and empty. Unless the projective poem is in quest of self-discovery or is revealing some difficult, partly concealed terrain of the mind, it collapses into aimless fragments and fails to achieve form.

The projective mode is intermittent in the book; Olson employs parts of the method, but rarely is the whole poetic active throughout a poem. In fact, several poems in the volume seem to be wholly lyrical and traditional in execution, having little to do with the new conventions he was advocating for poetry. "At Yorktown" is one such lyrical poem, a landscape meditation in which the speaker regards the ordered appearance of the Yorktown battlefields. The poem belongs to this first section thematically, for it is concerned with the subject of violence and also with the condition of change. Nature has continued to alter the appearance of the present; only history aspires to freeze a particular moment in time. The speaker is aware of both perspectives as he walks the greens.

In "At Yorktown" and other brief, lyrical poems in this volume, his language is often too flat, even prosaic, to equal the euphonious lyrics of Pound and Williams. Olson's ear is tuned to a speech that is bitten-off or that juxtaposes a technical terminology with common speech; when the language manages a lyrical tone, it rasps more than soothes; it goes flat at junctures that are either surprising or merely disappointing. It is not a language that conveys coherent experience; the admixture of sounds and terms only fitfully renders coherence and more often must seek for it or force it from available fragments. Nonetheless, "At Yorktown" is a distinguished, even startling poem—its lyric falls off so often into the mundane that the disappointments to the ear become almost a satisfaction, for the lines end consistently in odd verbal decisions:

    At Yorktown the church
    at Yorktown the dead
    at Yorktown the grass
    are alive . . .

> at York-town only the flies
> dawdle, like history,
> in the sun . . .
>
> and time is a shine caught blue
> from a martin's
> back (AM, pp. 58–59)

Other poems of the first section are composed with a mixture of lyric and projective elements. The three-part "ABCs" poems, with their mocking reference to Pound's studies, attack both Pound and Williams as going in the wrong directions for a poet; Olson accuses Pound of monotony of theme and Williams of distortion. The third poem is dedicated to Rimbaud, whom alone the poet admires at the end. In "There was a Youth / whose Name was Thomas Granger," Olson sympathizes with a youth who has committed bestiality and is executed for his crime. The poem quotes passages from a trial held in 1642 that suggest at once the hostility of the court and its fear of this irrational act. Both man and animals are slain, as if to erase the last detail of the darkness of the unconscious. The final thought of the poem is the speaker's and implies his quiet regret over this fury and waste of life.

"The Praises" closes the section and celebrates the ideas of a few bold thinkers who were either persecuted or driven into exile as the result of their theories. The poem has the appearance but little of the deep excitement of Olson's more dramatic processual poems. In "The Praises" the suspense is neither so rich nor the invention so bold and articulate as in "The Kingfishers." But in his choice of "Praises" as the last poem, Olson's sense of an ending is sure and subtle, for the speaker, without direct admission, here celebrates a tradition he evidently aspires to in his own work: it is the theme of the whole section, for in each poem the speaker casts off a weight from his mind and thus clears it to seek his own vision. In this final poem, he praises the men who have perished, for their ideas survive. The poet must brave a civilization that has rejected change throughout its history; the poet is an apostle of change, of new directions.

Following the order of Olson's plan, "La Chute" begins the second section. In tone and simplicity of language, the poem resembles the songs of Blake. The poet calls for his lute and drum, the elements of his verse, which he has dropped among the dead. The poet is a survivor, one who has not fallen like the rest. He has resisted death; but more promisingly, he appears ready to begin over again, as though a change had brought renewal to the dismal scene. There is urgency in the command; the poet seems to taunt his listener. The language is deliberately spare and simple, giving the poem and the emotion it expresses a primitive quality. Olson had at one time planned but never wrote a book of translations of Mayan and Sumerian glyphs to be called *The Transpositions* and evidently had intended "La Chute" to be prefatory.[35] We have already noted that he regarded both Mayan and Sumerian cultures as having developed vital arts that showed humans in the center of the natural world. "La Chute" would seem to suggest the same condition. But the section itself shows the poet in the torment of attempting to enter the world surrounding him. The poems of this section are especially provocative and moving because of the drama of this confrontation: he struggles throughout the section with the task of raising each experience to his understanding.

The chief poem of this section is "In Cold Hell, In Thicket," in which the methods of "The Kingfishers" are again used successfully. This time the speaker is on the grounds of an old fort during a light snow. He has been walking in a thicket, where the snow apparently clings in precise patterns. The cold hell of the title is the emotional numbness he feels as he gazes upon this bitter reminder of death and bloodshed. The sheer size and multiple contours of this fort are something the speaker feels unable to comprehend fully. He is frustrated at the opening of the poem because the fort remains as it is without engaging his perception, by which he might then turn it into a form of meaning. He is shut out from an understanding of this object, and the feelings of obscurity and entanglement within himself are then suggested by his description of the thicket that surrounds him:

> How shall he who is not happy, who has been so made unclear,
> who is no longer privileged to be at ease, who, in this brush,
>   stands
> reluctant, imageless, unpleasured, caught in a sort of hell, how
> shall he convert this underbrush, how turn this unbidden place
> how trace and arch again
> the necessary goddess? (AM, p. 66)

The poem is divided into two main sections, and the first is further divided into three parts. The second part of the first section restates the speaker's need to understand how the things external to him at that point assault his interiors. The confusion of the moment frustrates him, and the speech is abrupt and nervous:

> The branches made against the sky are not of use, are
> already done, like snow-flakes, do not, cannot service
> him who has to raise (Who puts this on, this damning of his
>   flesh?)
> he can, but how far, how sufficiently far can he raise the
>   thickets of
> this wilderness? (AM, p. 67)

This is the torment of the poet, moaning with pain that what has
gripped him might possibly remain mute in spite of all endeavor. The
fort is silent; the creative form of its multiple particulars has yet to
emerge:

> How can he make these blood-points into panels, into sides
> for a king's, for his own
> for a wagon, for a sleigh, for the beak of the running sides of
> a vessel fit for
> moving? (AM, p. 67)

The question inevitably redounds upon the self that posed it:

> The question, the fear he raises up himself against
> (against the same each act is proffered, under the eyes
> each fix, the town of the earth over, is managed) is: Who
> am I? (AM, p. 67)

And to answer that question, in order to know what the fort truly means
to him at that hour of uncertainty, involves knowing the self's knotted
complexities:

> as in this thicket, each
> smallest branch, plant, fern, root
> —roots lie, on the surface, as nerves are laid upon—
> must now (the bitterness of the taste of her) be
> isolated, observed, picked over, measured, raised
> as though a word, an accuracy were a pincer! (AM, p. 67)

The second section of the poem opens "ya, selva oscura," alluding to
the second line of Dante's *Inferno* ("mi ritrovai per una selva oscura"),
in which the speaker of that poem also finds himself in a "dark wood,"
unable to extricate himself from a rough and stubborn thicket ("questa
selva selvaggia ed aspra e forte") leading only to that opening by which
he will make his descent into hell. In Olson's poem, the speaker discovers that hell "is not exterior, is not to be got out of." He will not be
escorted, as Dante was, to his own salvation. There are no clear bounda-

ries of heaven, hell, and purgatory in the modern world; there is no "outside," only further alienation or deeper obscurity than what the speaker experiences here. He remains in a vague paralysis at the fort site, "in utmost pain," aware of fragments of the fort's meaning:

> he looks around this battlefield, this
> rotted place where men did die, where boys
> and immigrants have fallen, where nature
> (the years that she's took over)
> does not matter, where
>   that men killed, do kill, that woman kills
>   is part, too, of his question (AM, pp. 68–69)

In the second and last part of section II, the speaker, reminiscent of Carlyle's Teufelsdroeck, realizes that if the hell is within himself, so might the heaven be:

> . . . a man, men, are now their own wood
> and thus their own hell and paradise
> . . . they are, in hell or in happiness, merely
> something to be wrought, to be shaped, to be carved, for use, for
> others. (AM, p. 69)

And, although this does not lessen his numbness of the moment, it encourages him to attempt the first step of clarification within, metaphorically expressed here as taking the first step across the field, the place where his feet were first halted:

> He shall step, he
> will shape, he
> is already also
> moving off
>   into the soil, on to his own bones. (AM, p. 69)

In the closing lines of the poem, the speaker now freely moves toward self-revelation as having exited from a wilderness, that thicket grown large, now behind him. The terms of this confrontation, the fear and resolve to meet it and transform its particulars into understanding, lead him to a larger epiphany—existence itself is a continual confrontation of such wildernesses:

> He will cross
>
>   And is bound to enter (as she is)
>   a later wilderness. (AM, p. 69)

And it is here that we finally perceive the poem's intention—to dramatize the stages of dialectic in these vivid metaphorical terms of wilderness, fort, and movement across snowy fields. The speaker has faced the nothingness of a strange historical landmark and has been seized by its power to negate all that he knew of himself before, and as he writes in this torment of uncertainty, the becoming, or enriched understanding, emerges from within and enables him to move again and even to await the next confrontation of the nothing.

Playing over the surface of these thoughts are allusions to other influential events which deepen and enrich the substance of the lines, without necessarily adding further clarity to them. For it appears, from frequent allusions to a woman in the poem, that the hell of the speaker is made more poignant by some unhappy separation, a sudden and permanent break in a relationship which leaves the character vulnerable and that much more isolated, hence more open to the disequilibrium of the experience the poem describes.

Finally, in a characteristic use of myth to enlarge the topic of the poem to its widest possible range of meanings, Olson makes reference to the Egyptian sky goddess Nut, whose breasts are outlined by the stars. Each morning she gives birth to the sun god Ra, who travels the sky until he becomes lodged in the branches of a tree, where he then reenters the womb of Nut to be reborn again. The situation of entanglement in branches, seaweed, or thickets is archetypal, Jung observed, of the cycles of death and rebirth[36] and is a further dimension of the dialectical rhythm of conscious and unconscious states in "In Cold Hell, In Thicket."

The poem is as varied in appearance as "The Kingfishers." Each of its five printed pages (in *Archaeologist of Morning*) is different, as though different poems had been mistakenly stitched together. The first page has a conventional appearance, with all of its lines beginning at the left margin. The next page indents most of its shorter strophes; the next has three different shapes, one airy and fairly scattered, the second closely formed at the left margin, the third indented further in. The fourth page is again turbulent, the margins jagged, and the final page terminates its movement in the center with a triplet.

But the language has such quickness of pace that unless attention is directed specifically to the incongruous shapes, one overlooks them. What one does notice is the achievement of another dictum of Olson's projectivism, that one perception lead quickly to the next until all are exhausted. The argument of the poem may not be fully understood as one reads it, but the reader is borne so swiftly through its passages that they seem to make full sense.

In cold hell, in thicket, how
abstract (as high mind, as not lust, as love is) how
strong (as strut or wing, as polytope, as things are
constellated) how
strung, how cold
can a man stay (can men) confronted
thus? (AM, p. 66)

What is the question? What do the interjections say? The question
lacks defined reference. Confronted with what? But the sense is still
apparent, even if it can not be articulated. Somehow, the question asks
how a man (or men) can remain poised in a certain kind of confusion.
That is almost enough. The rest of the question, the experience it specifically refers to, will be provided in the remainder of the poem. The
interjections "as high mind" and "as love is" refer presumably to being
abstract; "as strut or wing" refers to strength. But they depart so widely
from the direction of the question that they distract from more than
clarify what is being asked. Unless of course we realize that the questioner is expressing himself through the intensity of his visual associations—he cannot let the terms he uses stand by themselves, he must
charge them with images. The question is asked in some desperation;
the questioner is an intense witness to experience. The two are welded
into an effective opening; they are the facets of a single voice that com-
pels the reader to enter the poem and seek a clearer understanding. The
speaker is about to dramatize the issue of his question, and the reader
will become the captive monitor of the event.

The other poems of the section also explore emotional duress; the
poems are shorter, the foci smaller, the arguments more directed and
controlled. "Move Over" (AM, p. 71) is homely in its simplicity; it
marks the loneliness Olson felt in moving to Washington, D.C., in
1947. He misses New England's countryside, "my true love's green . . .
despite her merchants and her morals." The change of pace is refresh-
ing. The poem is light and simple after the weight of "In Cold Hell."
The changes in rhythm from poem to poem, as Olson arranged them,
are clear and effective. "A Round & A Canon" (AM, p. 72 f.) is slightly darker in mood but still playful. Two images dominate the poem's
two numbered sections. The first is the image of the speaker's daughter,
as he swings her back and forth. The other, linked by memory, is of a
bird ascending and being struck and killed. Olson had witnessed the
killing of a frigate bird while in Yucatan, and the image of the large

bird being brought down by stones haunts a number of passages in his writing.[37]

But in the next poem, "The Moon is the Number 18" (AM, p. 74 f.), the emotion turns finally into torment and despair. The title concerns the eighteenth card of the Tarot, the moon card, portending death. Olson had toyed with prediction from Tarot cards and foretold the death of his mother to the day and hour. In this sparely written, moving elegy, the speaker imagines himself among the "blue dogs" depicted on this card, observing the forces of fate as passively as these totem animals. In the *Origin* edition of this poem, a crude sketch of the moon card followed the poem.

And in "La Torre" (AM, p. 76 f.) there is frustration and anger, an impatience with brooding and lamentation. The speaker thrills at destruction, claiming that "When the structures go, light comes through." The poem is a celebration of courage before a crisis; its lines hark back to the opening of "In Cold Hell," for it answers the question raised there by remarking, "In the laden air / we are no longer cold." The speaker builds a new tower in place of the old; his resilience anticipates the note of courage sounded in the closing poem of this section, "An Ode on Nativity" (AM, pp. 81 ff.). The turbulence of mind in the first part of "La Torre" is expressed through the spatial structure, a staggered descent of irregular stanzas. Whereas four of these clusterings make up the first part, in the second part a single, ordered stanza located at the left margin of the page expresses a resolution.

But these are again poems blending lyric and projective techniques. The plan of each section was to open with a brief prefatory poem and follow with a fully rendered projective poem of sustained length and successive shorter poems that closed on forceful statements. Indeed, that symmetry is visible throughout the volume. "Section II" closes with "An Ode on Nativity," a poem written for his daughter, which again explores a difficult change of mind expressed through projective technique. The poem is in the tradition of birthday meditations, in which the poet discovers himself at a juncture of his life and must find the resolve to go on. The feeling of desolation and the poet's confidential reverie with his daughter recall the situation in Coleridge's "Frost at Midnight."

Olson was born December 27, and in the poem he is reminded of Christ's life and suffering and of the redemption he has promised. But when we consider the poem in the context of the section, in which many difficult experiences have been endured, it is evident that the adversities

here recalled from his youth, the painful disappointment, memories of
a stubborn grandfather, and his own torments, lead finally to a greater
resolve: to refuse the redemption Christ offered and to pursue life for
its own sake. The poem ends on a strident note of resolution that brings
the threads of the whole section, from "La Chute" and "In Cold Hell"
to "La Torre," together:

> The question stays
> in the city out of tune, the skies
> not seen, now, again, in
> a bare winter time:
>
>   is there any birth
> any other splendor than
> the brilliance of the going on, the loneliness
> whence all our cries arise? (AM, p. 84)

In the third and final section of the book we find the program of the
poetic articulated from various vantage points. Olson is argumentative:
either the scenes are of combat and struggle, or they demonstrate the
virtues of direct perception and keen attention. The section opens with a
startling preface, "The Leader" (AM, p. 85), in which the poet Orpheus is slain and devoured by maenads. The poem is in plain speech,
with hardly a figurative word used, as though it were meant to be an
impartial report. The poem seems to warn us of the depth of the poet's
responsibilities: Orpheus does not falter, even when he knows what im-
pends. He is likened to Christ, except that Orpheus is intent to live, not
to transcend his existence: "he not loving anything but / his own life,
that generousness, that he give / with no expectation of anything back."

"The Leader" signals, in other words, the preoccupation of the final
section: what the poet must do with his life and what he must always
expect as a possible consequence of his acts. It leads us into the next
poem, "To Gerhardt, there, among Europe's things of which he has
written us in his 'Brief an Creeley und Olson' " (AM, pp. 86–94), in
which the poet summons his friend to join him and reminds him of his
duties as a writer. "To Gerhardt" is typical of a certain stance Olson
took toward his closest friends: in letter form he cruelly chastized and
upbraided, in order to free the friend from what he felt was closed-
mindedness. Olson is hardly tactful in these tracts; his attacks on Vincent Ferrini in the early *Maximus* poems were meant to instruct this
modest poet in the ways of projectivism, but they resulted in angering
him and hurting his feelings. The angry letters Olson fired at Cid Corman

were likewise more vicious than explanatory, and more than once Corman had to take his own firm stand against his overbearing friend.[38] Olson clearly had this contentious side to him, but the critical attack is muted and more generalized in "To Gerhardt."

"To Gerhardt" must be placed with "The Kingfishers" and "In Cold Hell" as among the fully rendered projective poems of his early years. It has breadth of thought and is rich in mythic allusion, but the speaker is not a discoverer as he is in the other poems; he has become an angry disciple whose advice has become imperious. Half of the discourse of the poem is an assault upon Pound, whom the speaker dismisses at every turn of his argument; at the same time, he offers America to the young German poet, not as a subject but as a location in the world where others are also inventing. The company, not the continent, is what the speaker proffers Gerhardt. "Place as a force is a lie," he tells the German poet; there is no reason to stay in Europe and continue to exist under the dead weight of an empty historic tradition: ". . . man has no oar to screw down into the earth, and say / here i'll plant, does not know / why he should cease / staying on the prowl" (AM, p. 87).

The poem becomes wearisome for lack of a change of tone; the anger goes deep. The discipleship to Pound dissolves in the course of the argument, as the speaker taunts and nags Pound to speak or act. The poem both invites and repels Gerhardt; Olson is angry, not hospitable. Fear and daring are missing from this poem; these are the qualities that make the speakers of the earlier poems so attractive and compelling.

But the speaker crumbles entirely in the next poem, "A Po-Sy, A Po-Sy" (AM, pp. 95–100), where vitriol dominates. The poem is, in appearance at least, cast in the projective mode, but the angry attacks on Pound give the poem no shape or coherence. The speaker mockingly imitates the style of Pound's Rome Radio broadcasts during World War II and has him utter many nonsensical claims in a thick dialect. The anger is without focus, as though Olson felt required to exorcise the influence of Pound by such taunts.

But the third section of the volume is weakened perhaps by the difficulty of its intent: Olson is attempting to show a connection between poetics and ethics. Pound is accused of a villainy of neglect; he is accused in "A Po-Sy" and "To Gerhardt" of closing his mind and refusing to pursue experience in his poetry. He has somehow deeply offended the speaker by his stubborn refusal to change himself. We can infer the ethical ideal from these accusations, but it is a dull exercise; the poems are not models of the alternative Olson bids his older rival to follow.

"A Po-Sy" is the formless and imageless detritus of projective strategy.

The final short poems deliberately alter the direction away from angry venting. The poems are an orderly anatomy of the ideal poet: in "A Discrete Gloss" (AM, p. 101 f.), what he should see as he looks upon the world; in "Concerning Exaggeration, or How, Properly, to Heap Up" (AM, pp. 103 ff.), how he should regard his whole self ("I am not my parts. I am one system"); and finally, in "Merce of Egypt" (AM, p. 106 f.), the full participation of the poet needed in expressing his understanding. None of the poems shows an aggressive use of projective techniques. There is overall an appearance of conventional free verse, with long verse paragraphs and no unusual spacing of words or lines. In "Concerning Exaggeration," there is slight experimentation with staggered and indented stanzas, but the poem is arranged conventionally for the most part.

The anatomy of the poet in the final poems illustrates the doctrine of objectism. Olson manages a clear and figurative exposition in these poems, but none is an instance of the bold invention we find in his best work. Olson's genius is fully active in the poem that speculates about a possible doctrine or that actively prospects in the mind in search of one. But the poems in which he can comfortably declaim from a position of certainty inevitably lead him to reduce the tension and nearly desperate variety of his poetic structure. But such poems have a specific function in the context of the section: each fleshes out a point of his conception of the responsible poet. It is perhaps unfair to ask that they achieve voluptuous form; at the same time, it is disappointing to read such patently thematic poems in a volume celebrating uncertainty and discovery.

The closing poem "Knowing All Ways, Including the Transposition of Continents" (AM, p. 108), gathers up the strains of argument developed throughout the book and resolves them into a new dedication to the art of poetry; the poet refuses to burden himself with the unchangeable disharmony of social life: "I have had all I intend / of cause or man." The poet resolves to discover what is human within himself and how that humanness absorbs the world around him: "the unselected / (my own) is enough / to be bothered with. Today / I serve beauty of selection alone."

The poems of *In Cold Hell, In Thicket* are a bold undertaking by an innovative, deeply earnest poet of the mid-century. We can begin to sense a basis on which to evaluate his accomplishments as a poet of the short forms. Clearly, the poem that dramatizes an epistemological event of great moment reveals Olson at his best; it points to the lasting value of the projective technique as well. The poetic is especially suited to the mapping or charting of the flow of thought and feeling in a moment of deep transformation. But it is also evident that Olson did not sustain projective technique throughout his book. Perhaps he understood some of its limitations. There are instances where the thought does not leap or change direction with any insistence; his quieter, more subdued verse commentaries shrink back to more conventional free verse strategies. His thematic poems, where he argues points of his poetic or of his objectist doctrine, are completely crafted from the techniques Pound and Williams had formulated. Finally, we can see what becomes of the open poem when the mind is not responsive but virulent: the form of the poem is shattered and the lines are leaden and uncommunicative.

The three sections of the volume contribute to a plot of sorts, a "growth of the poet's mind" perhaps, but, more notably still, the structure of the volume bears an interesting resemblance to the plot of his austere drama *Apollonius of Tyana*. In the play, Apollonius must separate himself from the burdensome influence of "place," discover the world on his own, and return to the original embrace enriched and contemplative. This is the threefold development of *In Cold Hell, In Thicket*, presented with greater intensity and a larger range of emotion and argument. And like the play, the poems track the waking life of the speaker. They give us the patterns of his conscious thought, what dilemmas and other concerns he is most alert to as he seeks to grow and change in his awareness. It would be the burden of *The Distances* (1960) to chart the other surfaces of the mind, the dream state, the more recessed terrains of the self's interiors.

In Cold Hell, In Thicket was the only book of short poems Olson was to finish and see through publication while he was rector of Black Mountain College, the place that has come to be synonymous with his writings and influence on other poets. After 1953, the fortunes of the college so adversely changed that in two years it was barely alive, and another year later its demise was informally decided over beer one afternoon.[39] From the latter part of 1956 onward, Olson resided in Gloucester except for a two-year teaching post at the State University of New York at Buffalo (1963–1965) and a briefer stay at Storrs, Connecticut, in 1969, just prior to his death. *The Gloucester Guide*, published in 1973, points out Olson's residence at Fort Point as a landmark of the town.

The Distances, emerging from the first years of his Gloucester residence, departs from the exuberance and broad imaginative feeling of *In Cold Hell, In Thicket*. Its title reveals the themes and general disposition of the book: the poems restlessly contemplate the wide rifts between the lonely subject and the whole dense world of objects surrounding it. The poems here depict that "later wilderness" mentioned in *In Cold Hell, In Thicket*, which the speaker struggles to clarify.

Ten of the twenty-one poems in the new volume are from *In Cold Hell, In Thicket*, including "The Kingfishers" and the title poem. The last eleven poems are new. Olson chose what was best in the first volume and then built upon that base. The later volume is unified by many intersecting themes, but there is a hinge between the old and the new poems. The latter half of the book is characterized by a more petulant and aggressive voice. The poet, lost in the wilderness of the former volume, was absorbed with his own struggle to emerge from confusion. But in the new volume, a sense of ever-increasing distance bears down upon him exactly as he exercises and deepens his consciousness. The progress of these poems is toward isolation, until, in the final poem, he at last stands in elemental relation to earth; a man facing the inanimate stone, commanding it to arise and embrace life.

The first of the new poems, "Letter for Melville 1951" (AM, pp. 32 ff.), is a breezy frontal assault upon scholars' centennial celebration of Melville's birthday, which Olson angrily denounced as an exploitation by careerist professors. The poem has an almost childish belligerency about it; Olson hates the thought of an organized conference in the first place, but he also accuses the attending members of generalizing and trivial arguments about the author. Olson is possessive of Melville and seems unable to tolerate the idea that he could be discussed in the atmosphere of an official ceremony. The poem is actually a letter to the Melville Society rejecting its invitation to the ceremony, in which Olson surveys the details about Melville's life and work that he feels will most certainly be overlooked by the other scholars.

The poem is phillipic, too breezy and niggardly to pass as searching criticism of the academic process, but it anticipates later and more virulent attacks upon academicism by other poets of his circle. It is notable as a kind of early signal of the growing disaffection of some American poets who felt that the universities had become citadels of official critical cant.

The self of these poems has rejected the influence of Europe and the university, and in "I, Mencius" (AM, pp. 115 ff.), another angry poem, Olson again rejects his mentor Pound. This too is an attack, but the anger is more articulate and intense here than in "A Po-Sy' and "To Gerhardt." It is the drama Olson loved best, where the son challenges the father for majority. Here Olson writes with his fist and hotly condemns the older poet for failure of nerve, for accepting prizes, and for what Olson seems to think is a cheapening popularity:

Charles Olson at the back of his apartment at 28 Fort Square, Gloucester, Massachusetts, in 1969, a year before his death. *Photo: Gerard Malanga*.

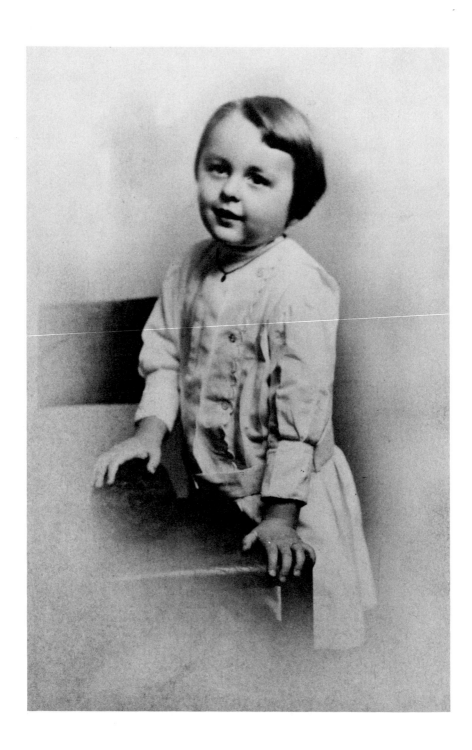

Olson young, Olson old. The child's dress was typical portrait attire early in the century. The other portrait is of the visionary Olson at his prime, circa 1963. *Courtesy of the Literary Archives, University of Connecticut Library.*

The Olson family in Worcester, Massachusetts, 1927: Charles Joseph Olson, Mary Theresa (Hines) Olson, and son Charles. At seventeen, Olson was already as tall as his father; at maturity he stood around 6'7". *Courtesy of the Literary Archives, University of Connecticut Library.*

The scholarly young Olson prior to his graduation from Classical High School, Worcester, circa 1928. Olson's student years were marked by many academic awards and honors. *Courtesy of the Literary Archives, University of Connecticut Library.*

Olson in his cottage at Black Mountain College, circa 1953, at work on *The Maximus Poems*. *Photo by Jonathan Williams, courtesy of the Literary Archives, University of Connecticut Library.*

Four basic shapes of the projective poem. 1. Language densely clustered at the left-hand side of the page. The shape, based on a poem in *The Maximus Poems: Volume Three*, p. 14, stresses an objective, immediate perception of experience, without leaps to the imaginary or to memory, dream, or speculation. 2. Language pushed to the right of the page, where the thought processes are taken directly from dream, and the argument is rich with speculation and synthetic musing. Based on the closing movement of the long dream poem "As The Dead Prey Upon Us," in *Archaeologist of Morning*, p. 171. 3. The rhythmic shift from close observation to sudden perception is scored visually in these strophes placed opposite each other down the page. This spatial rhythm is maintained throughout most of the elegy "The Death of Europe," in

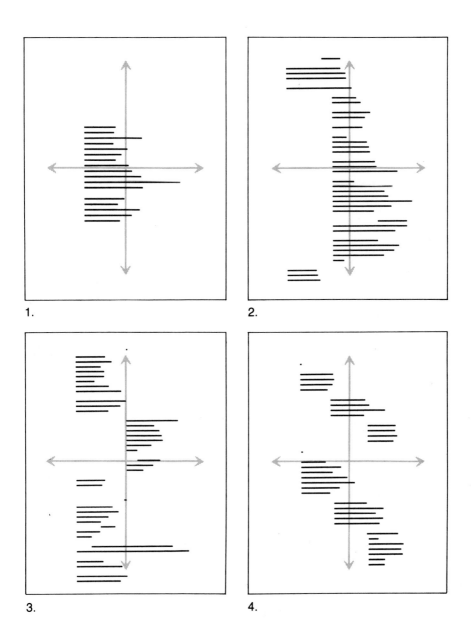

1.

2.

3.

4.

Archaeologist of Morning, p. 124. 4. Like a staircase, these strophes move simultaneously down and across the page as the thought tends toward deeper introspection in an effort to resolve the conflict within the thought. From parts 4 and 5 of "I, Maximus of Gloucester, to You," in *The Maximus Poems*, p. 3.

IN COLD HELL, IN THICKET

in cold hell, in thicket, how
abstract (as we are, as not lust, as love) how
(as struts that polytope, as things
constellated) how
strung, how cold
can a man stay (can men) confronted
thus?

language even, bitter, words
taste like paper wars, get raised up
(in a child's attic) to be knocked down by fire
from a spit-hardened fort, fronted
as we are, here,
from there must go

a man, as his acts must, as there is always one thing
himself, he raises
on a reed he raises his
or, if it is me, what
he has to say

what has he to say?
In hell it is not easy
to know the tracery, the markings
(the canals, the pits, the mountings by which space
declares herself, arched, as she is, the sister
awkward stars drawn for teats to pleasure him, the brother
who lies in stasis under her, at ease as a monarch or
a happy man)

How shall he who is not happy,
who is not clear, who is not at ease, who stands
reluctant, imageless, unpleasured, caught in a sort of hell,
how shall he convert this underbrush, how
the goddess?

The branches made against the sky are not of use, are,
like snow-flakes,
already done, do not
him who has to raise
but how far sufficiently far? the thickets of
this wilderness

How can he change, his question is
these black and silvered things, these
awkwardnesses
into panels, into sides for a king's,
for his own
wagon, for a sleigh, for the beak of, the sides of
a vessel fit for
moving?

Drafts of the openings of "In Cold Hell, In Thicket" and "I, Maximus of Gloucester, to You," the first poem of *The Maximus Poems*, showing Olson's careful revisions, especially his attention to placement of language on the page. First versions of poems were composed on the typewriter, followed by handwritten concisions and recastings.

I, MAXIMUS, OF GLOUCESTER, TO YOU

Off-shore, by islands, hidden, in the blood
jewels and miracles, I, Maximus,
a metal hot from boiling water, tell you
what is a lance, who obeys the figures of the present
dance

1

the thing may lie
around the bend/of the nest
(second, time slain, the bird! the bird!
there! (strong) thrust, the mast, flight

                              (o the birds the kylix)

of Padua, sweep low, o bless
the roofs, the old ones, the gentle steep ones/on whose ridge-poles
the gulls sit, from which they depart,
                              And the flake racks
my city!

2

love is form, and cannot be without
important substance (the weight
say, 58 carats, each one of us, perforce,
goldsmith's scale:
                    feather to feather added
                    and what is mineral, what
                    is curling hair, the string
                    you carry in your nervous beak, these
                    make bulk, these,
                    in the end,
                    are the sum

                    o my lady

                              (o my lady of)

                              good voyage,

                              in whose arm,

                              with whose left arm

no boy, but a carefully carved wood, a painted face and schooner,
a delicate mast, a bow-sprit for

                    forwarding

Although Olson remarked that the typewriter was a machine for exact scoring of the
poet's intentions, these revisions suggest that he worked at typographical arrangement
more freely with pen in hand. *Courtesy of the Literary Archives, University of Connecticut
Library.*

Copies of Olson's first sequence of *The Maximus Poems*, published by the Jargon Press in 1953, were featured at a Jargon book exhibit. *Photo by Jonathan Williams, courtesy of the Literary Archives, University of Connecticut Library.*

One of several crowded walls of Olson's Fort Square apartment on which he posted notes of his research for the *Maximus* sequence. Notes shown here concern the settlement of Dogtown; the photo in the center is of one of the original prostitutes of Dogtown. *Courtesy of the Literary Archives, University of Connecticut Library.*

The car referred to in "my wife my car my color and myself," the oblique closing line of the *Maximus* sequence. *Photo: George Butterick.*

Robert Creeley at the door of his home in Bolinas, California, 1972. At one time Creeley sported a black patch over his missing left eye, the result of an automobile accident in his youth. He divides his time between teaching in the northeast and living on the seacoast north of San Francisco, near the home of Donald Allen. *Photo: Gerard Malanga*.

Robert Duncan in the dining room of his ornately furnished home in San Francisco, 1973. Duncan's baroque imagination was a new input to the Black Mountain movement, which was overwhelmingly the effort of New Englanders. Now one of the central figures of contemporary poetry, Duncan remains perhaps the most articulate spiritual poet of his time. *Photo: Gerard Malanga*.

Cid Corman was the backbone of the Black Mountain movement in the early years with his magazine *Origin*, which helped launch Olson and the figures of his circle. Until recently Corman lived in Kyoto, Japan, where he established a small-press archive and bookstore. *Courtesy of the Humanities Research Center, University of Texas at Austin.*

Paul Blackburn traveling in Puebla, Mexico, in 1967. Blackburn was often lured to Mediterranean cultures, from which he derived some of the inspiration for his superbly lyrical poetry. *Courtesy of the Special Collections, the Library of the University of California at San Diego.*

Denise Levertov was the only woman to join the Black Mountain movement. She has since plotted an individual course in poetry as an activist and feminist. *Photo by Pam Csik, courtesy of New Directions Publishing Corp.*

Ed Dorn, the most prolific of Olson's Black Mountain student poets, now teaches writing at the University of Colorado at Boulder. *Photo by Jenny Dunbar, courtesy of the poet.*

John Wieners, in some ways the most elegant and musical of the younger Black Mountain poets, in front of the Grolier Bookshop, Cambridge, Massachusetts. *Photo: Gerard Malanga.*

From left to right: Joel Oppenheimer, Allen Ginsberg, Michael Rumaker, and Jonathan Williams celebrating the twenty-fifth anniversary of the Jargon Society at a party in the Gotham Book Mart, 1976. *Photo by Shelley M. Brown, courtesy of Jargon Archives.*

that the great 'ear
can no longer 'hear!

> o Whitman,
> let us keep our trade with you when
> the Distributor
> who couldn't go beyond wood,
> apparently,
> has gone out of business

.   .   .   .

We'll to these woods
no more, where we were used
to get so much, . . . (AM, p. 116)

A number of the new poems cluster around the theme of death, and
they range from elegy to exorcism. "The Death of Europe" (AM, pp.
123 ff.) is a moving farewell to his friend Rainer M. Gerhardt, the
subject of his earlier criticism. His death is equated with the death of
the continent; only Gerhardt seemed alive among the ruins of that civilization. But, as he concisely words it, "the ground is now the sky." As
in the earlier poem, Olson reminds him of his summons to America:

O, Rainer,
you should have ridden your bike
across the Atlantic instead of your mind, (AM, p. 126)

Olson refers in this passage to the magazine Gerhardt had produced in
Germany, *fragmente*, which had published some of the new American
poetry. Near its close the poem makes this simple and tender statement:
"O that the Earth / had to be given to you / this way!" (AM, p. 128).
Others of the death poems are an attempt to exorcise the influence the
dead have on him. In "A Newly Discovered 'Homeric' Hymn" (AM, p.
164 f.), Olson warns against sharing the cup with the dead; they bring
a liquor to the feast that can only turn one away from life. One must
"Hail them and fall off." In his elegy to Gerhardt, Olson makes a similar statement when he describes his friend's death as a "false peace" and
says that the living must continue to try to gain understanding. "Beware
the dead," he warns in his "Hymn," they guide the soul falsely.
A more anxious exorcism occurs in the following poem, "As The Dead
Prey Upon Us" (AM, pp. 166 ff.), one of the most remarkable elegies
of modern poetry, written about his painful memory of his deceased
mother. The dead, he remarks at the opening, have entangled "the nets

of being," and he must now wake them and demand his freedom from them. The poem develops from a dream of the dead rising and assuming life again. His mother is once more seated in her chair as the poet returns in the evening. The weight of grief is suddenly felt, in the symbolism of the dream, as the crushing burden of a neglected automobile that lies over him. Other images are thrust into the nightmare of this situation, each of them enacting some confused memory or feeling the poet has about his mother and her death. After each has been felt, the burden is slowly lifted from him. "I ask my mother to sleep," he says at the end; only then is the automobile "hauled away." Finally, in "Moonset, Gloucester, December 1, 1957, 1:58 AM" (AM, p. 173), he completes this exorcism by a command: ". . . Rise / Mother from off me / God damn you God damn me my / misunderstanding of you." With that ghost exorcised, "I can die now I just begun to live."

Two other dream poems are in this collection, "The Lordly and Isolate Satyrs" (AM, pp. 161 ff.) and "The Librarian" (AM, pp. 189 ff.). The first is a strangely provocative image of demigods who have emerged from the water and sit reposefully upon large, muscular tails on the beach. The humans who watch can only feel their small size and distance from these curious giants. The satyrs seem to have seized the beach for the moment, although they threaten no one nor seem to recognize others are present. The poem appears to have dredged an archetype from the mind: the figures are like sea horses but have human shape as well; they have come from the ocean and pause momentarily on the edge of human understanding. They will return, and all that the observer in this poem can do is quietly marvel to himself at the strangeness that so closely underlies the ordinary reality of the day.

In "The Librarian," another dream poem of stunning detail, the persona returns to Gloucester as a stranger and sees various figures of his life: his deceased father, a youth who had at one time made advances to his former wife, his daughter standing across the Cut, where the Annisquam River flows into the harbor of Gloucester, but none recognizes or notices him. He moves in exile among them, and the distinction seems lost between who is alive and who dead.

In the closing poem, "The Distances" (AM, p. 177 f.), the urge is now to draw new connections between the self and experience. The other poems are like the moltings of the psyche, which, once exposed to the direct air of this final poem, needs desperately to embrace life, to wake up the stubborn objects that defy us. The poem rapidly develops a series of polarities which it then works back and forth as the meaning of distance is nervously considered. The polarities are between vitality and death, between the passionately alive and the inanimate. The first polarity is between the lusty Zeus and the severely disciplined Augustus; later the polarity widens between the two as they are regarded in the museum of the monastery of La Cluny, where Zeus is "a god throned on torsoes [sic]," and the young Augustus is "made for bed in a military camp." The dream is that these two poles of emotion can "be enclosed," so "that the impossible distance / be healed," not only between these two different creatures but between humanity and the grim, inanimate stone: "I wake you, / stone. Love this man" (AM, p. 178).

The new poems of the volume seem particularly to brood on death and to struggle against it but nowhere more so than in a macabre passage in "The Distances," the incident of "a German inventor in Key West." The allusion is to Karl Tanzler, an eighty-three-year-old x-ray technician, who fell in love with a sickly young Cuban girl. After her death he removed her body from the grave and preserved it in paraffin; he then kept her in his house for eight years, during which time he was forced to replace parts of her body with plaster casts. According to local newspaper reports, he serenaded her each night on a homemade pipe organ. When police arrested him in 1952, they found the corpse dressed for bed and her hair decked in fresh flowers. He told the court at his hearing that he was building a plane and that as soon as she returned to life, he planned to fly her back to Germany.[40] These grim details are severely understated in the one lyrical phrase that sums up the incident toward the end of the poem: "the girl who makes you weep, and you keep the corpse live by all / your arts."

Tanzler's story provides a close analog to the myth of Pygmalion and Galatea. Like Tanzler, Pygmalion worships a creature of his own devising, an ivory statue of Aphrodite, which he slept with, according to Robert Graves, for a period of at least eight years, possibly longer.[41] Aphrodite entered this image, and the divinely animated statue became Galatea, such a transformation as Tanzler himself apparently awaited in vain:

> Death is a loving matter, then, a horror
>   we cannot bide, and avoid
> by greedy life
>   we think all living things are precious
>   —Pygmalions (AM, p. 177)

The Distances is a difficult book of poems to judge in any final sense. The petulance of some of the poems is counterbalanced by the moving elegiac language of others. The carping of some passages is as true of the self as are the generous thoughts of others in this volume. *In Cold Hell, In Thicket* contains perhaps his boldest departures from convention, and they make that book strong. These great leaps of poetry are contained in the new volume and give it their weight; the new poems are jaggedly constructed documents that continue the sensitive mapping of the self.

Many sides of the question of distance are taken up in these poems, from dreams of isolation and confused regret, emotional farewell, angry rebuttal against foes, and rejection of old masters to that final eloquent prayer for unity and harmony between humans and earth. Once more Olson brings all the resistance he can summon to the otherwise accessible generality that man longs for transcendence. The spiritual progress of the volume is halted at every turn, and each moment of hesitation or frustration is examined carefully by an ambitious poem.

The other sense one has of this book is that Olson has come to the boundary of the short poem; his thought chafes against its limits. The internal complexity and movement he gives to these shorter works threaten to overweight them as vehicles. His poetic apprenticeship has ended, and the form of the poems strikes one as almost lazily etched in as the words struggle to burst into larger combinations.

4. The Maximus Poems

o tansy city, root city
let them not make you
as the nation is
  —The Maximus Poems

I looked up and saw
its form
through everything
—it is sewn
in all parts, under
and over
  —Maximus Poems IV, V, VI

 I pass between
these stone soldiers, remembering
my dreams I continue to walk into the alley
of Fort Square. . . .
  —The Maximus Poems: Volume Three

The Maximus Poems (1960), *Maximus Poems IV, V, VI* (1968), and *The Maximus Poems: Volume Three* (1975) comprise Olson's master work,[1] which he began at the start of his poetic career, in 1947, and continued to add to till the end of his life.[2] He undertook an actual draft of the poem, however, somewhat hesitantly in his first years at Black Mountain College, where his time was divided between writing and the duties of teaching and administering. During the closing years of the college's life he turned more and more of his attention to this long poem, for it quite possibly sustained him in this period of considerable hardship. From 1956 to 1960 Olson completed the last section of *The Maximus Poems*, after carefully researching the earliest history and settlement of Gloucester. By 1963, he had finished a second triad of *Maximus* poems, very different from the first, and he wrote the poems in the final volume from then until his death in 1970.

The long poem has been the mark by which various American poets have proved their talent and their intelligence in the twentieth century. And many have acknowledged that their lineage is from Whitman and his prodigious poetic monument *Leaves of Grass* (1855–1892). However, poets in his tradition have first labored, sometimes indifferently, in the short lyric, serving their apprenticeship there before launching a work of size. Pound began with the conventional short lyric, wrote voluminously in it for a brief term, but with the line "And then went down to the ship," commenced a poem requiring fifty years to complete. Hart Crane composed a more modest but excellent sequence, *The Bridge*; and Louis Zukofsky recently concluded work on his own long objectivist cycle, *A*. In 1946, closer to Olson's time, William Carlos Williams published Book I of *Paterson*, a poem he too would continue writing till the last days of his life.

It is an unavoidable conclusion that Olson began the *Maximus* sequence in imitation of Pound and Williams; a lesser poet than Olson would soon have abandoned the project or produced a listless and inferior imitation of *The Cantos* or *Paterson*, but Olson intended to outdo his elders. The *Maximus* poems do borrow heavily from both works, and the evidence of this is a feast for his detractors.[3] But as more critics come to examine the *Maximus* poems, we are discovering that the work measures up to the stature of its great predecessors. It is a distinguished and beautifully crafted sequence of poems, which, viewed in their totality, make evident that Olson brought a new and distinctive imagination to American literature. This is especially true of the second and third volumes, where the work is inspired with Olson's genius and eccentricity.

The long poem was a fulfilling form for Olson and for many other poets of this century, although few have distinguished themselves by their attempts. Nonetheless the lure of a form without prior structural principles but of infinite extensibility is unmistakable in our era, and it is worthwhile to inquire briefly into the attraction this form has for poets. One of the conditions modern poets react most passionately to is a sense of the disunity of experience, which, whether expressly formulated or not, is generally attributed to the effects of industrialization and advanced capitalism. Together they have hastened a fundamental restructuring of Western society, transforming it from a feudal and agrarian order of existence into the sophisticated, technological system it is today.

The fertility of the romantic tradition derives from the passion and upheaval these profound social changes have provoked; the literature of the past two centuries has largely been the record of ethical, esthetic, and moral adjustments to the new technology. Of the long poems by the first English romantics (Blake's *The Four Zoas*, the great sequence Wordsworth planned but never finished, Byron's *Don Juan*, and so on), each has as its central purpose the desire to gather up the shattered world and find its living connections once more. It is the function of the long poem or "neo-epic," as L. S. Dembo has called it, just as it was of the classical epic, to portray the wholeness of the world, and this task has clearly been taken up in the twentieth century by American poets of great conviction, for the fragmented condition of experience has not changed very much over the last two centuries.[4]

By contrast, the short lyric appears to be the form for a stable world, where the subtlety of the most fleeting emotion may be captured. Its very brevity tacitly suggests that the attentions of the poet are not fixed intensely upon some one large issue tormenting him, such as the metaphysical dislocation of an age, but may luxuriate freely upon himself and others of his world and upon a wide range of limited subjects. Regardless of the content of the short lyric, it is poetry of the moment, where the greatest ache is made bearable through lyric deliverance. That each poet of the long poem began by writing short poems is one more indication of the complexity of the age, for it would appear that at least for a time he was able to sustain his faith in the order of his life, which he celebrated through the short lyric. Just as fundamentally, however, he passed beyond that faith into a void, where he must seek new bearings for his existence, and that search is a process of thought and articulation requiring the length and breadth of the long poem.

This is essentially Olson's own development. The body of short poems served him as a medium for expressing states of mind; they begin and end just there, with the exploration of evanescent mental changes, even though some of the experiences are of the greatest seriousness. But the *Maximus* poems emerge from some area of mind beneath evanescence, among his more enduring and persistent concerns. That point is proved by the long period over which they were written; it is a point which every long poem seems to prove about its author's mind. And the changes that take place within the unfolding sequence capture the author's own growth and change, so that the poem becomes a joint expression of the subject and of the author's life as it is lived in contemplation of his subject.

Each of the six books of *The Maximus Poems* and *Maximus Poems IV, V, VI* has its own organizing theme, and all six books fall into two natural triads, which are also thematically organized. The recent appearance of *The Maximus Poems: Volume Three* (1975) now completes the work. The posthumous editing of this volume leaves open the question what final design Olson intended for this last volume, but the body of poetry itself indicates quite clearly that no firm division into books was planned. Thus, we may talk of the first two volumes of the *Maximus* poems as first and second triads and consider the final volume as a long undivided sequence. We might note at the outset of our discussion that the structure of the work progressively tends toward less ordering of parts. The final volume is quite different from the first in terms of form and procedure: unlike the well-planned divisions and thematic unities of the first volume, the third is a weave of ideas, moods, items of research; little of this late work can be submitted to classification or category.

The title alludes to Maximus of Tyre, a Neoplatonic philosopher of the second century A.D., who resided in a coastal town of ancient origins and is thus parallel to Olson's modern Maximus, who is a resident of a coastal fishing town. The Mediterranean of that period was the great sea, just as the Atlantic has become the great sea of the new millennium. Both men are secular, but the reach of their thought is toward the spiritual. Olson takes the identification no further. But he invests his persona with a mind of broadly synthetic thought and with knowledge of myth and history like that of the persona of *The Cantos*. The protean consciousness of Maximus, sometimes becoming the mind of Gloucester or of Gravelly Hill in Dogtown, resembles the elastic identity of Paterson in Williams' sequence. The epistolary style of the poems in the *Maximus* sequence, however, is uniquely Olson's poetic device; it is the loose form in which so much of his work has been cast. It recalls, as well, the epistolary literature of island-bound or itinerant missionaries and mystics, who used the letter form as the vehicle of their revelations.

In the ten letters that compose Book I, Maximus confronts the town of Gloucester as a multitude of particulars which he will attempt to perceive as a form. In the opening letter, addressed to Vincent Ferrini, poet and editor of the Gloucester literary journal *Four Winds*, Maximus states his love of this neglected suburb of Boston, which had at one time been the most productive fishing port of the world. The general shabbiness and deterioration do not deter Maximus; rather, the dream of a new *polis* appears to him, and Gloucester becomes the humble substrate of the ideal city. Maximus comes to it as a sword newly tempered and sharpened, an instrument of war and of reform, and this missionary of unity plans to use himself for both. But the metaphor subtly shifts, and the "lance" of the opening now becomes a feather, which Maximus carries to the town of Gloucester to add to its emerging form:

> . . . I carry you a feather
> as though, sharp, I picked up,

in the afternoon delivered you
a jewel,
        it flashing more than a wing,
than any old romantic thing,
than memory, than place,
than anything other than that which you carry

than that which is,
call it a nest . . . (M1, p. 4)

The emphasis of this opening poem is on the making of some continuous formal entity out of the disarray of particles that compose Gloucester. First the sword is thought of, perhaps the sword of Mercury, a healing weapon by which to sever the corrupted limbs and foulness away from the otherwise living substance of the town; but now in this second metaphor, Maximus is the mothering bird, who brings a feather to help bind up the loose particulars into that ancient symbol of wholeness, the vehicle of new life, the bird's nest, itself circular, cup-shaped, crafted out of the lifeless oddments the eye of the bird can see drifting over the surface of earth. It is the perfect parallel to the poet's own mental process, where the eye of the imagination espies the casual drift of things on the surface of the mind and binds them into poetry. Hence, Gloucester is absorbed into a complex metaphor by the force of this protean implement, and the town is at once a thing which Maximus stands outside of and the substance of his own interiors, which he must order and clarify, as Olson would labor to do in "In Cold Hell, In Thicket," written a year after "I, Maximus of Gloucester, to You."

The desire is to make Gloucester become continuous with himself, so that there are no longer barriers of subject and object between them: if this can be achieved, then the dream of the new *polis* will have been realized. The first poems are a bid for entry into a walled objective world by a returning exile. Such was nearly the case for Olson personally. He returned an older man to what had been the family's summer residence during his earliest childhood and the scene of many of his fondest memories. We should note here, too, that the historical Maximus was of the city of Tyre, a name derived from the Greek word *tyrsis*, or "walled city."[5]

Maximus strives to regain some higher, tempered form of innocence by his return to Gloucester, after having been expelled, in the Blakean sense, from its garden and tried by the world. He remarks in the short second section of the poem, "the binding force of form is love," and then catalogs the materials of the form as:

> feather to feather added
> (and what is mineral, what
> is curling hair, the string
> you carry in your nervous beak, these
>
> make bulk, these, in the end, are
> the sum (M1, p. 1)

But the sum will have been to make all Gloucester the bulk to be held together by the binding principle of love:

> (o Gloucester-man,
>   weave
>   your birds and fingers
>   new, your roof-tops,
>   clean shit upon racks
>   sunned on
> American (M1, p. 3)

The intensity of Maximus is beautifully reflected in his closing lines as he urges all Gloucester to yield to the braided, woven design of transcendent unity, and his own speech is a weaving of the metaphors of such joinery as early shipbuilding and the nest-making of the bird:

> in! in! the bow-sprit, bird, the beak
> in, the bend is, in, goes in, the form
> that which you make, what holds, which is
> the law of object, strut after strut, what you are, what you
>   must be, what
> the force can throw up, can, right now hereinafter erect,
> the mast, the mast, the tender
> mast!

> The nest, I say, to you, I Maximus, say
> under the hand, as I see it, over the waters
> from this place where I am, where I hear,
> can still hear
>
> from where I carry you a feather (M1, p. 4)

A contrary theme is also present in this poem, but it is left unemphasized for deliberate reason: it will become the dominant consideration of the second book. Its subject is what has destroyed the community: the destructive force of capitalism, which reduces all things to the status of commodities and raises a few individuals into positions of absolute power.[6] And Maximus regards the people of Gloucester as having been corrupted by the commoditization of all aspects of life:

love is not easy
but how shall you know,
New England, now
that pejorocracy is here, . . . (M1, p. 3)

The old customs of the fisherman have given way to the new cheapness of postwar America:

how shall you strike,
o swordsman, the blue-red back
when, last night, your aim
was mu-sick, mu-sick, mu-sick
And not the cribbage game? (M1, p. 3)

This is not so trivial a complaint as it might seem. Olson's Maximus is
the apostle of total awareness, and the glutting of the sense of hearing
with the "mu-sick" of the juke box has made the ear a crude instrument.
Elsewhere in the first book of *The Maximus Poems*, he complains of the
loss of hearing in all the din of advertising jingles and loud popular
music. In "The Songs of Maximus" (the title itself is significant), Maximus complains that there are

No eyes or ears left
to do their own doings (all

invaded, appropriated, outraged, all senses

including the mind, that worker on what is
And that other sense
made to give even the most wretched, or any of us, wretched,
that consolation (greased
lulled
even the street-car's

song (M1, p. 13)

Thus Maximus is not merely being petulant when he complains that
the fishermen neglect the quiet of a cribbage game for the juke box;
rather, the range of their awareness, the subtlety of hearing, if allowed
to be impaired, will result in less skill to strike the cod. The undermining of skills and trades by the cheap, harsh products of popular culture—this is the larger theme of Maximus' complaints. Near the close
of the first letter, Maximus cries out in a despair equal to Lear's rage
against betrayal,

                    o kill kill kill kill kill
                    those
                    who advertise you
                    out) (M1, p. 4)

The first ten letters are really a reconnoitering by Maximus, a reading
of the exact condition of his city and an assessment of the task that lies
before him. Maximus begins his residence in and penetration of the
mysterious unities of the town in full self-consciousness; it is a frustrating self-awareness, for this is the very thing he would transcend in
order to join his townspeople in a higher, selfless polity. And the disarray of the town is his own; to aid in the reformation of the one is to
heal the other; hence the anguish at finding Gloucester corrupt and
fractured.

"Letter 3" states the theme of recovery in the most direct terms:

    Let those who use words cheap, who use us cheap
    take themselves out of the way
    Let them not talk of what is good for the city

    Let them free the way for me, for the men of the Fort
    who are not hired, who buy the white houses

    Let them cease putting out words in the public print
    so that any of us have to leave, . . .

        .   .   .   .

    in the present shame of,
    the wondership stolen by,
    ownership (M1, p. 9)

And the ideal is again stated, made richer by the context of this
struggle between commoner and patrician:

    As the people of the earth are now, Gloucester
    is heterogeneous, and so can know polis
    not as localism, not that mu-sick (the trick
    of corporations, new[s]papers, slick magazines, movie houses,
    the ships, even the wharves, absentee-owned

        .   .   .   .

    o tansy city, root city
    let them not make you
    as the nation is (M1, pp. 10–11)

"The Songs of Maximus," the next letter, pursues this theme further, that a cheapness and squalor pervade the spirit of Gloucester in the form of "gurry," fish offal:

> And I am asked—ask myself (I, too, covered
> with the gurry of it) where
> shall we go from here, what can we do
> when even the public conveyances
> sing? (M1, p. 13)

The gurry is grave fill, and the citizens in their present state are in a living death, their sensory life nullified:

> how can we go anywhere,
> even cross-town
>   how get out of anywhere (the bodies
> all buried
> in shallow graves? (M1, p. 13)

Letters 5 through 7 attack Vincent Ferrini himself for creating a journal, *Four Winds*, that is merely another literary magazine that could be printed anywhere in the country. It is not born and bred of the things in Gloucester; it is not part of the nest, or *kylix* (cup) of the town's real form. "Letter 7" completes the criticism of Ferrini by discoursing on the men who have made things from the materials of Gloucester. The artist Marsden Hartley, who had painted Dogtown's landscapes and other scenes around Gloucester, is praised for his deliberation and criticized for occasionally exaggerating or misrepresenting the actual, at which thought Maximus turns against Ferrini again. The shipwright William Stevens is another example of the local craftsman, "the first to make things, / not just live off nature" (M1, p. 31). Al Gorman, a fish seller, and Mason Andrews, a street peddler, are recalled from childhood as the crusty eccentrics of the town, authentic townspeople whom Ferrini would ignore in *Four Winds*, but who are included here.[7] The point of the poem is that Ferrini should not adulterate the content of the city but dwell exclusively on its particulars. "Such transubstantiations," Maximus reminds him, are "not permitted" (M1, p. 33).

The complaints against Ferrini's journal spring from the conviction that only immediate experience is a subject for art. "Tyrian Businesses," the next poem, turns to the percipient, who must work to draw in the experience around him: he must be a good dancer. As Sherman Paul has observed, this poem was written at the same time Olson wrote an essay on dance technique, "Syllabary for a Dancer."[8] Olson had high regard for dance and, as we noted previously, he took dance lessons as a youth and participated in several recitals at Black Mountain College. Dance aroused the interoceptors of the body and expanded one's consciousness. The poet, he remarks in this poem, must learn to "dance sitting down." But he distinguishes this dance among phenomena from the jitterbugging "children, / who want to go back, who want to lie down / in Tiamat" (M1, p. 35).

The second half of the poem is a dance of the mind among words in a dictionary, which he draws out and weaves together like a rite of bibliomancy. "Metacenter," "nasturtium," "*Tropaeolum*," "totipalmate"— words run across in thumbing the dictionary—the imagination will bind into a form. The nasturtium is a tropical plant, genus *Tropaeolum*; totipalmate birds are of the genus *Phaëthon* and inhabit tropical seas. The totipalmate frigate bird Olson came to admire while in Yucatan.

But the section begins with a fragment from Webster's definition of "heart." Maximus shifts next to a reference to Mme. Chiang Kai-shek, alluded to in the first section as that "international doll" who insisted on silk sheets during her visit at the White House. What have these to do with one another? The heart is possibly the key: it is the seat of vanity as well as courage. Mme. Chiang is vain, so is the totipalmate bird also mentioned in this section:

> it plucks its tail to free the handsome green eye from
> redundant feathers Which, then, it switches
> to admire itself, as an Egyptian lady
> must have looked fixing herself
> by polished stone (M1, p. 37)

The nasturtium, another item mentioned here, is an emblem of courage, its leaves resembling shields and its flowers, "gilded helmets spattered with blood and punctured with lances."[9]

Vanity and courage are passions struggling in the heart; Maximus switches the discussion to the seemingly unrelated relationship of mass and gravity, terms found in another dictionary entry on "metacenter" and related to the buoyancy of a boat. When mass is above the center of gravity, the vessel is stable; when below, unstable. When they are in equal relation to each other, the craft is said to be "neutral," or, as Maximus remarks, "When M & G are coincident, / it is not very interesting" (M1, p. 36). We are left to infer how the two pairs of terms relate, but it would seem likely that we are being asked to consider the buoyancy of the heart in this instance, where the relation between courage and vanity can determine the stability or instability of a person's character.

These key terms, vanity and courage, mass and gravity, lead us into the prose narrative near the conclusion of the poem. The story, based on Olson's actual experience, relates how a Gloucester schooner captain, Cecil Moulton, endangered the lives of his crew by requiring them to salvage driftwood for a garage he was building. A storm was developing at the time, and as Maximus recalls, "there seemed no reason to think the 'Hawes' would weather that one" (M1, p. 38). Still, he remarks, "none of us thought of the danger, even the skipper himself" (M1, p. 39). Moulton's greed and recklessness suggest, at first glance, Ahab's obsession with the whale, with Maximus now the Ishmaelian narrator of this real episode of a captain's disregard for his crew. Moulton's greed and feckless daring literally disturb the buoyancy of the *Doris M. Hawes*, which lost its props after plunging onto a drift plank. Given its curious imbalance of vanity and courage, the captain's heart has clearly shifted the metacenter of his craft, as Ahab's vain but courageous heart brought the *Pequod* to its end. Thus, the pairs of terms are indeed meaningfully linked to each other. We have been given a sort of rebus to decode, but all the connections we need are provided in the terse digressions and commentaries accompanying these clues.

The final passage of the poem continues the rebus with two more terms, "futtocks" and "fylfot," just across from each other on the same page of the dictionary. The wandering eye or finger chooses two terms, but then this "commissure" is made: futtocks are the curved wooden members that form ribs (like the ribs that cage the captain's heart?) in the ship's hull; and the fylfot or swastika is the Sanskrit sign for good luck. The futtocks support the hull from staving, as they did possibly in the *Hawes* episode, and the crew's survival was partly a matter of luck. The *Hawes'* propellers were mangled by the drift plank, bent in such a way perhaps as to suggest the tipped-back edges of swastikas.

This poem shows us the act of making a poem literally from words found at hand, while at the same time bringing Gloucester experience into its form. Maximus has danced in his own mind, amid experience and the meaning of words, and the poem he makes is an example for Ferrini to follow.

"I had to clobber him," meaning Ferrini, he says in the next poem, but the lecturing is over. Instead, "Letter 9" turns upon the pleasure of spring in Gloucester and of the "news" that Creeley has finished printing Olson's first book of poems, *In Cold Hell, In Thicket*. He compares himself to the season: both are producing. The poem is a celebration of high spirits. Maximus is his own best instance of the poet he has been describing to Ferrini:

> I measure my song,
> measure the sources of my song,
> measure me, measure
> my forces (M1, p. 44)

And in the closing poem, "Letter 10," the preoccupation with self and art is discontinued as a new subject veers into focus: the history and settlement of Gloucester. Maximus opens the poem with a fundamental question: what was the city founded for, an ideal or a commercial venture:

> on founding: was it puritanism,
> or was it fish? (M1, p. 45)

The founders of the settlement, John White, who organized the Dorchester Company that subsidized the first fishermen, and Roger Conant, the first governor, are brought into the argument. Conant abandoned the settlement after three years, leaving Gloucester to "the shrinkers." Conant left on principle; he sought to establish another community when it became clear that Gloucester was to be a commercial center instead. Maximus inherits the drab town that was to have been the pilgrims' haven.

This poem is a hinge to the next sequence, but it is also a fitting close to the first. Not until Maximus has clarified his own stance toward the city through the first nine poems does he turn to the larger question of Gloucester's present condition. The examination of origins is the beginning of the quest for its possible redemption.

The second book, containing Letters 11 through 22, was published in 1956, three years after the first.[10] Maximus continues to examine the figures and events which transformed Gloucester from a modest experiment in communal living to an exploited, dependent canning and curing town, a capitalist investment. His self-consciousness is changed into an absorption with the past of his town, which forms a sort of bridge or connection (the first of several) by which he will dissolve the subjective barriers that isolate him from Gloucester. For it is in the history of the town, in its archives and biographies, that the perceptual process begins; somewhere in the historic past the design was whole, before it broke into the fragments of the present time.

"Maximus, to Gloucester, Letter 11" introduces us to the earliest years of Plymouth Colony and its satellite communities, including Gloucester. No sooner did the colony begin than counter forces started reshaping it. John Smith, admired in this poem for his leadership, "also got shoved aside" when the Puritans chose Miles Standish to accompany them to North America instead; he was cheaper to hire than the more accomplished Smith. The fishermen arrived, and an industry, the first in America, therein had its formal beginnings. The community which the pilgrims of the *Mayflower* had desired was already being undermined by this new interest, which was not communal but private and individual. John Winthrop, the elected governor and staunch Puritan who crossed the Atlantic with the Bay Colony settlers, had called the congregation bound for Massachusetts "a city upon a hill," already a *polis* in themselves, but no sooner had his ship the *Arbella* landed than the settlers dispersed too widely to form a close-knit community. His phrase "a city upon a hill" becomes a refrain of the second book of letters.

Letter 14 resumes the theme of exploitation by a merchant class whose increasing cupidity is seen in the differences between John Hawkins (1532–1595) and his son Richard (ca. 1562–1622). The father had traded in the Indies and remained fair-minded; the son rationalized the pursuit of property in the New World, and his toneless pragmatism is quoted with interjections by the enraged Maximus. As Maximus penetrates this early example of sober rapacity all the way to the son's demise in a Spanish dungeon, the consciousness suddenly contracts in an astonishing leap to the present. As he writes, Maximus associates the name of Richard Hawkins with Romulus and Remus and the establishment of Rome by fratricide, after which Romulus filled the walled city with "fugitives and criminals," and obliquely alludes to that tale in this one casual observation:

And now the shadow

of the radiator on the floor

is wolf-tits, the even row of it

fit to raise

feral children. (M1, p. 65)

The letter ends by regarding Hawkins as a modern analog of the rapacious Romulus, who had caused so much terror at the beginning of that earlier city:

> You will count them all in,
>
> you will stay in the midst of them,
>
> you will know no law, you will hear them
>
> in the narrow seas. (M1, p. 66 f.)

"Letter 16" leaps forward to the closing years of the eighteenth century to follow the further disintegration of the community from new
commercial developments. The issue lying beneath the surface of the
letters in Book II is that while the Puritans chose to settle in New
England and create "the city of God," rooted within their own devout
religiosity was the impetus to succeed individually; and since all walks
of life were honorable in the eyes of the Lord, the businessman had
divine justification to pursue success, even if that success came by captur-
ing markets and means of production, monopoly ownership—the way
in which communality is undermined and dissolved. As Maximus comments in this letter, the seeming benevolence of such a faith imposes
worse hardships than more obvious social villains do, since the seemingly
good citizens are "always damn / Safe" within their unimpeachable
orthodoxy.

"Letter 16" concentrates on two supposedly virtuous men who perpe-
trate evils upon a naive society. The first is Nathaniel Bowditch (1773–
1838), son of a Salem cooper, whose knack for figures led him to organize an insurance company in Salem. By that stroke he began, according
to Maximus, the movement of money away from "primary production
& trade" and allowed it to feed upon itself, to become that powerful
abstraction of finance, interest, which Pound had cursed and derided so
often in *The Cantos*. The other figure in this letter is Stephen Higgin-
son (1743–1828), a Boston merchant and unscrupulous peddler of arm-
ament, who helped suppress Shay's Rebellion. He is quoted praising the
virtues of industry and frugality of Cape Cod fishermen, applauding
their capitalist mentality against the less thrifty habits of the simple
Gloucestermen.

Two complete versions of the final book of the volume were written
over a period of seven years, from 1953 to 1959. When Olson wrote to
Corman in July of 1953 that he had completed a new group of poems
taking him to "Letter 33," he was referring to the original version of
Book III, which by September he would decide to cancel.[11] In 1956,
only the second book was issued by Jonathan Williams, under the title
The Maximus Poems / 11–22. In the first version Olson felt he had en-

gaged an unmanageably large theme, touching upon too many subjects at once. And at some point after September, he wrote a new "Letter 23," which introduced the theme of fourteen Dorchester fishermen coming to Cape Ann to establish a fishery. This was to be the new, better focused topic of the third book. The other poems of the book were all composed after Olson had left North Carolina in 1957 and settled permanently in Gloucester. The new "Letter 23" is pivotal: in introducing the new theme of the Dorchestermen, Olson achieves a subtle synthesis of the issues and concerns Maximus has expressed earlier. The Dorchestermen who came to fish are emblematic of the struggle and defeat of others who wished to remain free and independent in the new colony. By his close look at the precise details of the conflict between the fishermen and the pilgrims, Maximus finds in a single image all that he has been arguing in the previous poems.

"Letter 23" recounts that at the very beginning of Plymouth Colony, the pilgrims' ship *Charitie* reached Cape Ann five weeks prior to a second, the *Fellowship*, carrying fourteen Dorchester fishermen. A pilgrim fishing stage had been built and abandoned until the next fishing season, and the Dorchestermen took it over and began fishing from it. The next season the pilgrims returned, but instead of welcoming or accommodating these new citizens into their community, they routed the fishermen by military means. Maximus observes in the fishermen's struggle "the whole engagement against (1) mercantilism . . . ; and (2) against nascent capitalism except as it stays the individual adventurer and the worker on share—against all sliding statism, ownership getting in to, the community as, Chamber of Commerce, or theocracy; or City Manager" (M1, p. 101). As some individuals aggressively move to own and control all the available goods and property, they begin the process by which a community becomes stratified into a class system based on privilege and power; the original parity of relations is thus ended.

"Letter 23" concludes Book II, but in its mention of the fourteen Dorchester fishermen we are introduced to the subject of Book III, the inexorable transformation of Gloucester fishermen from self-employed independent seafarers to corporate drudges. Letters 24 to 37 closely examine relevant details of those fourteen men's coming to Cape Ann in 1623. The fishermen had discovered the world's most bountiful fishing ground, but the moment this fact is made known, the struggle to "cash in on it" begins. The event is proof of the great fertility of the new continent, but as "Letter 32," "Capt Christopher Levett (of York)," goes on to observe,

> . . . About seven years
> and you can carry cinders
> in your hand for what
>
> America was worth . . .
>
> .   .   .   .   .
>
> . . . We know
>
> what Levett Smith or Conant
> didn't, that no one
> knew better
> than to cash in on [the fish]. . . . (M1, p. 135)

The first triad of the *Maximus* sequence begins with the high expectations of a returning exile; his earliest letters announce a program of reunification. But as Maximus considers the condition and complex past of his city, the dream of unity perceptibly fades, and the tone of delight and anticipation turns to despair and occasionally bitterness. The first triad is really about the failure of the dream of a transcendent unity, even though Maximus himself has been lifted from his subjectivity through his intense concentration upon Gloucester's misfortunes. And he has used the sword of the first letter much more than the feather; for the task was to disentangle the essential Gloucester of the dream from the thicket of its moral history.

Finally, we should note that the overall structure of this volume, in contrast to the succeeding volumes, is linear and relatively easy to grasp. Although the poems are dense with meaning and are complexly interconnected, it is clear that Maximus is slowly advancing toward a specific goal: to become a part of his subject by enmeshing himself with its historical background. As George Butterick has observed, the poems reveal "a kind of systematic progression, if on the level of scholarship and reference alone. The earliest poems contain nothing of the history of Gloucester save that known from having lived, as Olson did, in the town, hearing stories from Alfred Mansfield Brooks." The later poems begin "what increasingly becomes the narrow investigation . . . of the land, sea, and sources around him . . . his direct, single-minded investigation and possession of the city."[12]

Two broad categories of content dominate this volume: Maximus' feelings and attitudes and the historic data he seeks to draw into his consciousness. In the next volumes, the strategies of the quest become more complex; Gloucester is separated into other categories of content which must also be examined and sustained in Maximus' attention.

Thus, the first volume should be understood as a preliminary stage of a process or event; the whole of the *Maximus* sequence is, in effect, a drama: a modern mystery play, in which the vision of a spiritual earth unfolds through "acts," the three volumes of the sequence. In this (admittedly risky) comparison of forms, the first volume of poems gives us the complication, where Maximus, who pursues the vision, is frustrated with the confusion and decadence he espies in Gloucester; his inspection of history takes him no closer to his goal. The next "act" is the center of the drama, where Maximus plunges into the vortex of his subject and the revelation of a cosmos is achieved. The third, unfinished volume is putatively the resolution of the play, the return to sense after the trance of the vision has lifted from him. He walks through Gloucester with the traces of a mythic reality clinging to the objects he observes.

The second triad, *Maximus Poems IV, V, VI*, was published eight years later, in 1968, and fundamental differences in subject and treatment distinguish it from the first volume. The poems of the first triad have a finished appearance: the format of the book, size of page, type faces, paper stock all contribute to suggest a work of polish and deliberation. The second triad is in direct contrast: the paper has a rough, mat finish; the type is large and practical; the format is crude and simple, with overlarge unnumbered pages. Except for bold dashes, the symbols used are from the typewriter: asterisks, slashes, etc. These characteristics suggest a poet's notebook, a work in progress, something hastily, even carelessly thrown together, with notes to the poet left in, jottings from library catalogs, bracketed comments usually confined to rough drafts.

The poems abandon most of the recognizable conventions of versification. Many are centered on the page, and it appears to be a rule that initial words of a strophe are capitalized; some lines are conventionally punctuated, and many of the pieces are titled. Beyond these few rules, the poems sprawl on the page in whatever form the material determined at the moment. The language is unusual and difficult; it is a style of great density of allusion and detail, flat and prosy in places, cautious in its use of imagery and metaphors. The attention shifts continually from subject to subject or from detail to detail, and many times the transition or the logic of the change is outrageously subtle or private. Rhetorical devices are at a minimum. The first triad, itself complex and unconventional, seems modestly traditional compared to the second.

But even with these various difficulties in the way of the reader, the second triad is livelier, bolder, more imaginative than the first. The single greatest effect that Olson achieves here is of essence, of the pleasure of perception with a minimum of rhetorical formality. The poems sustain moments of clear understanding, and where they end or die out, there is merely the blank page to turn to find the next poem stripped down to the bare essentials of an epiphany, occasionally with a few words to connect it to the larger sequence. These jottings of thought are all that Maximus has hastily recorded as he meditates on Gloucester and the mythic reality he perceives surrounding it.

The organization in these three books cannot be described by means of conventional categories. The poems have been arranged in such a way as to create a field of dynamic linguistic entities, each enriched by the collective meaning of all the others. The concept of the field enables the poems to coexist in a mass without becoming fixed into hierarchical relationships, which, as Olson had argued often, is precisely the failing of most other means of organization, particularly of the organic. Olson fought against Corman's attempt to give *Origin* an organic structure for the principal reason that to do so meant to arrange things according to their functional importance, which is merely an expression of subjective priorities.[13] Direct perception is of things that are all equally extant to the percipient; to judge the quality of existence of each of them is to mediate the perception by arbitrary categories. Moreover, the ordering of experience in the organic mode, the chief metaphor of the romantic period, makes attention selective, so that the rendering of a complex thing becomes intense in one aspect, cursory and vague in another. The field, on the other hand, allows the artist to perceive a complex continuity, so that at any point of his experience of the field he can render with intensity.

But Olson invented a verse field in the second volume out of necessity—he wanted to free the rest of the sequence from the plot he had been developing in the previous volume. The first ten poems successfully created the open character of Maximus and established the drama that was to unfold in the remaining volumes. But the sudden and intense absorption with Gloucester's history had rendered a different kind of persona than Olson had originally intended. Maximus was no longer the prospective adventurer; he had become a historian whose investigations were leading to a methodical interpretation of the moral history of the city. The work had begun to take on some of the characteristics of Pound's *Cantos*, at least to the extent that a persona presumed to judge history by moral and ethical standards. Maximus had been made an authority on matters which Olson personally felt uncertain about. After finishing "Letter 23," a pivotal poem in the first volume, he wrote Corman that he feared he had lost his direction in the sequence.[14]

In his own copy of *The Maximus Poems 11–22*, he scrawled an intri-

cate series of notes of self-criticism, expressing his doubts about his work
thus far:[15]

> watch 23 r (+check over 11–22) to make sure the clear
> stain of polis is on anything . . .

> polis as such stopping expressing itself as 'eyes' or
> whatever 'message' +started coming out of its ears (or
> like a crack across the mouth instead. . . .

He felt he had fallen into the very trap his theoretical essays had warned
other writers against: he accused himself of "failing to *saturate*" each
word with the sense of *polis* in favor of trying to prove an economic
argument.

His poetic objective was not merely to "keep up a sequence of subject
or complete anything," and he told himself not to "worry about *present*
in subject: the poetics is enuf." His notes then narrow down to the essential conflict:

> watch fish +Gloucester: that they aint deadheading
>   all ready < + that the
> reason is yr own failure to shoot them through with what
> I above call the polis of the poem + the poetic
> isn't it that yr economics is an unlived area—
> a numb point+therefore you better keep yr mouth shut on it.

In a summary of the poems thus far, he writes:

> striking thing of I [the first ten Maximus poems] is that
> except for "Songs of Max"
>   +"Tyrian Bus[inesses]"
> *all* every page is Gloucester polis . . .

> of II is, except for #11
>   p. 10–11 (on Northward) [i.e., final section of "the
>   Song and Dance of"]
>   p. 13–14 on buttocks [i.e., Letter 14, "Maximus, to
>   Gloucester"]
> #15
> #17 LA COSA
> #18 The Twist
>
>   rest is
>   high-fallutin
>   big shot stuff

fancy
+
wide

"Historie,"
instead
of
live
warm
stupid
Gloucester

He never deleted the matter he objected to, but the notes articulate Olson's change of attitude toward the poems of the first volume. Change is perhaps not the right word; it is more likely that Olson recalled a different concept of history which the writing of these poems had temporarily displaced.

In 1947, he wrote a prose fragment entitled "Notes for a lecture at Pacific Northwest Writers Conference," in which he stated that "my own interest in document stems from a need to have experience stripped of . . . inadequate personal interpretations. . . . I want it exposed to us . . . so that . . . we can begin to uncover where we are."[16] "Historie," which he accused himself of writing in his *Maximus* poems, was any manipulation and selection of events that gave an illusory flow and sequentiality to actual processes.

In another fragment entitled "Notes for Poetry & Art," he wrote that "Experience, like matter, is discontinuous, and the act of writing is the act of object. . . . It is an essential act, to align experience, and by words alone to create such space around the words that they become a thing as solid in the mind, or the ear, as a stone or cowslip in the hand." He desired a new method for his poems that emphasized a narrative of impeded, resisted motion, not the sense of flowing events found in conventional historical accounts.

In 1953 he prepared a series of lectures to be given at Black Mountain College's "Institute of the New Sciences of Man." In one entitled "The Science of Mythology," he seized upon a particularly vivid distinction between flowing and resistant narration: "Is narrative born in the river valley cultures? The running river suggests the running events of narration." In contrast, what he calls the mountain cultures had "chronicle . . . *logoi*" and preceded the river cultures. "*Narrative* now . . . must restore such resistance [found in the art of mountain civilizations] (such cloggings) in order to allow in the rude force of life which the Greek mythological system obscured." According to Olson, the Greeks had woven the fragments of earlier more primitive myth into a highly systematic view of early history and had obscured the distinct identity of the mythic figures, just as conventional historiography attempted to systematize events of the recent past.

He summarized these views in another brief statement, "An Essay in the Direction of a Restoration of the act of MYTH":

I   Greek mythological system as such a beautiful wall in
     the way of act now as the Greek metaphysical system
     is in the way of the act of intellect:
     (a) the degree to which the Greeks synthesized all
          myths into a universal system, & so lost the
          original local act & force of each: (// to Plato &
          Aristotle) . . .
     (b) the degree to which *narrative*, as a continuity & a
          binder, worked, in Greek & then Roman hands, *against*
          or to remove the original *magical* naivete or purpose
          out of which the tales & personages arose. . . .

One must tear off "the face of all systemic Greek myth, in order to make the live forces embedded in it once more clear so that their relevance to the act of myth now may be made clear." He applies the same criticism to systematic historiography, which he feels has denied the full identity of particular events. "Documentary," on the other hand, "takes as *serious* any human experience (this is also bound to a clearance from the other Greek system, especially the 'logic' of that system), and so restores to narrative by way of an assumption of the *magical* force of language a *particularism* & a *naivete* which (it is my assumption) was at root to the original act of myth anywhere—AND IS SO NOW, ALSO ANYWHERE."

The problem with the final poems of the first volume, as Olson understood it, was that Gloucester's history had been rendered a system of events rather than a cluster of objects; he had substituted an interpretation for the direct perception of his subject. If the *Maximus* sequence were to be extended to another volume, a new approach to the materials of Gloucester was needed, one that would succeed "to the degree that it tears off the face" of whatever system he had thus far imposed upon the events.[17]

To that end, Olson began reading Whitehead once more, in 1956, but this time with great interest, especially the forbidding cosmological essay *Process and Reality*, a book which became increasingly important to him in the remaining years of his life. We have already touched upon the major theme of this work in a previous chapter, but it is especially relevant here to recall that in this book, Whitehead describes the material universe as an infinite field of particles, called occasions, which collect into formal entities through a universal cohesive principle. Occasions converge and exist formally whenever an "eternal object" enters into them as a binding agent. The "eternal objects," the qualities by which we perceive things, such as color, mass, and texture, constitute the potentialities of the field, its dynamic principle. All the particles of the field are flowing into forms either by prehending other particles to themselves or by being prehended.

It was this cosmological model that Olson then radically simplified and expressed in his poetry. In *Maximus Poems IV, V, VI*, Olson frequently cites Whitehead's thesis; for example, in "A Later Note on Letter #15," referring to the first volume of *Maximus*, he paraphrases Whitehead's conception of the dialectic of matter as a law of the new reality:

> . . . Whitehead's important corollary: that no event
> is not penetrated, in intersection or collision with, an eternal
> event
>   The poetics of such a situation
> are yet to be found out (M2, p. 79)

Whitehead's cosmological argument appealed to Olson as a thrilling feat of vision; it pushed back for him the limits of potential cognition. In an unpublished essay entitled "THE AREA, and the DISCIPLINE of, TOTALITY," Olson persuades himself that the mind is capable of an infinite breadth of attention, an awareness vastly more extensive than we would normally think possible. In his description of the wide grasp of the mind, he is essentially refashioning the mind of Maximus, which he will present in the poems of the second volume:

> It could be put this way: any phenomenon, to be experienced, takes precise engagement; and that the experience of several phenomena increases the precision brought to bear. . . . And the reason is very much tied to field—to that which I have called the virtue of totality: that experience is such (is so rich), that the more kinds of experience one includes (the more phenomena and actions) the finer and faster is the attention brought to bear on all succeeding ones, and, by the brilliance of memory, on what has been known. This constellating of experience and attentions is such a

breeder of values that one can say that just here is the gain which has undone all hierarchy—that just here is where the discovery of value now can be said to lie, in this increase of the precision of attention by the width and depth of the phenomena allowed in to demand attention. The mind of man, it turns out—and the soul— is as capable of stretch (of the unusual sort of extent the Scots keep the Anglo-Saxon word streek to cover) as his energies have shown themselves to be capable of in racing ahead with the machine.

Stance is very much a source and result of such maximal attention. And space could be called the inclusion of all the possible stances to all the possible facts or objects or acts which I am here insisting is [sic] the phenomenal man is required to include within himself. Thus any one of us is the morality of the amount of space we then do dispose. And that the qualitative measure becomes again the precision with which the whole organism of the individual has brought itself to bear on each individual fact and over them all. With this important difference: that the number of them declares, at a certain point, the quality of precision any of them can get, that constellation.

Maximus is the "phenomenal man" whom we will see confront every aspect of his subject simultaneously: he has ceased to organize his perceptions and present them in an orderly discourse. Olson has, in effect, decided to shatter the "plot" of the first volume and to let the main subject, Gloucester, become an island of floating particles of meaning in Whitehead's cosmic field. Olson will thrust his persona, the "phenomenal man," into the center of this swarm of particulars, and the poems will record the creative interaction resulting between them.

We can now understand the design of the printed book: the unfinished, in-process look of the pages, the large leaves, the workbook appearance express the nature of this poetic composition. The poems are the partially stated connections between objects in the Gloucester field; they are "soundings" or, for that matter, the "field notes" of its metaphysical and cosmological exploration. The infinite potentiality and complexity of the field make any one effort at best a fragment of understanding; and the final books are just this, the partial filling in of a vast totality.

The second triad of books achieves subtle shape from the rhythmic sweep of Maximus' attention; he is a "Drummond light" as he explores the larger historical pattern of Gloucester's remote past, settlement, and present configuration, the cultural conditions which shaped her industry and architecture, the minutiae of daily experience felt directly by citizen Maximus. All are part of the field, since no object is ever subtracted from the sum. The past is really a stage of combinations, as is the present or the future, and all are present in one form or another at any one glance at the whole field.

But we have still to describe how the poems of the second volume have been organized. There is thematic sequentiality among groups of poems, but such sequences terminate at a point where the poet's preoccupation with a particular subject is exhausted. The sense of a poetic field is conveyed through the implicit connectedness of all the poems as they engage one overall subject through a seemingly haphazard, often desultory progress. Another quality of the field is the spatial relation of the poems—we find them in one book, occurring for the most part on continuous pages. The less apparent and more profound quality of the field arises from the properties of the poet's consciousness: the individual scraps and fragments of the poet's thought are linked together by a complex of associations, refrains, echoes, paraphrases, key words, and summaries.

But Olson may have captured the organizing principle of the poems best in a two-word construct that occupies its own large page in the volume: "*tesserae* / commissure" (M2, p. 99). The first term is the Latin for "squares," the individual pieces used in making mosaics. The second term refers to joining things together. Hence the poems, as individual compositions, are things being brought together to form a mosaic, one not laid out on a single plane but folded into a book. The poems are placed one on another, but the mosaic "field" they constitute emerges as we read them in series. To think of the poems as the *tesserae* of a mosaic agrees closely with what Olson called "resistant narration," a story told by putting events together without transitions.

The second volume is intended to be one field of continuous thought, but we may still discern certain categories of content that reveal part of the order of this work. These categories function as "subfields" in the larger poem and are the result of having divided the subject of Gloucester into its essential facets. For the purposes of a general anatomy of the volume, we may assume there are six main subfields active throughout the poems: (1) the history of Gloucester; (2) the geography and geology of Gloucester; (3) the origins and history of Dogtown and to a lesser extent its geological features; (4) the marine and fishing history of Cape Ann; (5) individual figures of Gloucester and Dogtown; and (6) myth and ancient history. None of these subfields is located in a single place; the poems that constitute one subfield are scattered among all the others.

The history poems explore the founding and settling of Gloucester, the rise of social classes, and the origins of capitalism, which are all themes of the first triad, but they are distributed throughout the volume and suggest no pattern of development or chronological order. The early poem "DECEMBER, 1960" begins with the first settlement of the coast of Gloucester, but near the close of the volume other poems concern the Revolutionary War and the fortunes of what was later known as Fort Defiance, the remaining battlements of which Olson could see from his apartment in Fort Point. There is no overall pattern to the poems, but particular historic subjects are taken up for two or three poems in series and then dropped.

History is not a plot in the poems; it enters the work as the personal memories and associations of the speaker. This gives the poems continuity with the larger work; as Maximus glances to a new area of Gloucester, the historic detail shifts accordingly. The quality of these poems varies widely, from statistical detail to vividly rendered narratives. Few of them would survive independently outside the volume itself, but their loose structure and generally prosaic language are balanced against their structural function in the larger sequence.

In reading through these narratives and fragments one must infer their relation to the surrounding poems. The reader is continually challenged to seek connections between fragments that have no seeming link. But the task gives a certain pleasure, especially if the reader is persuaded that the *tesserae* have a final, perceptible configuration. Maximus assures the reader that "commissure" is his own intention, as in this brief poem from Book VI:

> All night long
> I was a Eumolpidae
> as I slept
> putting things together
> which had not previously
> fit (M2, p. 157)

A Eumolpidae, a fitting allusion in the poem, was an initiate of the Eleusinian Greater Mysteries.

The geography and geology of Gloucester are new subjects in the *Maximus* sequence and represent the persona's deepening investigations. These poems are for the most part plain and unprovocative, but they contribute to the whole poem by introducing areas of experience usually excluded from a poetic work, giving the poem a ballast of resistant, unusual content that deepens the impression of actuality. The attention to technical features of the terrain is part of the risk Olson is willing to take both to diversify the whole and to strain the formative powers of his composition.

The poems on Dogtown's origins and terrain are more successful as creative works, inspiring Maximus into dazzling leaps of thought in order to claim the place as the center of a new cosmos. This too is a new but inevitable subject of the sequence, for some of Gloucester's fishermen were driven to this bare ground to try farming after their first livelihood was taken away from them. Marine and fishing history is also dealt with, largely through the presentation of documents and paraphrased accounts of shipwrecks, near disasters, and feats of bravery and skillful navigation, while the personal commentary on any of these events is kept to a minimum. Individual figures vary from the eccentric millionaire Jack Hammond, whom Olson had known personally, to personages who either figure importantly in the early settlement of Gloucester and Dogtown or are important to the poet in the context of any of the subfields thus far described.

Finally, there are the poems specifically concerned with myth and ancient history, by far the largest category in the volume, where the thought and lyric creativity achieve the greatest effect. Olson was a serious student of mythology, but his use of this material in the first volume was spare and cautious compared to the luxurious breadth of allusion found in the second. The mythic content of these poems is worthy of its own broad study, and we may only touch upon significant features of it here.

We may note at once that the poems draw from a wide variety of mythic systems: Egyptian, Assyro-Babylonian, Phoenician, Greek, Indian, Chinese, Teutonic, Celtic, and American Indian. Further, the poems make sustained allusions to creation myths, divine combat, gigantomachy, and a series of individual mythic heroes and warriors, particularly Zeus, Herakles, and Enyalios. The diversity of borrowings is in no way an effort to systematize world mythology; figures and events are taken out of their original contexts and used as they are needed in particular poems or junctions of the larger sequence.

Olson's use of myth varies according to context, but throughout the volume we can distinguish at least three different ways in which this literature is invoked: (1) as encoded historical document; (2) as "eternal objects" or as the permanent forms of human experience; and (3) as archetypes of the unconscious.

We have already seen in chapter 2 how Olson's discussion of Melville turned upon the thesis that myth is essentially historic, that the genius of Melville lay in his capacity to go beyond the limits of Western memory or thought to levels of the primordial past for his plot about Ahab and the whale. Essentially, this is Olson's ambition in using scattered mythic fragments. In conjunction with actual historic record, most frequently in his references to Herodotus and Homer, Olson pieces together the narrative of human migration, beginning with the breakup of the Mesopotamian river cultures and proceeding through the slow trek westward to the founding and settling of North America. Migratory history is the largest frame in which to cast the identity and history of Gloucester, and as close analysis of the Herakles myths will illustrate, by the heroic exploits, travels, founding of cities ascribed to this most famous hero of Mediterranean civilization, myth is indeed the record of migratory peoples.[18] Each of the mythic heroes treated prominently in the *Maximus* sequence is a figure in whom a whole culture's experience has been embodied, from Osiris to Odin. A particular exploit of any one of them serves as a narrative link in the history of the spread of Western civilization.

Olson's use of myth as "eternal objects" is less vigorously asserted in the poems. We find it in poems that scan the geography and coastline of Gloucester and in poems which allude to the city of Tyre and Phoenician history, which Maximus parallels with the history of Gloucester and Cape Ann. It is not that history repeats itself through Tyre and Gloucester but that events and objects cohere similarly across time. Hence, Maximus the persona confronts a city in the twentieth century which, with only accidental differences, the earlier Maximus experienced nearly two thousand years before. Rise and dissolution of civilizations occur as permanent forms of events—even though the details that are swept into these forms may greatly vary. Not only does Maximus equate himself with the earlier Tyrian Maximus, but in the closing poems of Book V he finds affinity with the Phoenician poet and mythographer, Sanchuniathon (misspelled in the text Sanunchthion).

But these historic and mythic parallels have the most evident function of articulating the processes of reality as Whitehead had perceived them. The historic and mythic elements are cited to show the presence of the eternal among the scattered objects of the present time. Gloucester is itself rooted in the eternal; it grows out of an earth that has no past or future, only forms of events that recur whenever eternal objects come to reside in them.

This view of historic process is particularly evident in a poem entitled "Bk ii chapter 37," which parodies the language of a guidebook, as Maximus assumes a prosaic tone of voice and details the features of Gloucester for the tourist on foot:

> I. Beginning at the hill of Middle Street the city
> which consists mostly of wharves & houses
> reaches down to the sea. It is bounded
> on the one side by the river Annisquam,
> and on the other by the stream or entrance
> to the inner harbor. In the Fort at this entrance
>
> are the images of stone . . .

But as the monotone passage continues, the sights he mentions progressively transform Gloucester into an ancient citadel, a composite of Tyre and other Mediterranean cities:

> . . . and there is another
> place near the river where there is a seated
> wooden image of Demeter. The city's own
> wooden image of the goddess is on a hill
> along the next ridge above Middle Street
> between the two towers of a church called
> the Lady of Good Voyage. There is also a stone image
> of Aphrodite beside the sea. 2. But the
> spot where the river comes into the
> sea is reserved for the special
> Hydra called the Lernean monster,
> the particular worship of the city,
> though it is proven to be recent
> and the particular tablets of Poseidon
> written on copper in the shape of a heart
> prove to be likewise new. (M2, p. 84)

From the style and numbers of the title, we might infer a reference to 2 Chronicles of the Old Testament, since it alone runs to thirty-six chapters. The poem is thus a new final chapter for 2 Chronicles, a wry invention of further details of the apostasy that followed the dissolution of David's house. The guide has swept the tourist through the city and through time to reveal to him the multifoliate textures of the eternal present. Shortly after, Maximus exclaims in a single couplet the course of his thought: "my memory is / the history of time" (M2, p. 86).[19]

But the subtlest and most provocative use of myths lies in their revelation as archetypes of the unconscious. Olson read widely in the psychoanalytic treatment of myth. Among the collection of his books now housed in the University of Connecticut's Olson archives, fourteen volumes are by Jung alone. Many are heavily marked with his notations and marginalia, particularly *The Archetypes of the Collective Unconscious, Psychology and Alchemy, Psychology of the Unconscious,* and *Symbols of Transformation.* Other works in his collection include studies by Carl Kerenyi and Jung's student Erich Neumann (*The Great Mother: An Analysis of the Archetype*) and a wide variety of other psychological studies, including a number of works by Freud, Otto Rank, and Geza Roheim.[20]

The majority of these works assert that myth is psychic history, that it recounts the human struggle to acquire consciousness. The monsters, heroes, and gods that abound in myth are the images that have been thrust up in the struggle of the human mind to rise from passive unconsciousness to a condition of self-awareness.

In *The Origins and History of Consciousness,* a bold study which seeks to synthesize the various arguments of Jungian writers, Erich Neumann concluded that world mythology is the ill-assorted fragments of a continuous narrative relating the evolution of man's consciousness.[21] World myth unfolds a drama in which the infant psyche separates from the unconscious, or Great Mother, matures in exile, and eventually slays the unconscious, parental forces that struggle to retain authority over it. The heroic psyche inherits an uncertain realm where the immortal unconscious forever threatens to rise and renew the combat.

Neumann's thesis goes too far when it stresses the necessity of man's seeking total domination over his unconscious mind. Olson would have argued that this is the error Ahab commits and that the West has continued to commit at all levels of social life. Rather, the ego should remain in creative combat with the uroboric unconscious, knowing when to reconcile itself with this force and when to fight against its sudden encroachments. The unconscious is bivalent: it is destructive as well as creative and renewing. For Olson, the uniformity of social life, mass behavior, nationalism, and indoctrination is the sterile side of unconsciousness. Delight, surprise, astonishment, transformation, energy, and intuitive wisdom are its vitalities. Neumann argued a linear evolution of consciousness, whereas Olson imagined a dialectical progression. Neumann insisted man is moving away from the authority of his uncon scious psyche, learning to harness and control its forces. But throughout Olson's writing it is evident that he imagined the ego enriched itself through periodic immersion into the unconscious. The image of cyclical dissolution of the ego pervades the poems of the second volume of the *Maximus* sequence.[22]

Olson was familiar with the studies of archetypal myth when he wrote *Call Me Ishmael*; his argument about *Moby-Dick* depends upon our accepting Ahab as a version of the primordial ego seeking its majority through combat with the whale. Several years later, in preparing his lectures for the "Institute of the New Sciences of Man" he sketched out a bold argument about myth and the unconscious entitled "The heart of the art of experience is the archetypes." Among his notes he observed that the test of any story is the "degree to which it accurately obeys to and discloses the unconscious, enables the person to bring the figures, events and objects of their unconscious (the archetypes) up into consciousness." But this should not be taken to refer only to the use an artist may make of his personal dreams; rather, he means the content of embedded experience that is present collectively in the human mind. The unconscious, he argued, is common; the "home" of the unconscious is "any one of our selves." In the years which followed, his interest in archetypal content for art both deepened and advanced to the conclusion that the archetypes documented humanity's progress toward awareness.

When we turn to the second volume of the *Maximus* sequence, we find a determined and extensive use of mythic archetypes; their appearance throughout the three books of the volume ranges from fragmentary allusion to developed narrative. And the loosely arranged order of archetypal reference in the volume suggests that Olson was recapitulating the history of human consciousness in Maximus' struggle to extend and liberate his own mind.

The discourse that arises from Maximus' immersion into the welter of Gloucester's content stirs the latent memory of humanity's original quest for knowledge. Repeatedly throughout the second volume Maximus is aware of the self-devouring serpent that encircles the earth, the uroboros or Great Mother, which primordial man had overcome and pushed out to the farthest edge, to free some center ground in which to make a cosmos. That center is where the ego still resides, its cosmos continually imperiled on all sides by the presence of this devouring spirit. But the poems of the volume not only recall the ancient mythic archetypes but extend them into the present age. It is apparent that Maximus resumes the conflict between ego and unconscious when he seeks to wrest Gloucester from the coils of a serpentine uniformity which he calls "the nation." Gloucester is a possible cosmos which threatens to dissolve into the torpid condition of mass society, and Maximus regards himself as the heroic ego that will attempt to drive the destructive uroboric forces of society back to a distant edge once more.

This drama of the liberation of Gloucester recapitulates the acts of the whole lineage of mythic heroes, from Gilgamesh onward. And as Joseph Fontenrose argues in *Python: A Study of Delphic Myth and Its Origins*, the heroes who combat the various forms of the devouring serpent, here dealt with as Typhon and Python, attempt either to drive off or injure the immortal monster or steal her "cosmic milk."[23] In each of Herakles' battles, the bivalence of the offending monster is made clear: the oppressor is both death and life, as with Geryon's cattle, whose milk is the vital food with which a human cosmos is nurtured into existence. Hera herself succors the infant Herakles at her breast and is in that capacity the fertile mother of consciousness; but she also thwarts him thereafter and seeks his death by siring the monsters Herakles encounters. To be a hero is to have won the struggle, to have taken the food and avoided the poison or flame. The hero in any case is always the metaphor of the renewed and successful consciousness.

The *Maximus* sequence preponderates in such combat heroes, all of whom have encountered the monstrous dimension of the dark and succeeded in revitalizing themselves from it. As the second volume opens, Maximus has leaped from a porch into the snow, recognizing as he runs through the streets that war is the condition of the earth, as it is the condition of his own mind.

> Where it says excessively rough moraine,
> I count such shapes this evening in the universe
> I run back home out of the new moon
> makes fun of me in each puddle on the road.
> The war of Africa against Eurasia
> has just begun again. . . . (M2, p. 1)

And in the next poem, "Maximus, From Dogtown — I," the great devouring serpent Okeanos is seen encircling earth, with man both taking his succor from it and continuing to defend the right of his own illuminated space.

> deep-swirling Okeanos steers all things through all things,
> everything issues from the one, the soul is led from drunkenness
> to dryness, the sleeper lights up from the dead,
> the man awake lights up from the sleeping (M2, p. 2)

The poem illustrates this combat with the dark in the story of James Merry, a brash young sailor who practiced bullfighting with a young calf he was raising in one of the tiny rock-walled pastures of Dogtown. As the bull calf matured, it became a more formidable opponent to Merry, but he boasted one evening that he would take the calf in a fight the following morning. Merry then drunkenly stumbled to the pasture to fight the calf privately, but he was found in the morning fatally gored. Maximus celebrates the prime of the brash youth and his daring and places his struggle in the long tradition of mythic contests between spirited mortal heroes and savage monsters, figures emblematic of the rivalry between conscious and unconscious mind. And he sees in the incident both sides of the Great Mother, for in death the youth has joined the fertile mother again in harmony.

> Only the sun
> in the morning
> covered him
> with flies
>
> Then only
> after the grubs
> had done him
> did the earth
> let her robe
> uncover and her part
> take him in (M2, p. 6)

Death and life are juxtaposed in this as well as in all other such con-flicts of mythic literature. Maximus defends Gloucester essentially as a realm of consciousness which the nation threatens to devour. But he also seeks the renewal of cosmic Gloucester from the fertile darkness of the collective unconscious.

This brief anatomy of what we are calling the six major subfields of the volume commits the very error the poem has successfully tran-scended: we have substantially reordered content for logical discourse. But the subject matter of any one category entangles itself in the others to such an extent that only through the most deliberate scrutiny does a category of content become at all discernible. And this is of course Olson's intention: a discrete subject is merely an arbitrary distinction by fiat of our mentality; it doesn't exist in nature nor does it function dis-cretely in the human mind that claims to isolate it. Consciousness is con-tinuous, although it is made up of the discontinuous objects of experi-ence. In dissolving the form of the poem to talk about its parts, we lose all the technique and genius that has made the poem intensely real and dramatic: throughout the desultory, seemingly slipshod order of events, a modern pilgrim's progress is occurring; enlightenment in its freshest, most contemporary terms happens convincingly to a protagonist who attempts to experience the world that exists beyond abstract order and classification.

Before turning to the third volume of the sequence, we should attempt to summarize the entangled narrative of the second. If the whole sequence is an allegory of a person seeking understanding, Volume Two is the center of the drama; it is the middle term of the dialectic of knowing, the negation of what Maximus thought he could know through the ordered history he constructed in the closing movements of the first volume. Volume One begins with Maximus' initial perception of Gloucester; the content of the poems is poised between the speaker's self-conscious entry into the city and the lore and record of the past which he interprets. But in Volume Two his awareness of Gloucester dissolves as he willingly submits to an infinite welter of things that surge through his frame. The echoes we hear from the poems of the first volume are what remain of self-conscious knowledge after we have moved into the unordered phenomenal welter. The poems of Volume Two are a marbling of both prior understanding and its deeper, richer negation through new experience.

But negation is a bridge to a new synthesis of thought forming throughout the three books. The opening poem of the second volume, "Letter #41 [broken off]," alerts us to the beginning of a momentous undertaking humorously declared as Maximus leaps from a porch in Gloucester and runs home under the new moon. The leap is from the known and familiar into the warring opposites of his psyche. The house at Kent Circle is on the west side of the Cut, where the Annisquam River flows through Gloucester to the sea, but Maximus compares his crossing to the migration of humans across the Orontes River, where Typhon had cut a trench in the earth trying to escape the scourging of Zeus. Before the end of the poem the two banks of the Cut are again the open seams of a once continuous earth. The poem literally breaks off at the final word, Gondwana, the mother continent which broke into the present separate land masses. Continental shift, human migration, the dialectic of experience are the themes Maximus pursues after leaping from a porch into a snowstorm. The scene is based on an actual incident, the St. Valentine's Day snowstorm of 1940, which occurred just prior to the poet's departure for New York to seek his livelihood.

Book IV begins, then, with the intimation of human origins, the primal factors that have determined the course of history. The major theme of Book IV, the history of awareness, is further defined in the next poem, "Maximus from Dogtown — I," which vividly reenacts James Merry's fatal challenge of a bull calf. This act, as we have noted, is a vortex of ancient combat myths, which figure in the initial struggles of the ego to gain autonomy. Around this event a narrative is woven of Egyptian and Greek creation myths which function as more elaborate allegories of the emergence of ego awareness. The Egyptian creation myth in particular shows Nut, the Great Mother, absorbing the sun, her offspring, each evening. Ra, the emblem of fledgling awareness, rhythmically submerges and dissolves into its opposite, the dark, and is reborn in the cycle of each day. Like Merry the sailor, the sun succumbs to the omnipotent darkness. The poem makes extensive allusion to Neumann's *The Great Mother: An Analysis of The Archetype.*[24]

Another concern in Book IV is with the geological and social origins of Dogtown and Gloucester. Merry's occupation as a sailor introduces the key subject of Book V, the westward migrations of humanity, as explorers first roamed the coasts of the Mediterranean and the Black Sea, and then the Atlantic, until settlements ranged over the surface of the planet. The death and reunification of Merry with the earth foreshadow the basic issue of Book VI, which terminates the sequence with its visions of a unified and harmonious cosmos, at the center of which stands Gloucester. The last book begins with this simple preface: "The earth with a city in her hair / entangled of trees."

It is significant that Olson chose to end this volume with an allusion to the close of Melville's *Moby-Dick*, where Ishmael clings to the "coffin life-buoy" and travels a strangely benign sea for several days, living to tell the drama of Ahab and the whale. Olson may have intended a similar fortune for Maximus, who seems himself an "orphan" of the world. The Maximus who leaps from a porch in Kent Circle into the phenomenal abyss now carries his transformed consciousness further out into uncertainty, the condition that Olson said any person of achievement must agree to live within.

The volume cannot be judged merely as a collection of poems. Taken from their context, some of these entries are virtually meaningless. What would we make of the following couplet, for example, if we were to see it by itself?

>   128 a mole
> to get at Tyre (M2, p. 80)

Yet, put into its place as the second "poem" of Book V, it rings with associations and possible meanings. Even then, we must carefully comb the other poems to learn that "128" is Route 128, the state highway that links Boston and Gloucester. A "mole" is a jetty or stone causeway. Route 128 crosses the Annisquam River and terminates in the center of Gloucester. And finally, Gloucester is the reconfiguration of the ancient city of Tyre, another harbor city, with causeways and linkages to the rest of Phoenicia. Book V explores migratory history, and, in a way, the few terms of this couplet manage to encapsulate that very subject. Gloucester, as it is taken in these poems, is a form wrought by epochs of civilization and borne westward by tides of migration.

Other poems are fully developed and can be interpreted without referring to their context in the volume. There are a great number of such poems ranging from short lyrics to reveries, narratives, and long, complexly structured monologues. But it would be a meaningless exercise to isolate these poems and judge the entire volume by them alone. The least fragment contributes to the whole; in some cases, the tags, couplets, notations are more intriguing than some of the longer poems. The work must be understood as a composition of many different parts, in which no one category is a basis for judging the whole.

We must take the volume as it was intended: one work of many "commissures." It is therefore to be judged as a single, extended poem. It is a projective poem which seems to have excavated every nuance of meaning from the poetic Olson had formulated. If we must make final estimates of the worth of the poetic ideal, there is no better criterion of performance than the work gathered here. It is Olson's monument to projectivism. Both the first volume and the third are variations on the mode; they depart from it in various ways: toward too much order in the first volume or to no plan of order in the third. The middle volume strikes a delicate balance between experience and relation. The poet is able to convey to us the sense that he rushes to experience in each of the poems, but their subtle juxtapositions in the volume also show us his understanding and his craft in shaping the work into a perceptible form. That is why, in reading the middle volume, it is difficult to think of poems individually or to try to remove them from their contexts as favorites to be salvaged. The pleasure of any poem in the volume comes both from its own masterful evocation and form and from its exact placement among the other poems. The work is suitably compared to mosaic in this respect: that only the final configuration of all the pieces produces the desired effect. Unlike mosaic, however, the individual pieces of the middle volume are themselves intricately rendered, unique works.

But can the projective poem be extended to this enormous length and succeed as a work of exhilarating perception? "The Kingfishers" partly succeeds because of the brevity of its difficult circuitry. The reader is put through considerable leaps of thought, but he can go back and carefully survey the ground if he has lost his way. In the second volume of the *Maximus*, the way is long and the cues of connection are not pronounced. The foreground is so crowded with detail that the reader never glimpses the whole subject of the work. Narrative does not sweep us forward, as it does in other poems of this length. We must infer a narrative, even struggle for one, as though we were made to cross a mosaic floor on all fours and guess what figure the tiles make up.

But these complaints do not account for the real excitement one experiences in reading this work. Even when we acknowledge the frequent dullness of passages, the unreasonable difficulty of allusions, the purely personal details to which we have no access, the long catalogs of facts and minutiae, all of which clutter up and destroy a smooth flow of language and "plot," the discovery of the poet's control over his material at any juncture is a pleasure that beckons us onward.

The delight of the work comes from our very exasperation and doubt about the poet: just as the seeming disarray is about to make us walk away in disgust, we are suddenly caught up with the surprise that order is possible, even majestic. The language suddenly gives way to a vision of forgotten ideals. The poet is too prospective to declare himself outright; instead, he has let the fragments speak of an earth that has meaning and spirit. The statistics and archival records are made to express the yearning of a citizen to make his tiny coastal settlement rise above impersonal uniformity. A crochety, at times inarticulate stammering of memories and mythological oddments is the language he has chosen to communicate the loneliness of the age, as a society presumes to exist without roots in the past or a conscience about the present. Man, taken as a creature with few skills and a capacity to consume goods, has been shrunk to a fraction of his real worth. This is the lamentation of the vast body of contemporary critical thinking; in this volume of jagged scrawls and tracts, the image of the contemporary human as a stubborn, even desperate soul in search of a new Eden is rendered with poignance and uncanny reality.

The feverish assortment of details to make such a world passes before the reader's eye. It is a poem about building, in which the construction happens almost word by word, as though the total structure could not be visualized until it was complete. The poem is a vast junkyard of discarded visions and experiences which the poet has scavenged in an age that has rejected them from its rational scheme—it celebrates the crude, the organismic, the impractical, the reckless, wild, primitive, useless objects of life, out of which Maximus has fashioned a picture of the world as it might be—in which all these neglected things have value again.

The final part of the sequence, *The Maximus Poems: Volume Three*, was never completed. Olson had begun work on this last book as early as 1963 and wrote poems for it as late as three months before his death. When his papers were purchased by the University of Connecticut, the center piece was a bulky manuscript of drafts and work sheets labeled "Volume Three." The poems were in no particular order, many were still in obvious stages of revision, others were written in such haste by the poet that passages remain undecipherable. When George Butterick and Charles Boer agreed to edit the final volume, the position of only two poems had been indicated by Olson: the first and the last. As a result, we will never know the extent to which the poems would have differed had Olson lived to finish them and refine the order and appearance of the final volume. In all likelihood he would have deleted many lines and even whole poems from the present text, and I also suspect that the order of some of the poems would have been different as well. The movement of the poems lacks the leaping thought and brilliantly executed form of the earlier volumes; the pace is smoother and more regulated, the themes cohere more placidly, even the energy is less intense.

But Butterick and Boer nonetheless produced a useful and necessary text of poems arranged chronologically. Olson was in the habit of dating most of his manuscripts, even the most trivial jotting. The largely chronological order of the previous volumes suggests that Olson would have continued to place poems of the third volume in similar order. The real editorial guesswork involved in producing this text lay in deciding the typographical form for poems taken directly from holograph manuscript. Often the size of the manuscript paper seems to determine the crowding or clustering of lines that Olson might later have rearranged in typescript.

One of the freely arranged poems of the volume, and one of the best as well, is the long untitled tract (M3, pp. 117–121) that begins "I have an ability." It is set in conventional typography for several pages and then curls round in a "j"-shaped curve on one page and turns in circles on the next. According to Butterick, Olson's explanation was that he had run out of space on his paper to continue dropping down the page line by line.[25] But the words themselves begin to suggest some determinacy in this formation, a result either of Olson's wittingly exploiting the necessity or of his having had this form in mind from the beginning. Again, the question remains unanswerable, and the editors have wisely chosen to remain faithful to the texts as discovered.

The uncompleted condition of the work makes tentative any discussion of its intent and form. But we may assume that something substantially like the text as published would have appeared as the closing movement of the *Maximus* sequence. There is little in Olson's papers to suggest that he ever intended to divide the poems of this volume into separate books. The "Editor's Note" to the Viking/Compass edition indictates that in only one instance does Olson refer to the poems as "Volume 3 or Books VII and After." The poems themselves suggest no intended divisibility as those in the previous volumes do. There is instead the feeling of a continuous flow of thought across the length of the work, as though the steady progression of the sequence sought still greater liberation from structuring.

And there are other significant changes we may note based on the content of the poems. We have already observed that the subject categories of the first volume are Maximus' self-consciousness and the history of Gloucester. In the second volume, this self-consciousness all but disappears as the subject divides into interacting subfields. But in the third volume these various subfields are much less active; in fact, we may say that the categories are reduced to a simple tension between Maximus' self-consciousness and a mythic perception of his subject.

Relatively few of the poems are directly concerned with Gloucester's history and geology; still fewer with marine history, Dogtown, or particular figures. At the same time, the use of myth and ancient history has become bolder and more intense in this volume; the references to myth are drawn from wider, more remote sources, as though the mythic potentiality of Gloucester were more vividly perceptible to the persona. And the persona is himself changed in this work: a new quality of brooding self-analysis has entered into the poems unlike any other voice in the sequence:

> Wholly absorbed
> into my own conduits to
> an inner nature or subterranean lake
> the depths or bounds of which I more and more
> explore and know more
> of, in that sense that other than that all else

closes out and I tend further to fall into
the Beloved Lake and I am blinder from

spending time as insistently in and on
this personal preserve from which
what I do do emerges more well-known than
other ways and other outside places which
don't give us much and distract me from

keeping my attentions as clear (M3, p. 191)

There is a move toward the simplification of experience in this volume, almost as though Olson had consciously intended that his sequence would fulfill itself in the synthesis or third term of the dialectic we have been tracing through his poems. A sense of becoming charges the language of his best poems—as though the mastery of attention had the power to call forth the rest of the mystery any object conceals in itself.

The poems no longer strive to master the intricacies of physical phenomena; it is as though the immersion of Volume Two had satisfied or educated Maximus; now the phenomenal structure of Gloucester is examined for its potential spirituality—Maximus no longer requires the *polis* of collective human awareness; his meditations have led him to a state of mind where contemplation of the divine is all-engrossing; it is the source from which the real emanates. Maximus is no longer the village explainer but the solitary dreamer of the spirit from this shore so stubborn and resistant to his pleas for change. In "*Poem 143. The Festival Aspect*," he refuses "all false form," which would include the various abstract conceptions of divinity in Western religions (M3, p. 73). But the poem goes on to celebrate the possibility of living in a condition in which the divine and the physical are one realm, as seen in the lotus flower, the blossom of which is matter itself.

This sense of becoming, the emergence of vision and belief, is further developed through Maximus' meditations on the soul. As we have discussed in chapter 2, the reaches of Olson's thought took him to the verge of stating that man's transcendence is to the anonymity of matter, which the soul struggles to achieve and the mind to prevent. But in a difficult meditation that begins with the poem "*February 3rd 1966 High Tide 10.6 Feet/8:43 AM*" and extends over several more days, there is a sense that his own mind may now permit that final submission to mystery which the soul yearns to enter:

And I heard the soul, I had successfully walked
round the Three Heavens——the Three Towns, the
trimurta
          And was, in this last month and this
winter seeking
another step (or objecting, in my soul & to my soul
at fate, I was indeed *planning*
to walk around the higher world, to go as my cormorant flies
if such a short distance when those words
of the soul——how could the heaven of the soul itself say
'That is no way for thee' how could I
be left
as the cormorant
with no more flight than
our own Rock? . . .

                .   .   .   .   .

. . . and what is the 'prison' the soul says
you shall stay in?
              It is none, my Island
has taught me. (M3, p. 116)

The island, Ten Pound Island, lies offshore in the center of Gloucester harbor, and its rocky surface is a constant metaphor of the density of the real which is here sought.

In a later poem near the end of the volume, "I live underneath" (M3, p. 228), Maximus is able to say, "I am a stone, / or the ground beneath." He then compares himself to the stone walls that range over the hills of the Connecticut countryside, emphasizing the degree to which he has felt himself move toward and into matter. But even in this late poem there is the rich implication that matter is an acceptable realm of the soul only as it reveals its divine embrace. The closing lines of the poem, "the initiation / of another kind of nation," remind us that Maximus pursues the possibility of a *polis* that is spiritual awareness, hence the "initiation," which is an entry into the mystery. The initiates shall form a nation to take the place of the larger, purely political entity. As the first poem of the volume announces, Maximus seeks to "write" a republic, to envision in poems the rising form of a divine consciousness.

The mythic poems attempt to see matter as divine form; they are the voice of thoughtful synthesis. These are not urgent statements of belief but are cast in a meditative language that is serenely inventive and sure. And they are among Olson's finest poems; the breach between the mythic and the present is filled by these feats of creative attention. Olson achieves a visionary lyricism, but the difference between his verse and that of the English romantics is that the ideal is not rendered as though abstract but is perceived as the principle of physical existence itself. Divinity is not only form; it is sensory impact and force of objects; it is motion and the processes of phenomena. Observation is devotional, and when the mythic dimension of an object is perceived, attention is "participation mystique" (M3, p. 174).

In this instance, for example, the Hindu God Ganesa (Ganesh), part elephant and part man, is imagined as the force clearing the harbor of Gloucester each year to renew its "form" again:

> Gloucester is
> sea-shore where
> Ganesh
> may be
> dropped rubbish
> into the Harbor cleared away
> yearly, to revive the Abstract to make it possible for form
> to be sought again. Each year form has expressed itself.
> Each year it too
> must be re-sought. There are 70 odd "forms", there
> are 70 chances at revealing
> the Real. The Real
> renews itself each year, the Real
> is solar, life is not, life is 13 months long each year. Minus
> one day (the day the sun turns). The Sun
> is in pursuit of itself. A year
> is the possibility, the Real
> goes on forever (M3, pp. 89–90)

As Maximus declares in another poem, "only / the divine alone interests me" (M3, p. 198). And in closing another poem he dedicates it to the Gloucester painter Fitz Hugh Lane, "in hymn & Celebration / of Idris Ragged Arse Gloucester / and / the Everlasting only worth the life" (M3, p. 200).

But the mythic poems represent only one strain of thought running through the volume; indeed, the serenity and musing of Maximus over the terrain of Gloucester is but one of many stances he takes to his subject. In others, he rages against political incompetence, the bulldozers of progress, the lack of concern for historical preservation, the continuing commercial decadence of the city. And there is fitful resumption of his research into the geology of Cape Ann, its history, and the continuing saga of fishermen, but these occupy him less and less in the course of the poems. The poems move collectively toward a sense of isolation from others, of a life lived more in contemplation than in any other act: "I am a poet / who now more thinks than writes" (M3, p. 227).

The last poem of the volume was jotted hastily into the margin of a book he was reading just before his death: "my wife   my car   my color   and   myself." They would appear to suggest what things his consciousness was diminishing to: his wife, Betty, who had died of an auto accident in 1964, to the profound grief of the poet; the car that she drove; the color of his skin, which must have shown the extent of his illness from cancer of the liver; himself, the source of consciousness throughout the long poetic odyssey of this sequence.

But the final volume has more the sense of just a collection of late poems than it does of a sequence coming to an end. There is a labyrinth of refrain strewn throughout the work that is intended to create the effect of continuity and structure, but a conceptual framework is missing. The themes of the sequence appear to come unraveled here as Olson writes from day to day. The original manuscripts of the poems show a haste and compulsion to write, but the craftsmanship is deteriorating. Errors are left uncorrected, spacings occur without evident strategy, passages are overwritten or left unfinished. It is what we should expect to find, however, in a manuscript the poet had not revised or shaped yet.

But a deeper disharmony is perceptible in the poems, which revision would not have overcome. The vision itself is coming apart in the volume. The mythic poems emphasize a cosmic order and the turn of the poet to its spiritual design, but a contrary shift is also occurring, where Maximus becomes a nocturnal pedestrian of Gloucester's streets, observing the senseless destruction of its historic houses and the spread of new commercial interests. Maximus seems unable to hold the two halves of his experience together: his mind drifts into arcane formulations of the spirit in nature as his anger mounts at the sight of the drab, dispirited void of modern, commercial Gloucester.

The republic he seeks to build out of the energy of the spirit invites him to transcend the unalterable stolidity of what is now merely a tourist trap. The vision has become private once more; Maximus is at once serene in his imagination of a celestial order and bitter in the knowledge of his failure: that no amount of meditation and discovery can alter the fate of his subject. A later poem in the volume, "DECEMBER 18th," reflects this torment in spare phrases:

. . . oh Gloucester

has no longer a West
end. It is a
part of the
country now a mangled
mess of all parts swollen
& fallen
into
degradation, . . .

.   .   .   .   .

what was Main
street are now

fake gasoline station
and A & P supermarket

construction (M3, pp. 202, 203)

In closing he admits that

the fake
which covers the emptiness
is the loss
in the 2nd instance of the
distraction. Gloucester too

is out of her mind and
is now indistinguishable from
the USA. (M3, p. 204)

These admissions bring us back to a Gloucester first observed in the opening poems of Volume One. A circuit has been completed, in which the fallen city is confronted, its redemption urgently sought through argument and prayer, and the fallen city recognized once again. The poet has discovered heaven in his quest, but the earth of his concerns remains an unchangeable house of mourning. What the human race makes of the world is shallow and stifling; only in matter and spirit does beauty seem perceptible to him. The poet has come to espouse the most primitive values: mystery and the eternal. Toward the end of the volume, he imagines himself walking in "Tartarian-Erojan, Gaean-Our-anian time," that he is "a stone, / or the ground beneath" (M3, p. 228).

But we should not conclude that the sequence terminates in bitter re-jection of its theme, the redemption of life. The recognition of the third volume is that the redemption is more difficult than he had imagined. The hope endures that renewal of existence is still possible, but the dream and the reality have become ever more distant from each other. The sequence has a tragic form, like *Moby-Dick*. But here the protago-nist is no villain; he is the hero, an Ishmael, whose quest is to liberate existence through his compassion and faith. Gloucester founders like the *Pequod* on the tides of the century, as Maximus' long discourse trails off and he himself seems to disappear in the closing words of the last page.

The third volume concludes one of the extraordinary long poems of American literature, which comes closer to articulating a vision of Amer-ica than any other since Whitman's *Leaves of Grass*. It is still too early to make precise judgments of the whole poem's accomplishment, but as a drama of human consciousness seeking to know the world around it, the poem is a faithful testament of its time. The twentieth century should rightly be called the "Age of Awareness." Consciousness, its con-dition, origin, history, social use, development, and control are the major issues of the modern period. Olson's greatness as a poet will have to be measured by the extent to which he not only examined but responded to and enriched the meaning of this word in his *Maximus* sequence.

5. Olson and the Black Mountain Poets

> please *hear* me. I am giving you a present. It's
> yrself.
>
> > that's what a poem is, a conjecture abt an experience we
> > are, for what reason, seized by—BUT I MEAN SEIZED. It
> > has to be something on our mind, really on our mind, at
> > the heart of us—where it hurts
> > > —Letter to Cid Corman, January 26, 1953

Olson and Modern Tradition

But now the perspective must broaden to include the poets who felt some sense of renewal or redirection in their poetry from their knowledge of and contact with Olson. Indeed, to conclude this study without casting attention to the impact of Olson's work on others would be to leave him in a false isolation from the poetry of his contemporaries and successors, which bears the mark of his ideas and style, sometimes slavishly, sometimes with delicate subtlety and precision. But my map of literary connections and patterns is at best tentative and unfinished, more a periplus of new territory than a chart of well-known terrain.

The waves of Olson's influence spread out to ever younger poets and to students of his poems and prose; his ideas and his style of lyric have become part of the unwitting technique of novice poets surfacing in the ephemeral reviews of today. But a careful scrutiny of the work of poets who knew Olson directly or read his writings carefully gives us the clearest sense of the enormous impact he had on the poetry of his time. In tracing this impact on the work of the mid-century experimentalists, Robert Creeley, Robert Duncan, Denise Levertov, Paul Blackburn, and others, I have found it necessary to review the span of each poet's canon, simply because their work is not known widely or in detail and because to engage in a discussion of specific facets of their poetry without the context of their work at hand would be meaningless. This chapter is intended, then, to serve two purposes: to give a broad, unrefined measure of Olson's influence on other poets and to achieve some preliminary overview of what their work is saying.

To understand fully Olson's place in literary tradition as well as the influence he had after the Second World War, we need to review some events in the history of imagism—particularly Pound's contributions—which both inspired and frustrated Olson. Only recently have critics and literary historians begun to see the importance of imagism as a separate part of modern poetry. In the complex ferment that generated the imagist poetic, the work of Eliot came to represent the achievements of the whole modernist movement.

Following World War I, the mention of Eliot's name in a critical essay was sufficient to evoke all the disturbing and satisfying qualities of modern poetry. While Pound's verse had come to be identified with the seemingly impenetrable obscurities of his early *Cantos*, Eliot's poems found their way into college classrooms and popular anthologies. William Carlos Williams and other poets who closely followed the imagist poetic remained obscure until the closing years of World War II. The sudden flurry of activity in the American arts in the postwar years drew public interest to the whole range of American expression and to the work of the newly repatriated Pound.

Eliot's domination of the literary scene was so broad that to launch a new movement required, almost of necessity, the rejection of all that Eliot stood for. Such is the dialectic of literary tradition that a friend and colleague of Ezra Pound, one of the great innovative forces of the modern period, was singled out as a principal obstacle to the making of a postmodern poetic. Pound became the central figure of the postwar avant garde, a group who saw themselves as postimagists, inheritors of Pound's poetic.

For Robert Creeley the resurgence of Pound's authority was the surfacing of a continuous poetic tradition in America that had become obscured not only by Eliot's great fame but by the prominence of the southern agrarian poets, Robert Penn Warren, John Crowe Ransom, and Allen Tate. "The actual tradition," he commented in an interview, "was still operating in the poetry of say [Louis] Zukofsky and [Charles] Reznikoff and George Oppen, but I feel that the continuity is there, suffers no break, keeps going."[1]

Many postwar poets rejected Eliot for reasons other than his prestige. Discussing Eliot's poetry in *The New Poetic*, C. K. Stead distinguishes between the early stages of Eliot's career, when he wrote nondiscursive poems from a poetic that was built on imagism, and his later works, chiefly the *Four Quartets*, which are experiments in baroque structures of imagery and are deliberately discursive. Stead is unhappy with the later poems not only because they adhere to a rigid symmetry of parts but because Eliot denied himself the use of his uncanny powers to report the exact details, the look and feel of daily life, that his genius as a poet depended upon. The quietist sentiments of the later Eliot involved him in renunciations of "the love of created things in order that [he might] be possessed of the Divine Union"; as a result, Stead remarks, "poetry is rarely achieved."[2] This direction of Eliot's verse and his turn to orthodoxy in religion and politics ran contrary to the aims of new American poets who wanted poetry to be critical and to have a full range of experience and emotion again.

Eliot's early works remain among the finest examples of modern poetry; his critical pronouncements about the "undissociated sensibility" agree with many of the theories of the postwar avant garde poets. The methodology of "The Waste Land," with its expression of a state of mind through all the uttered fragments of a dying culture, its use of myth and ritual as narrative devices, and its creation of a central intelligence in Tiresias, broke fresh ground. The brooding consciousness in *Paterson*, Olson's Maximus, and Pound's persona of the *Cantos* have roles similar to that of Eliot's Tiresias. But in the late 1940s and early 1950s, Pound and Williams seemed to younger writers to have kept the imagist poetic intact through the intervening decades of rival doctrinal vogues.

Imagism was an attempt to reverse all those tendencies toward morbid subjectivity that even Matthew Arnold complained of in his preface to the 1853 edition of his poems. Pound had begun his career by imitating the English decadent poets, who were, if anything, turned more inward on themselves than were the French symbolists, and it is perhaps because of both the introspection and the vagueness of his decadent masters that he abruptly bade farewell to them in "Hugh Selwyn Mauberly."

The alienation of artists in the nineteenth century had, according to Pound's critiques of the esthetic situation of 1910, led them to seek the protective retreat of longing daydreams. As a consequence, English decadent poetry had become laxly uncritical, the image lost in flimsy impressions and trite lyrical phrases.

Pound argued that the poet must turn surgeon, clean his instruments, and start afresh by excising dead language from his own speech. The ego that had emerged so boldly at the beginning of the nineteenth century in romantic poetry had by the 1890s retreated from the world. As Hugh Kenner remarks,

. . . it was English post-Symbolist verse that Pound's Imagism set out to reform, by deleting its self-indulgence, intensifying its virtue, and elevating the glimpse into the vision.[3]

Edmund Wilson's inquiry into the nature of symbolist literature, *Axel's Castle* (1931), ends with a firm prejudice against this body of art that had rejected the world at large and chosen morbid self-scrutiny instead:

> I believe therefore that the time is at hand when these writers, who have largely dominated the literary world of the decade 1920–30, though we shall continue to admire them as masters, will no longer serve us as guides. Axel's world of the private imagination in isolation from the life of society seems to have been expoited and explored as far as for the present is possible.[4]

But the artist who retreated into his psyche to explore the murky depths of his awareness increased his sensitivity to the outside world. Art had taken a new stance on experience during the symbolist retreat, Wilson reluctantly admits, and the poet or novelist who patiently examined the disarray of his thinking and memory acquired a keener eye for the nuance and ambiguity of ordinary reality:

> This new language [of the symbolists] may actually have the effect of revolutionizing our ideas of syntax, as modern philosophy seems to be tending to discard the notion of cause and effect. It is evidently working, like modern scientific theory, toward a totally new conception of reality. . . . Though it is true that they have tended to overemphasize the importance of the individual, that they have been preoccupied with introspection sometimes almost to the point of insanity . . . they have broken out of the old mechanistic routine, they have disintegrated the old materialism, and they have revealed to the imagination a new flexibility and freedom.[5]

As Kenner explains, the thing worth salvaging from the English post-symbolists was their tendency to render directly an object or emotion, an erratic strength of their best poetry. Hulme, wishing to make the break with the entire romantic tradition, had already suggested a line of dry, ironic impassiveness, but Pound evidently saw a greater potential in the nondiscursive pictorial mode of the decadents: it at least pointed one finger to an objective world.

Imagism had its beginnings in reaction against hazy subjectivity—it is a distinctly American movement. As European art sank deeper into introspection and evasive language, American poets insisted, as Wilson did later, on clear-sighted gazes. The few prescriptions that Pound and Richard Aldington offered in the name of imagism were too preliminary to provide poets with a clear sense of the new poetic. Imagism was general enough to be taken in several ways, each of which tended to spawn its own minor tradition in poetic history. As Kenner relates the event, Pound had rigorously edited H. D.'s "Hermes of the Ways" and scrawled at the bottom of the page "H. D. Imagiste."[6] Pound took away the unnecessary transitions and interpretative words that surrounded the images of the poem, but the editorial principle by which he made the reductions was not immediately apparent. Either he pared away all that was not pictorial, leaving only images, or he took away the discursive embellishments of conventional sentence structure, leaving a parataxis of imagistic phrases.

Of all the poets who attempted to write in the difficult medium of purely graphic language, Williams and H. D. distinguished themselves as masters. Williams' closest colleague in his formative years was not Pound, who had left the country, but Alfred Stieglitz, a highly accomplished pioneer in photography.[7] Although Williams corresponded with Pound throughout the 1910s and 1920s, he more or less shared the American "esthetic movement" with Stieglitz, who achieved with his camera what the poets were seeking to achieve in their verse, the energized image. Stieglitz was too diffident for Williams to join with him closely; the general practitioner and poet of Paterson experimented largely on his own. The lack of a varied social life with other writers may have deterred Williams from experimenting more boldly with the length and variety of measures possible in the lyric yet may have caused him to perfect the imagist poem to its furthest limits.

No sooner had the pictorial element become a principle of composition than Pound began to talk of a "doctrine of the Image," or a way in which to discriminate between what was merely a picture in verse and the imagistic poem.[8] The former is a wrenching of adjectives to obey some referent, an objective landscape or an invented one, but an image is the result in language of a moment in which experience has cohered into understanding. The merely pictorial could arrive at fragments of representation; the image, on the other hand, is taken as the climax of many uneventful encounters between the subject and the world, where the mundane suddenly reveals its density of meaning. In Pound's famous imagist poem "In a Station of the Metro," "The apparition of these faces in the crowd" is the circumstance experienced over and over again as one makes daily use of the Metro. But "Petals on a wet, black bough" is the image, the meeting of experience and understanding at an unanticipated moment. The crowd becomes the image of flowers radiating from a single branch. The dull repeating reality which tends to suppress emotion and awareness is illuminated in a flash of revelation: it ceases to be disjointed and becomes organic, fruitful, and luxurious.

Pound's excisions from H. D.'s poem were an effort to locate the images, the periods of real illumination, and to raise them above any syntactical suppression. There should be a minimum of structure for a poem that operates by scintillating illuminations. But imagism became for lesser writers a poetic of fragmentary ideas. Amy Lowell took personal possession of "free verse" in Boston, and its innovative possibilities found their way into midwestern poetry and contributed to a strident form of poetic realism, more prose than verse, which began appearing in Harriet Monroe's magazine *Poetry*. Carl Sandburg and Edgar Lee Masters were the foremost practitioners of this perishable mode.

Although Olson's theoretical and artistic work is rooted in imagism, his writings wage a continuous struggle against Pound's authority. The breach in their relationship in the spring of 1948 left Olson on his own, and it appears from his correspondence of the next few years that he continued his education as a poet by first rejecting the meaning that Pound originally had for him. "After 1917," he told Creeley, "the materials of history which [Pound] has found useful are not at all of use. . . ."[9] There was, however, an ambivalence in his blame, a reluctance to condemn Pound outright. His attitude was always shifting between respect and caustic rebuff as he searched for some direction beyond Pound.

The result of his efforts was a set of new emphases in poetry which reoriented imagism. Whereas Pound had forced the doctrine of the image to one extreme of its power in order to express an economic theory, an "ego-system" as Olson once described it to Creeley, Olson countered with essays on the primacy of objects.[10]

The spare lyric technique which Kenner says was Pound's particular concern in the early years is lost in Olson. Instead, he was chiefly concerned that the poem show all the processes of its creation. Robert Duncan, in his essay "Notes on Poetics: Regarding Olson's 'Maximus,' " offers an essential summary of Olson's contribution to poetic tradition: "The point: just as the ear and eye have been incorporated in the act of making in language, the locomotor muscular-nervous system is being called into the adventure."[11]

If the imagist poem was the immaculate setting of a perception, Olson's projective poem reenacted the difficulties by which the perception was wrenched from the intellect—false starts, digressions, and all. Pound's *Cantos* makes the world and its history a subject, but *Maximus* clings to the particulars of Gloucester, whatever the other preoccupation of the moment might be.

Robert Creeley touched on the main points that distinguish Olson from Pound in an interview with the British poet Charles Tomlinson. When Tomlinson asked him, "I take it we're really back now to what Williams was doing. Olson's work, perhaps, is a continuation of what was implicit in Williams' sense of the line, in his insistence on the line," Creeley responded:

> Yes. Except that I remember asking Olson what his own feel-
> ings were about Williams. They were quite different men. I think
> Olson always did respect Williams and his work, but Olson wanted
> something that could encompass a whole cultural reality, whereas
> Williams, I don't think, until the late instance of *Paterson*, was
> really interested in this. He was much more interested in what we
> perhaps could simply call a projected impression, but defined with
> all possible intelligence of that perception. Olson, however, wanted
> something that could encompass and deal with all the variability
> of presence in a total social organism. Now, in that sense, he's
> much more akin to Pound. I think Olson found Pound to be the
> most definitive of the poets prior to himself, at least in the Amer-
> ican scene. But Olson has always been irritated by the fact that
> Pound's back wall is, let's say, fifth century B.C. He goes right
> there and stops. Olson himself wants to push it back at least to
> the Hittites and the Sumerians, wants to think of organizations
> of intelligence as pre-Socratic. Also his sense of economics is very
> distinct from Pound's. His sense of the social complex is very
> distinct. His background curiously includes, for example, having
> been chairman for the foreign language groups for the Demo-
> cratic Party—I believe it was during the second time Roosevelt
> ran for President. So he was concerned with correcting what he
> felt to be the errors of Pound's attitude. He wanted to see the
> organization of the poem become something more than an ego
> system. That again is a qualification he makes of Pound.[12]

Olson restated imagism by bringing into it an expanded awareness of being, rich in the minute particulars of organismic response. American poetry needed a fresh new controversy in which to draw sides and do battle, and with this newly shaped poetic set against the drab state of American culture, Olson stated convictions about the artist's freedoms that other poets shared and could rally around. His poetic of breath and sound is a celebration of life in the first years of the nuclear age, when, as Jonathan Schell has remarked, "unprecedented wealth and ease came to coexist with unprecedented danger, and a sumptuous feast of consumable goods was spread out in the shadow of universal death."[13]

Olson's polemics reminded poets of a stance they could take in their art against the imposing forces of business and government. Creeley has commented on his own experience as a poet of this era:

> I think that in 1945, remembering that that's an arbitrary date, a war had ended, and men of my particular generation felt almost an immediate impatience with what was then to be regarded as a solution. Many of us had been involved in this huge global nightmare, and we came back to our specific personal lives, situations, feeling a great confusion and at times a great resentment about what had been given us as a rationale for all this. So we had that reason to move upon something—upon a clarity that could confront these dilemmas more adequately than the generalities we had been given.[14]

Creeley and Olson wanted poetry to be the center of a larger movement among the arts toward less "structured" forms of self-expression; jazz, orchestral composition, abstract expressionist painting, theater-in-the-round, ballet, architecture, and design had already abandoned traditional structural principles. Except for jazz, leading figures in each of these fields congregated at Black Mountain College to teach new techniques to their students. In Tomlinson's interview, Creeley described the convergence of artists at the college while Olson was rector:

> There was [interaction between writers and painters.] Very substantially. Not with Albers, but with the people who came in the fifties, primarily for summer teaching—Kline, Motherwell, de Kooning, Vincente, Guston, and so on, the painters that became the so-called action painters, the abstract expressionists. All of them at that time were, with the possible exception of de Kooning and Kline, just beginning to get some kind of recognition. That was a very volatile time in their own lives. The fifties, early fifties, for these painters is an extraordinary period. There was, yes, a close rapport.

When asked if "their mode of operation [had] anything to do with the way poems were beginning to be written at that time," Creeley responded: "Not actually as an example, perhaps, but it was a reassuring parallel."[15]

A movement in the formal sense of poets sharing their ideas and agreeing on certain intentions for their work came about through Olson's early efforts. The "Projective Verse" essay served as a manifesto declaring the basic tenets of the new poetry. Once Corman's journal was actually launched, with Olson's work prominently represented in it, Olson felt personally responsible that every aspect of the journal's editing should declare in print the ideals of the new poetry. And when Corman became less inclined to conform to the increasingly authoritarian role Olson had assumed with him, a new journal, the *Black Mountain Review*, was begun at the college with Creeley as editor.[16] Mary Novik, bibliographer of Creeley's works, has observed that these two early journals were part of an effort to create a network of outlets for the new poetry:

> The success of *Origin* was the wedge needed to open up the hoped-for alternative publishing system which centered from 1951 to 1954 in *Origin, Fragmente, Vou, Contact, CIV/n, Black Mountain Review*, Contact, Divers and Jargon Presses, and was pulled through to 1957 almost unassisted by Jargon, *Origin*, and *Black Mountain Review*. The last issue of *Black Mountain Review* in 1957 announced the San Francisco and New York Beat poetry renaissance and ushered in an expansive writing underground allied with the international avant-garde. City Lights, Grove, New Directions, and numerous small presses, along with *Evergreen Review, Yugen, Big Table, Measure*, and a flock of little magazines, advanced the new poetry to its presentation as an open alternative in Donald Allen's *The New American Poetry: 1945– 1960*—where it revealed itself as a poetry which defied limitation.[17]

A structure to the movement is very apparent in retrospect: it had its theoretical platform in Olson's essays, a series of official organs for the dissemination of its ideas and work, a base of operations in Black Mountain College, and an anthology that gathered up the variety of its participants. Even now, after the poets of that experience have become widely dispersed, and some have died, Robert Creeley remains a tireless apologist for Olson's work and the ideas that sustained the group of poets who initially formed around him.

As in any literary movement, there was a hierarchy of friendships among the Black Mountain poets. Of the ten poets Donald Allen listed in this category, Robert Creeley (b. 1926) and Robert Duncan (b. 1919) were closest to Olson, both in their admiration for him and in the extent to which they shared some of his ideas about writing. Personally, Olson was closer to Creeley perhaps than to any other man in his life.[18] Yet it is a sign of the isolation American poets suffered at this time that during the first four years Olson and Creeley knew of each other they never met face to face.

"The Creel"

Creeley began a literary career with some reluctance; in interviews he has frequently commented on the aimless character of his early life, when he raised and trained pigeons and had "no real sense of being a writer in any way; it was just an imaginative possibility that I really wanted to try to get to."[19] Except for a brief experience writing for the Harvard undergraduate magazine *Wake* from 1945 to 1948, Creeley had no "literary life" till he became acquainted with Mitchell Goodman and his wife, Denise Levertov, in 1949, whom he joined a year later in France. Through them he met the writer Martin Seymour-Smith, who lived in Mallorca and who supported himself by tutoring Robert Graves' son William. In 1953, Creeley and his family moved to Mallorca from France to join Seymour-Smith in launching a literary press, but after producing one or two books the two disagreed over matters of format and taste, and Creeley undertook to launch his own press. With its Mallorcan printer, Mossen Alcover, Creeley's Divers Press became one of the distinguished pioneering small presses of the postwar era. It didn't live long, but during its brief life from 1953 to 1957 the Divers Press published the works of Olson, Paul Blackburn, Larry Eigner, Irving Layton, Seymour-Smith, H. P. Macklin (*A Handbook of Fancy Pigeons*), Robert Duncan, and others.[20] The press was essential to Black Mountain poets who had been denied publication by more established houses; it was also the press for an issue of *Origin* and for the complete series of *Black Mountain Review*, which ran from 1954 to 1957.

While Creeley was in Europe he published his poetry in a few American reviews and journals specializing in new poets, but by 1951 he had barely a dozen poems in print.

> I was writing a lot but I was not publishing. I mean, say a friend says, we'd like some poems, so you send *all* the poems you possess and they take, reasonably, two pages. Then there are the difficulties

with the printer and with the money; so if a magazine makes it,
it usually comes out six to eight months after your initial intention.
And that's because everybody was stuck with the *physical* problem
of getting work into print.[21]

In that year, *Origin* almost simultaneously helped to establish Olson
as a leading figure among the projectivists and launched Creeley's career
as a prose writer. The first issue was dominated by Olson's poetry and
the second by Creeley's short stories. It should be noted also that in his
letters to *Origin* Olson continually insisted that he and Creeley, not Corman, would preach the doctrine of objectism and projective technique.

When Divers Press produced the first issue of *Black Mountain Review* in the spring of 1954, the projective movement was jointly led by
Olson in the United States and by Creeley in Mallorca. Olson had invited Creeley to teach at the college, and in March 1954 Creeley came to
Black Mountain, meeting Olson for the first time and teaching his first
class of students the same evening. He remained at the college for three
or four months, then returned to Mallorca, but came back a year later
to stay.

With Creeley now on the teaching staff, and with Duncan shortly to
join forces with Olson, a group of poets of similar ideas found themselves centered, off and on, at one place, a college in North Carolina:
the group now referred to as the Black Mountain poets was comprised
of teachers and their students, with Olson serving as rector.[22] For a
movement that lived in the journals of the moment, it was an unusually
substantial setting.

The influences on Creeley have been various, but after his initial dab-
bling in the style of Wallace Stevens, there is a pattern.[23] Creeley's own
criticism and the transcripts of his many interviews provide us with a
uniquely candid record of the esthetic training and technical problems
of a contemporary poet working in the imagist tradition. He read widely
in Pound, in spite of (perhaps because of) F. O. Matthiessen's exclusion of Pound's work from his course in modern poetry at Harvard. But
it was Pound's prose, the criticism and the practical advice to poets, that
Creeley read and not *The Cantos*, which he found too demanding.[24]

Williams influenced Creeley's writing more directly. Creeley's lecture
"I'm Given to Write Poems," delivered in Berlin in 1967, is a thorough
examination of the meaning Williams had for him:

> I think the most significant encounter for me as a young man
> trying to write was that found in the work of William Carlos

Williams. He engaged language at a level both familiar and active to my own senses, and made of his poems an intensively *emotional* perception, however evident his intelligence.[25]

In the same lecture he listed Poe and Hart Crane as poets of the short lyric who had influenced him. Elsewhere he has mentioned his debt to such masters of the short *line* as Hilda Doolittle and Louis Zukofsky. From all of them Creeley has learned "an explicit possibility in the speech that I was given to use, who made the condition of being American not something chauvinistically national but the intimate fact of one life in one place at one time."[26]

He was already moving toward a style of short lyric when in 1950 he received through Cid Corman several poems by Olson. Creeley was trying to launch his own literary review, and Corman was merely passing along materials for his consideration. But Creeley promptly rejected Olson's poems with a short note observing that Olson was still "looking for a language." Whereas Creeley was paring his own language into brief, tersely worded lines fitted like blocks into tiny triplets and square quatrains, Olson's poems rioted on the page. The callow rejection Creeley mailed off to Olson provoked a barrage of letters in return, but thus their friendship began. It was the freedom Olson preached that Creeley needed to hear, yet he was cautious and slow to relax his strict sense of what the poem should be.

Creeley, like Williams before him, faced an unusual dilemma with the inherent brevity of the imagist poetic: both wanted to increase the subtlety and range of subjects of imagism. Williams' progress toward the long poem had been slow: he published the first part of *Paterson* at the age of sixty-three. His early experiments with loose verbal structures in *Kora in Hell* (1920) were accompanied by apologies and long defenses; only in his early prose did he allow the voice to assume some suppleness and comprehensiveness of statement. In the act of writing *Paterson*, his crisp taciturnity relaxed into more boldly conversational statements. A quick glance at the chronological sections of *Pictures from Brueghel and Other Poems* (1962) shows the lines extending more and more toward the right margin, first and most pronouncedly in the poems from *The Desert Music* (1954) and then in the staggered triplets from *Journey to Love* (1955). As editor of *Black Mountain Review* and earlier as a correspondent to *Origin*, Creeley had observed these advances, and with publication of *The Desert Music* he applauded Williams' mastery in raising the imagist lyric to a complex form.

But at Berlin, in the lecture "I'm Given to Write Poems," Creeley concluded by acknowledging his special debt to Olson. While Williams had provided an essential method of versification, he remarked, "It is really Charles Olson I must thank for whatever *freedom* I have as a poet, and I would value him equally with Pound and Williams and those others I have mentioned." And he added, "What Olson made clear to me during the late forties and early fifties was of very great use. I am speaking of the kind of thinking that is evident in his essay, 'Projective Verse,' written during the same time. . . . Olson made evident to me . . . that writing could be an intensely specific revelation of one's own content, and of the world the fact of any life must engage."[27] In all of the interviews included in *Contexts of Poetry*, Creeley restates his indebtedness to Olson for encouraging him to be freer in his verse.

Even so, it is clear that Creeley's style builds upon the exacting techniques of Williams and Zukofsky. His poems generally lack the excitement and boldness of statement of his mentors, but he has created a compelling character in the mass of his brief lyrics, a persona who craves the love of his wife, but whose loneliness is insatiable. Kenneth Rexroth succinctly defined Creeley's poetry: "It is about the inability to communicate, an inability due to corruption of the organs of reciprocity. For Robert Creeley the interpersonal 'force field' as they call it in physics is so distorted and damaged that only remote, token signals can be pushed across it with the greatest effort."[28] The rhythms of his lyrics are all of a piece, a breathless, halting manner of speaking appropriate to the persona's depths of longing despair.

Creeley's poems are concerned with the nature of relationships, what comfort and pain they cause the individual:

> I've been given to write about that which has the most intimate presence for me, and I've always felt very, very edgy those few times when I have tried to gain a larger view. I've never felt right. I am given as a man to work with what is most intimate to me— these senses of relationship among people. I think, for myself at least, the world is most evident and most intense in those relationships. Therefore they are the materials of which my work is made.[29]

In a later interview he remarked, "I like a family. I'm very involved with domesticity as a fact or as a condition of living."[30] But in this admission, which he has been urged to make frequently as interviewers inquire into the singleness of theme in his work, Creeley has confessed his disappointment that other forms of content do not enter his poetry. He has expressed dismay and even embarrassment from time to time that his poems have not taken into account the Vietnam War, for example, and other social and historical events:

As a younger writer I had been most able to work in a small focus, in a very intensive kind of address, so that I depended on some kind of intense emotional nexus that let me gain this concentration. But, literally, as my life continued and I continued to live it, I really had a hunger for something that would give me a far more various emotional state, that is, the ability to enter it. And also I wanted a mode that could include, say, what people understandably might feel are instances of trivia; that is, I really respect Duncan's sense that there is a place for everything in the poem in the same sense that Williams says—"the total province of the poem is the world"—something of that order in *Paterson* somewhere—the sense that poetry isn't a discretion, that it is ultimately the realization of an entire world. So that I felt the kind of writing I'd been doing, though I frankly respected it, was nevertheless partial to a limited emotional agency and therefore I wanted to find means to include a far more various kind of statement through senses of writing I got from Olson and Duncan.[31]

With the exception of a few early poems on various subjects, Creeley's writing quickly seized upon the theme of the desperate husband, his scrutiny of whom is without parallel in American literature. No poet or novelist has ever turned his attention to the nuances and subtleties of the suffering husband to the degree Creeley has. Nothing is excluded from his painful analysis: the poetry is a record of destructive impulse, abuse, moodiness, dispute, need, implacable solipsism, rancor, and possessiveness.

Creeley created a figure whose appetites for love are greater than a wife could endure or return; his loneliness is metaphysical, an exile of the soul, from which no easy rescue is possible. Such solitude merely redoubles the husband's dependency on the wife, as though it were solely through her that any transcendence of despair were to be hoped for. Creeley's love poetry is tragic: the lover's passion is deranged and repels the beloved.

His love poems bear some comparison to seventeenth-century English lyrics, particularly in their ardor and intensity. But his writing lacks the philosophical embellishments, the verbal wit, and the metaphorical exaggeration of the English poets. Yet it is apparent that Creeley, like the metaphysical poets, is expressing through love spiritual and psychological dilemmas of the self. The plain, modestly literal quality of his language partly conceals an allegorical dimension in his poetry. It seems unlikely that he could connote any mythos in these limpid, imagistic miniatures, but the emotional processes of these poems are too convoluted and rich to be taken merely as amorous complaints.

His poetry is even more closely akin to the short love lyrics of the English poet Robert Graves, whom Creeley came to know during his residence in Mallorca in the early 1950s. Graves' lovers enjoy happier relationships, but there is a worship of the female, even a devotion to her, that is similar to that of Creeley's despairing husbands. More importantly, Creeley evidently read Graves' formidable study of female mythology *The White Goddess* before publishing *A Form of Women* (1959), in a note to which he makes casual reference to Graves' study.

Graves is a serious student of mythology, and his work has been of interest to a number of contemporary American poets, including Olson, who quoted from *The Greek Myths* and *The White Goddess* in his *Maximus* sequence.[32] In *The White Goddess*, Graves shows that early societies were matriarchal and worshiped female deities, principally the white goddess, a lunar deity. And he insists throughout his study that the disharmony of Western social life is the consequence of a shift to patriarchal order and to male religions and that the redemption of man and culture depends upon restoring the white goddess to her original divine status. The poem as a form of expression, he argues, is a hymn to the superior female; the lyric is an act of male devotion.

It is doubtful that Creeley accepted or was even especially conscious of the full weight of Graves' premise, but the singular deference to the female in his own poetry would indicate that he was responsive to some of its implications.

When we compare Graves' study of the female in mythology to Erich Neumann's *The Great Mother: An Analysis of the Archetype*, we can perhaps imagine the middle ground where Creeley has rooted his mythic perceptions of woman. Neumann too concludes that early human society was matriarchal and that primitive religion preponderated with female deities, but he regards matriarchy as a stage in the evolution of consciousness, in which the ego in pursuit of an autonomous identity has not yet overthrown female hegemony.

Creeley writes of the male ego who is cast at the border of two realms, desiring both to submit to the uroboric love of the female and to continue as he is, solitary and uncertain of his existence. In "A Form of Women," he captures this state of imbalance with great concision:

My face is my own.
My hands are my own.

My mouth is my own
but I am not.

Moon, moon,
when you leave me alone
all the darkness is
an utter blackness, [33]

Most of the other poems in *A Form of Women* are studies of this ago-
nizing dual realm of awareness. In "The Three Ladies," Creeley explores the tripartite character of woman as virgin, mother, and destroyer.
"Ballad of the Despairing Husband" is the strongest poem of the volume and Creeley's most searching examination of this theme. The first
ten quatrains parody ballad style, which he charges with contentious detail; the persona exposes the failures of his marriage with witty confidence. But the poem then veers into a hymn to the wife in which the
ego crumbles from desperate loneliness. In "The Door," dedicated to
Robert Duncan, Creeley departs from the spare style of most of his other
poems and attempts a more visionary treatment of the female. She is in-
accessible, a mere specter beckoning the speaker to come into a garden
through a wall he is unable to cross. The poem's imagery is a constellation of medieval, seventeenth-century, and romantic clichés, all of which
course through the persona's speech uncritically as he attempts to articulate the difficult dream he has had.

Most of Creeley's poems have in common a loosely structured plot
based directly on his own life, the essentials of which are the dissolution of a first marriage, a profoundly tormenting experience, and the
recovery of mind and heart in a second marriage. *For Love: Poems
1950–1960* collects the poems published earlier as brief books.[34] Part 1,
compiled from *Le Fou* (1952), *The Kind of Act Of* (1953), and *The
Whip* (1957), is concerned with love and the happier circumstances of
the first marriage. In Part 2, which reprints all of the poems from *A
Form of Women*, love has soured into misunderstanding, and the memories of the marriage are bitter and painful. Part 3, consisting of new
poems, narrates the details of the second marriage, which the persona
enters with tempered emotions and less vulnerability. The marriages are
centers of tension. Early in Part 1 a poem is dedicated to Creeley's first
wife, Ann, and the last poem in Part 3 is devoted to his second wife,
Bobbie. The book is a progress, and the two marriages are the halves of
adulthood: the callow husband of Part 1 is awakened to the mystery and
depth of love through the loss of his first wife; but in Part 3 the mystery

is considerably diminished, and the ranges of feeling are smaller, more articulately rendered:

> Love comes quietly,
> finally, drops
> about me, on me,
> in the old ways.

> What did I know
> thinking myself
> able to go
> alone all the way. (p. 151)

In *Words* (1967), Creeley renews the theme of the two marriages and divides the two main parts of his book into recollections of the first marriage, grown more distant in his memory, and the new marriage with its mellowed emotion. The speaker seems content to live from moment to moment, unprovoked by violent emotion or fitful despair, as we see in these two examples from "A Place" and "Water (2)":

> . . . I am im-
> patient to begin again, open

> whatever door it was, find the weather
> is out there, grey, the rain then and
> now falling from the sky to the wet ground. (p. 85)

> Water drips,
> a fissure of leaking
> moisture spills
> itself unnoticed.

> What
> was I looking at,
> not to see
> the wetness spread. (p. 130)

"Some Afternoon" moves closer to self-contemplation and the fragments of immediate experience:

> Why not ride
> with pleasure
> and take oneself
> as measure,

> making the world
> tacit description
> of what's taken
> from it
>
> for no good reason,
> the fact only. (p. 60)

And he remarks that the familiar "faces / smile, breaking / into tangible pieces," leaving "Nothing left / after the initial / blast but / some echo like this." This poem presages the direction of Creeley's subsequent poetry: to get to the remote edge of feeling where unimportant events may be recorded in minimally imagistic statements. The poems of his later books diminish into couplets, then phrases, and finally a few words. The titles of his recent books are significant: *Pieces* (1969), *A Day Book* (1972), *Thirty Things* (1974).

The poems of *Pieces* range from a few lines to several pages but they have been composed as indefinite passages lacking bold beginnings and full closures. The intention is to find some means of writing the serial long poem through the mode of short statements, and to a degree the effort is successful. Creeley has managed to overcome the habit of his verse to leap and halt, but the effort requires his continual coaxing— many of the poems are notations to himself to remember the goal of his work: to include the trivial, to leave the thought half-spoken, to accept a variety of content and not close himself thematically again.

It is the work of a poet in deliberate transition to a more open stance toward composition, and his self-consciousness involves him in many practical, rather colorless instructions. Merged with these spare, didactic statements are the lyric returns to love and memory. The book is painful and fascinating to read, for the poems show the poet's insistent will to grow in his writing, to change old habits and extend himself into other experiences, and yet the psyche hesitates and rebels against such directions. Creeley was able to create the open long poem in one sense, but the content he gave it was erratic, changeful, even disjunctive. He had succeeded in making the short poem less formal and contained, but he failed to make it participate fully in the field relations of a sequence.

The experiment to make a long poem continued in *A Day Book* with even less success; the poems in the second section, for example, are merely random entries from day to day, and no full engagement of consciousness is perceptible in them. Thereafter, he more or less abandoned the long poem and pursued the possibilities of the minimal image free of any linkages.

In a recent interview, Creeley indicated he was involved in a project of writing one- and two-line poems to be published separately in a series of five hundred postcards.[35] His most recent book, *Away* (1976), is a gathering of work done over the last several years and seems intended to conclude the phase in which developed poems of some length were important to him. The book is not organized by any one theme, and the poems vary greatly in style and in quality.

In contrast to the reluctant, sometimes stuttering rhythms of his poetry, his prose is confident and elegantly specific and invents personae equal in their responsiveness to any that Olson or Duncan has created. Creeley's genius luxuriates in the conditions of prose: whereas the poems are for the most part intensely specific inventions, his prose operates by a casual brilliance of observation. In speaking of these two media in his career, Creeley has said,

> The differences [between poetry and prose] as they exist for me
> are these. Poetry seems to be written momently—that is, it occupies
> a moment of time. There is, curiously, no time in writing a poem.
> I seem to be given to work in some intense moment of whatever
> possibility, and if I manage to gain the articulation necessary *in*
> that moment, then happily there is the poem. Whereas in prose
> there's a coming and going. Much more of a gathering process
> that's evident in the writing. In fact I think I began prose because
> it gave me a more extended opportunity to think in . . . terms of
> something which was on my mind. . . .
> . . . I think that I was probably more articulate in prose than
> in poetry at first, in the early fifties, as the second issue of *Origin*
> will probably show. You can see from that kind of evidence that
> prose was much on my mind; I was more at home with its pos-
> sibilities at that time than I was with poetry's. In any case, prose
> lets me tinker, rather than work in the adamant necessity of its
> demand upon me. I come and go from it. I can work at many
> levels of response and can articulate these many levels—whether
> intense or quite relaxed or even at times inattentive. Prose, as
> Williams says, can carry a weight of "ill-defined matter." Well, I
> don't know if it's necessarily ill-defined but it can be random, and
> even at times indecisive.

He also found in prose the possibility of working at a single piece from day to day: "This sense of continuity, of having something there day after day was something I've had a great longing to have the use of."[36]

In the second issue of *Origin*, published in the summer of 1951,

Creeley was "featured" with letters to Corman, poems, and three short stories. The letters to Corman are amusing instances of Olson's influence: they are nearly exact imitations of Olson's letter style with their occasional bombast, folksy idiom, and bravura. They all but conceal Creeley's real modesty and candor. But in these letters and elsewhere in this issue, Creeley is applying Olson's projective poetic to the writing of prose.

His stories show clearly the mastery of projectivism in fiction—"Mr. Blue," in particular, is overwhelming in its narration by an individual whose jealousy and fear are never named or abstractly formulated but torture him through the multitude of his minute thoughts and sensations. "Mr. Blue" became, for Olson, the model of what the projective stance could rise to in the fictional mode.[37] Indeed, with "Mr. Blue" as the successful new modality, and the traditional form of short story he found in *New Directions 12* as the evident failure of art, Olson was provoked into writing his classic essay on responsiveness, "Human Universe."

Creeley's essay "Notes for a New Prose" was also included in the second issue of *Origin* and is his manifesto for a projective prose. Even the style is imitative of Olson's "Projective Verse" essay, but the argument he advances is less comprehensive:

> Perhaps it will still be necessary to point to the fact that, while poetry will be the clear, the fact of the head, prose will be the coming, and going. Around. It is there that it can hit, beyond poetry. It is not a matter of better, or worse. There is no competition.[38]

In an interview fourteen years later, Creeley continued to make the same claim for prose, especially as it applied to his own work:

> Prose offers me a more various way of approaching that kind of experience than does poetry, but then I do have the sense that Pound speaks of in *Make It New*, that one chafes if something in prose is of interest, to have it, frankly, in the articulation of poetry. . . .
> . . . Prose allows me a tentativeness which I much enjoy at times because it's a need. That is, I don't want to anticipate the recognition of what's involved so that prose gives me a way of feeling my way through things. Whereas poetry again is more often a kind of absolute seizure, a demand that doesn't offer variations of this kind.[39]

Creeley has often corrected interviewers who assume that he is "pursuing" prose; he prefers to think of himself as a "writer" using the mode that is demanded by his thought of the moment. But he is keenly aware of the fact that his success lies more fully in prose. In one instance he even mentions Duncan's perception that his "rhythmic articulation in [*The Island*] had really gone beyond what the poems prior to it had accomplished. And I would feel him right."[40]

Creeley's novel *The Island* (1963) describes his years with his first wife in Mallorca. The details of the narrative are from his own experience. Artie of the novel is the writer Martin Seymour-Smith, the hapless publisher who helped begin the Divers Press. The book is brief and well written. The plot structure and keen psychological probing make use of Jamesian techniques, but the substance of the character, the full view of his mind that we gain from his articulate attention to himself, are the genius of Creeley. The principal effect that the book achieves is a quality of concentration the narrator assumes from the outset and maintains to the finish: it is an astonishing capacity to look carefully, almost but not quite with dispassion, at the working of his own psyche, a feat of attention made more incredible by the fact that the narrator is watching himself deteriorate under the pressure of a wife who is ceasing to love him.

Creeley called this work "my first 'long poem'; it was the first piece of serial writing that went on for many days, weeks, and so forth. It taught me a lot; it made me impatient with other forms of writing for quite a while."[41] This is a fair assessment of the work, that it is a long poem and that it sustains a projective stance in its uncanny transformation of the most subtle movements of feeling and thought into vivid language. It is not projective in format, however; the delivery, the drawing of breath, does not show in its conventionally blocked, symmetrical prose passages. But this was neither a sacrifice of technique nor a departure from anything Creeley had tried to do in his verse: Creeley has never closely followed Olson's dicta on typography or breath-lines but has followed the stanzaic patterns of Williams' poems. However, the essential nature of projectivism as an exhaustive enactment of the things of consciousness *The Island* delivers with mastery.

In this first attempt at a sustained prose piece, Creeley depended on certain habits of imagination manifest in his verse: he divided the narrative into four sections of five chapters each, giving the novel a noticeable but not essential structuring. And he mediated the experience he described by the use of invented names.

Nine years later, in *A Day Book* (1972), none of these devices is present, and the prose passage that takes up the first half of the work goes beyond the novelistic limits of *The Island* to achieve more closely the sound and movement of an actual long poem. Free to be tentative, the serial form of the prose permits trivial and tentative thoughts their place in the work, and the prose is intended to be an inventory of the events that occurred in his consciousness from Tuesday, November 19, 1968, to Friday, June 11, 1971.

Verse rigidly precluded the trivial, as he had remarked in interviews, and it was that arbitrary editorial rule that allowed his lyrics to implode to unbearable densities of emotion which inhibited invention and excitement. Here, in this free and open prose format, the reader experiences the nuances of awareness as attention expands to complex speculations and then, as in the long poems of Pound, Williams, Olson, and Duncan, suddenly contracts to mundane immediacy:

> Watching the markedly tall man leaving the dining room—he makes the actually over-large hallway and stairs going up to the lobby seem of a size his own body is the measure of, i.e., it's his size, not the overly big space others make of it. Now there is an awkwardness in the size of this typewriter, the way the keys are placed almost 'beside it'—in front—so that its literal operation seems to be somehow in another place, as one types. The resistant difficulty it seems to make of the action of thinking, in words, that this form of writing seems to be—[42]

Like *Maximus Poems IV, V, VI, A Day Book* is without numbered pages. Only breaks in paragraph spacing, or notes, suggest that there have been pauses in the composition. Otherwise, the prose creates a dense field of related thinking and emotion that ranges from squibs on poetics and comments on friends to Creeley's inimitable absorption in the minutiae of experience, as when Bobbie Creeley returns home and he records his impressions of her entry. There is the free play of the intellect as words are punned, their meanings toyed with; there are erotic fantasies and dream narratives and even echoes of details first mentioned in *The Island*, by which even that narrative becomes an extension of the field within which *A Day Book* functions.

Presences (1976), Creeley's most recent book of prose, is a series of informal meditations on photographs of satiric sculptures by Marisol. Creeley continues to broaden the scope of his prose by playful leaps of thought and surreal juxtapositions, amusing anecdotes, dream narratives, and, in several passages, returns to the theme of marriage and the details of an increasingly cranky relationship with his wife. The verbal brilliance is powerful, but almost too consciously achieved, as though intended as a performance. The prose is occasionally wordy, the wit labored; Creeley nonetheless manages to make the guide often more compelling to look at than the exhibition.

It is through his prose that Creeley captures the fullness of an individual's consciousness; his poems are achievements of a different order. Their intensity and clarity are the articulations of certain halted events. In the prose, mind is allowed to flow in its own digressive course, and the effect Creeley achieves is one of instantaneity and real motion. His grasp of the nature of consciousness reaches to the depth of Olson's own work.

"Dunk"

Robert Duncan is in direct contrast to Robert Creeley. Whereas Creeley is so much the poet of reluctant desire, tormented with doubt and confusion, Duncan is confident to the point of swagger and can barely restrain himself from interminable effusion. Creeley's simple loneliness and shy emotions are the opposite of Duncan's frank disclosures of homosexual passion; in the more torrid of his early erotic poems he is the confident aggressor, the taker, the forceful suitor demanding abject passiveness in the lover. Creeley seems happiest when ruled by force. And where the tribulations of a minutely observed domesticity dominate the imaginative world of Creeley's poems, Duncan's poetry rivals Olson's in its broad range of myth, occult lore, politics, poetics, and personal experience. Unlike Creeley, who could put off writing for the more immediate pleasure of raising fowl, Duncan was impatient to establish himself and began publishing poems in college reviews at the age of eighteen. "By my eighteenth year, I recognized in poetry my sole and ruling vocation."[43] It is even worth contrasting their regional origins: Creeley is eminently the taciturn New Englander, native of the somber back country of Massachusetts; Duncan, on the other hand, is from Oakland, California. When Duncan joined the faculty of Black Mountain College, he brought a new regional sensibility to the group, which had up to then been dominated by New Englanders.

None of these opposites has prevented the two poets from enjoying a close friendship and a mutual admiration for Olson. Both have frequently paid written tribute to Olson, and each has expressed a genuine appreciation for the work of the other. And once more Creeley has performed the role of chronicler of the Black Mountain movement in describing Duncan's first contacts with Olson:

Olson had met Duncan when he had been out on the West Coast. I think in the late forties. He had been out there, and he had been introduced to Duncan, and he had had a very vivid impression of him. He said he went to a party, I guess, at Robert's place. And he found Robert sitting on a kind of velvet throne, looking like Hermes himself, or something. He was very amused and impressed by the incredible drama that Robert was able to make of the scene. . . . But I think Robert was so involved in his own scene then, or so involved with the center of writing he'd got to, that I don't think he had much interest in Olson at that point. Olson really comes into Robert's purview, so to speak, through *Origin*.[44]

Origin was clearly serving its purpose—to make poets of the avant garde aware of each other's work. Through its broad use of the "open letter," in which poets frequently published their correspondence to each other, the sense of a movement was clearly manifested. In the spring 1954 issue, Duncan expressed his deep admiration for Olson's latest work, *In Cold Hell, In Thicket*, and for *Maximus Poems 1–10*. In that letter he also pointed to the area where Olson was to be the greatest influence, his demand that a poet fashion his work from full awareness:

> A very structure of act, a speech as learned in the hand-ear-to-mouth as walking, an athletic language. Because all here is the purpose of the poet there is no discouragement: that you have such technical achievement compared to my often inadequacy there is every encouragement, heartening: to be free! an [sic] I am as I speak.[45]

Two years later, Duncan expanded his commentary on the *Maximus* sequence in his essay "Notes on Poetics: Regarding Olson's *Maximus*" in *Black Mountain Review*. He asserts that Olson's poetic introduced a new dimension of the self to poetry, namely "internal sensation." A mastery of ear and eye had already been realized in poetic tradition, according to Duncan, and it remained that a final mastery be gained of this other function, where the "inner voice" resides. Olson's *Maximus* succeeds in this articulation of neural and muscular responsiveness of the poet, as it does in expressing what eye and ear perceive. In conclusion, he writes, "On the level of reference, the gain from Whitman's address to his cosmic body to Olson's address to 'The waist of a lion / for a man to move properly' is immense."[46]

Scattered through Duncan's poetry, after the middle 1950s, are various allusions to Olson, all favorable in tone, relating either to the matter of poetics and Olson's importance to him or to actual poems by Olson, which Duncan liberally quotes. But with all this evidence at hand for us to argue the extent of Olson's influence upon Duncan, the younger poet's interests and dispositions make difficult the premise that he assimilated Olson's projective poetic.

Duncan often writes what he has described as "pretentious fictions," the allegorical narratives that appear in much of his poetry. This, and his penchant for being the center of various esthetic cults, prompted Olson to admonish him in his 1954 essay "Against Wisdom as Such." Duncan answered in self-defense a year later in "From A Notebook," where he remarked that he sought to revive the romantic spirit. "This is of course the radical disagreement that Olson has with me. In a sense he is so keen upon the virtu of reality that he rejects my 'wisdom' not as it might seem at first glance because 'wisdom' is a vice; but because my wisdom is not real wisdom." He then defines the state of his own poetic at the moment:

> He suspects, and rightly, that I indulge myself in pretentious fictions. I, however, at this point take enuf delight in the available glamor that I do not stop to trouble the cheapness of such stuff. I mean that it is, for a man of rigor, an inexpensive irony to play with puns on pretending and pretension. I like rigor and even clarity as a quality of a work—that is, as I like muddle and floaty vagaries. It is the intensity of the conception that moves me. This intensity may be that it is all of a fervent marshmallow dandy lion fluff.[47]

Projectivism tied the poet too directly to his world. Duncan's objection is that he wished to include the inventions of the imagination, spoofs, fancies, allegory, fable, all. His difference as a poet of the Black Mountain school is that he has been deeply influenced by English romantic verse, which amounts to heresy among American poets, many of whom cherish provinciality after so long a domination of their art by British standards.

Much of Duncan's poetry is in the loosely worded style of the visionary romantics, particularly Blake and Shelley, though some of his poems allude richly to Wordsworth's lyrics and to Keats' poems, especially the more euphonious lines of his sonnets. Blake's assumption of prophetic powers is a model for Duncan's hieratic pronouncements on the American condition. The elaborate allegorical structures of Shelley's political poems are reconceived in Duncan's art; the flair for exaggeration and the frequent use of satanic and erotic images Shelley poured forth are similarly intense in Duncan's tracts.

Duncan's explicit manifesto of his romantic stance is in *The Truth & Life of Myth: An Essay in Essential Autobiography*, revised from a lecture he presented in 1967. Reminiscent of Shelley's "Defence of Poetry," the essay argues that poets must open themselves to mythic reality if they are to extend the narrowing bounds of reality in contemporary society. The positivistic thought of the last several centuries has thrown a wall up against the deep past and the mythic consciousness found in the Old and New Testaments and the tradition of visionary poetry dating back to Homer:

> The very word "Romantic" is, in literary and social criticism today, pejorative. But it is in the Romantic vein—to which I see my own work as clearly belonging—that the two worlds, the lordly and the humble, that seemed to scholars irreconcilably at odds, mythological vision and folklorish phantasy, are wedded in a phantasmagoria—as Goethe called his Helen episode—the spiritual romance . . . and today, over a hundred years after the beginnings of the Romantic synthesis, our poetic task remains to compose the true ephithalamium where chastity and lewdness, love and lust, the philosopher king and the monstrous clown dance together in all their human reality.[48]

The essay makes many references to the English romantic poets, particularly to Blake's mythic poems, but, throughout, Duncan perceives no real separation between these poets and his American contemporaries. He manages a synthesis of his own between the remotely exotic imagination of early visionary poets and the poetic of immediacy Olson outlined. In one passage Duncan makes a concise recapitulation of Olson's essay on projectivism and incorporates it into his own system:

> But let us take just this concrete immediacy of the poem: I start with the word "Father", and since I compose by the tone-leading of vowels, the vowels are notes of a scale, in which breaths move, but these soundings of spirit upon which the form of the poem depends are not constant. . . . But I do not mistrust reality any more than I trust it: I seek it with an ardor that leads as it misleads.[49]

In a published chapter of a work still in progress and given the tentative title *Beginnings of the H. D. Book*, Duncan asserts his romantic conviction that "all things have come into their comparisons," suggesting that in the twentieth century the recognition has been made again that human life is gathered into the "cooperative design of all living things, in the life of everything, everywhere."[50] His commentary restates Wordsworth's perception of the "one life within us and abroad," and he goes on to assert that Freud, Marx, and Darwin each envisioned a oneness or global community in their theories. They voiced a key assumption of modern thought, that in nature's phenomena lie the terms for understanding human nature and even human culture. Myth, when either primitive (as in the culture of Australian tribesmen) or highly sophisticated, is the human understanding thrust outward into that larger nature. The human being is cast into a small awareness which he seeks to broaden through his guesses and intuitions; every art form is such a quest for meaning and experience. In this context Duncan discusses the work and thought of Hilda Doolittle and the whole imagist movement. He passes over the earliest stages of imagist poetry, the severely brief lyrics, to the point at which Eliot, Pound, Doolittle, and Williams all succeeded in creating a poetry which is essentially a rite of participation with history, politics, society, and the whole noumenal realm of vision.

He is principally interested in H. D.'s most ambitious poems, the World War II sequence entitled *Trilogy*. Here a series of motifs and complex mythic allusions is drawn into her agony over the experience of war in London. Duncan cites the longer poems of the imagists almost as though they needed to be thought of in terms of the wars in which they were written. Eliot's own rite of participation is "The Waste Land"; Pound's *Pisan Cantos* is a ritual meditation on World War II; and *Paterson* arises from the aroused conscience after war. Each of these longer poetic masterworks is seen by Duncan as a document of the poet's desire to enrich the actual by making vision and desire take form and reality in his work. The argument may not hold true for the despairing vision in "The Waste Land," but it is valid for H. D.'s *Trilogy*, which closes in a celebration of Christ and human transcendence. Duncan includes H. D. among the poets of the mythopoetic tradition, the romantic visionaries, those who dissolve "the boundaries of time" and seek to "extend the burden of consciousness" to include the larger world. As we shall see, Duncan wrote his poem "Passages" on the war in Vietnam, and Levertov was to follow with a war sequence as well.

For much of his career, Duncan has been trying to find a meeting point between a voluptuous lyricism gained from wide reading in Continental and English romantic literature, both early and late, and the American imagist poetic, which has insisted that the immediate world dominate the poet's utterance. The innate severity of imagist speech, with its attention fixed upon the material condition, often remains an indissoluble element in the flow of Duncan's "period" eloquence.

He has indeed made a synthesis of these tendencies in some of his poems, and he has worked in one vein or the other throughout his prolific career. But Duncan has followed a different premise from that of Olson, who first set out to denounce the "lyrical interference of the individual as ego"; Duncan's work derives from the sense that it is the lyricism of the individual ego that precipitates poetry.

Olson's theoretical writings, with their emphasis on the exact concrete details of experience, were just the checkrein Duncan needed for his habitual airy subjectivity. Olson (and Pound before him) built directly upon imagist precision, and with Olson the precision lay directly in the poet's translation of all his sensory changes as he experienced other objects. For Duncan, such accuracy was a skill he had not used before. Through Olson, too, Duncan was persuaded to allow more of the physical self to take part in his poetic discourse, as in "The Dance" and "The Song of the Borderguard." As he commented in his biographical sketch for Allen's anthology (where these two poems appear),

> Since 1951 my work has been associated in my mind with a larger work that appeared in the writing of Charles Olson, Denise Levertov, and Robert Creeley. . . . What released my sense of a new generation in poetry was first a poem (*The Shifting* by Denise Levertov) in *Origin IV*, 1952; then in 1954, thru *The Gold Diggers* a grasp of the art of Robert Creeley, where such minute attentions and cares moved in the line; and third, but from the first, the break-thru to a meaningful reading of Olson's *Maximus*, from which his *Projective Verse* and *In Cold Hell In Thicket* [sic] took on new meaning: that, for one thing, the task in poetry could be promethean.[51]

In the poems of *The Opening of the Field* (1960), Duncan digests the elements of projective composition almost one by one while returning intermittently to romantic versifying. After a spate of empty lyricism, we are caught up in his increasing awareness of the projective mode. In "A Poem Beginning with a Line by Pindar" (Part III of which is dedicated to Charles Olson), Duncan writes the first really open composition of his career. The self he creates is open to the complex impulses that direct his utterance: he is making into speech all the available contents of his immediate experience. A misread line from Pindar has engaged his wonder, and what Duncan utters draws out the web of sensation and idea which the misreading has aroused.

His poems of the late 1950s and early 1960s are alert to the processes of the whole physical entity. The dominant theme of this poetry is the creative process itself, the coming to speech of stray impulses, nowhere better presented than in the masterful open poem "An Owl Is An Only Bird of Poetry."

The turn to the organismic self led naturally to the larger autobiographical sequence "The Structure of Rime," which follows the stages of a poet's growth as he awakens to the mysterious cosmos. The early poems borrow plot from Dante's *The Divine Comedy*, as the speaker is led by unidentified guides to a psychological hell. The sequence of poems is scattered throughout *The Opening of the Field* and breaks off at the point where some larger understanding awaits him.

In *Roots and Branches* (1964) the sequence is resumed with a perception of order, the "inner view of things," which is likened to the tree Iggdrasil, whose roots and branches join all things together. In Parts XIV through XXI, the persona grows fearful of still deeper confusion until, with the final passage, he is "Lost in the hour-maze" but sees "the sun returning to the day" (p. 171). In the next poem, the last of the book, the sun is seen rising over the nation, illuminating it as well as the poet's vision.

In *Bending the Bow* (1968), "The Structure of Rime" moves to a point of fulfillment in the life of a poet, in Parts XXIV and XXV, and then the sequence dissolves into a new long poem that began earlier in the same book. Thus, Section XXVI of "The Structure of Rime" is simultaneously "Passages 20," an important juncture of the two long poems. "Passages 20" fuses two allegorical tales. The first is Maeterlinck's play *The Blue Bird*, in which two children search for the bluebird of happiness only to realize that they have had it all along and have just given it its freedom. The second is Charles Perrault's *Blue Beard*, in which the young wife opens the only door of a castle forbidden to her and finds the corpses of all her husband's previous wives. The poem suggests a fork in the road confronting the persona in his journey, one path leading to satisfaction and the other to terrifying revelation.

"Passages" is a bolder, more projective sequence than "The Structure of Rime." In the second poem, "At the Loom," Duncan explains the principles he will use in composing the work. As in the later books of the *Maximus* sequence Olson allows his persona to treat or ignore any part of his large subject, Duncan similarly uses the metaphor of a weaver who is free to introduce into the warp of his theme any and all "luminous soft threads":

> the thrown glamour, crossing and recrossing,
>   the twisted sinews underlying the work.
> Back of the images, the few cords that bind
>   meaning in the word-flow,
>   the rivering web
>   rises among wits and senses
> gathering the wool into its full cloth.[52]

In "Passages 4" he remarks, "I have in this my own / intense area of self creation," which the following poems pursue until "Passages 20," when the warp receives the themes of the prior sequence. "Passages 13" introduces the major theme, the war in Vietnam, so that with "Passages 20" we are brought up to the situation of the forked road, where the persona chooses unknowingly the road leading to terror and despair. The joining of the two sequences at this point is an instance of high craftsmanship, for the first sequence, stalled in indecision, gives way to the new sequence, which depends on projective principles more emphatically in addressing the topic of war and in which Duncan's imagination seems to open to its depths in the confrontation.

The later "Passages" probe the mythic reality of the war. Duncan drew anger from his intense convictions as a socialist poet and wrote some of his finest poems. In a recent continuation, *Tribunals, Passages 31–35*, his exalted speech creates a stately and gripping dirge that captures the stark horror of the long conflict in Asia. "Passages" is a worthy, thrilling achievement in the tradition of long, openly constructed sequential works.

Levertov

Denise Levertov and Paul Blackburn did not reside at Black Mountain College during Olson's rectorship and knew him only casually, but their work was published in *Origin* and *Black Mountain Review*, and their styles and techniques were influenced in part by the projective mode.

Denise Levertov was the only female poet to have entered into the decidedly masculine Black Mountain movement, and her participation in it is all the more interesting when we consider that she began writing as a "British Romantic with almost Victorian background," as she admitted in her note for the Allen anthology.

Under the self-scrutiny of much of her verse, Levertov has uncovered the blunt desires of her sexual nature and also her public concerns, which turned her to a radical, even anarchistic position against the American war in Vietnam. The tautness in her verse lies in the various transformations of identity, from tactful British womanhood to advocate of women's liberation, or from the cheerfully energetic housewife and gardener to political activist deciding, as in one of her best poems, between "death or revolution."

Her first book of poems, *The Double Image*, was published in London in 1946, and a year later she married Mitchell Goodman, an American who had attended Harvard with Creeley. After arriving in the United States in 1948, Levertov was drawn into the early stirrings of the movement with the publication in 1951 of her poem "The Bereaved" in the second issue of *Origin*, the "Creeley" issue. She appeared again in the sixth issue (Summer 1952) and then frequently thereafter. Among the influences of her early career, she has cited sources familiar among Black Mountain poets: "My reading of William Carlos Williams and Wallace Stevens, which began in Paris in 1948; of Olson's essay, 'Projective Verse'; conversations and correspondence with Robert Duncan . . . ; an introduction to some of the concepts of Jung; the friendship of certain painters such as Albert Kresch—have all been influential and continue to be so."[53] Her first American book, *Here and Now* (1957), shows very clearly the extent of Williams' influence on her poetry. The title itself reveals a concern with the precise language of imagism, and the poems are an effort to describe the objects of direct and simple perception. The book is a summary of her transition from an English poet to an assertive American poet learning "new rhythms of life and speech."

But as the Black Mountain movement began to dissolve into subsequent currents of new poetry, especially beat poetry, she began to reject some of the tenets of the avant garde she had become identified with, particularly the tendency of some poets to publish work that was misspelled, unpunctuated, casually written. In a postscript to her note in the Allen anthology, she wrote, "At the time [1960] I was reaching irritation to the printing of some poets' work complete with spelling errors, e.g., Peter Orlovsky's 'Frist Poem,' [sic], to the eulogizing of Jack Kerouac's poems . . . to the enthusiastic publication that was then taking place of anything any soon-to-be-forgotten imitator of Allen Ginsberg happened to scrawl on the back of the proverbial envelope. . . . I didn't like the sloppy garbage that seemed in 1959 to be suddenly appearing everywhere in his wake."[54] Her own verse of these years is neat in appearance, conventionally spaced and punctuated, and somewhat conventional in content as well: her poems turn upon minor discoveries in her observation of daily reality and rely frequently on the technique of surprising closure.

Her frustration in the late 1950s with the lack of a varied poetic content was similar to Creeley's: both poets had discovered that the six- or eight-line imagist poem precluded a great variety of subjects that require not only a larger space but a diction that must be allowed to vary between compression and expansion; the poet's feelings are more accurately registered in the changes of rhythm, in typography, and even in the silences of open forms.

At the beginning of the 1960s Levertov moved toward a more open style. In the essay "Some Notes on Organic Form," published in *Poetry* in 1965, she gives her own version of open composition:

> During the writing of a poem the various elements of the poet's
> being are in communion with each other, and heightened. Ear
> and eye, intellect and passion, interrelate more subtly than at other
> times; and the "checking for accuracy," for precision of language,
> that must take place throughout the writing is not a matter of one
> element supervising the others but of intuitive interaction between
> all the elements involved.
>
> In the same way, content and form are in a state of dynamic
> interaction; the understanding of whether an experience is a linear
> sequence or a constellation raying out from and into a central
> focus or axis, for instance, is discoverable only in the work, not
> before it.[55]

The books of poems she began publishing after *Here and Now* (1957) progress toward self-recognition. *With Eyes at the Back of Our Heads* (1959), her first really substantial book, describes her frustration with a vague sense of identity overlaying the real but remote truths of self. In "The Goddess" she sees herself violently released from banal assumptions. The figure of truth, she writes,

> Flung me across the room, and
> room after room (hitting the walls, re-
> bounding—to the last
> sticky wall—wrenching away from it
> pulled hair out!)
> till I lay
> outside the outer walls!
>
> There in cold air

lying still where her hand had thrown me,
I tasted the mud that splattered my lips:
the seeds of a forest were in it,
asleep and growing! I tasted
her power! (p. 43)

O Taste and See (1964) boldly explores the feminine psyche, revealing in the course of its many short poems a condition of disordered vitalities equal to what her male counterparts discovered in their own awareness. The final stanza of "Song of Ishtar," which initiates this book, beautifully sums up the theme of the volume:

In the black of desire
we rock and grunt, grunt and
shine (p. 3)

In "Hypocrite Women" the examination of self culminates in a frank disclosure of female sexuality:

Hypocrite women, how seldom we speak
of our own doubts, while dubiously
we mother man in his doubt!

. . . .

our cunts are ugly—why didn't we
admit we have thought so too? (And
what shame? They are not for the eye!)

No, they are dark and wrinkled and hairy,
caves of the Moon . . .   And when a
dark humming fills us, a

coldness towards life,
we are too much women to
own to such unwomanliness. (p. 70)

In later volumes, she has made the transition from personal to more public concerns, specifically the war in Vietnam, which has required her to experiment with the longer poem. In *Relearning the Alphabet* (1970) the short poem continues to dominate her work, but in at least two poems dealing with the war, "An Interim" and "From a Notebook: October '68–May '69," she has successfully constructed a sequence that captures the changes and subtleties of consciousness. In the first she studies her indignation and anger on learning of the suicidal fast of a war protester.

The second poem masters the projective mode, for in the process of articulating her political radicalism she is drawn into a close scrutiny of all that enters into her disposition to make her radical, including her keen sense of perhaps having been too remote from her precise surroundings:

> Learned—not for the first time—my 'roots in the
> 19th century' put me
>
>   out of touch. (p. 96)

To Stay Alive (1971) culminates in a long poem about the war entitled "Staying Alive." Each of its four parts chronicles developments of the war and her reaction to them. The poem is a complex, varied expression of the female sensibility driven to violent rage. It employs projective techniques, even while obeying Levertov's earliest habits to retain the conventions of punctuation and orthography, standards she has refused to abandon in her work.

"The Black"

Paul Blackburn's poetry first appeared in the "Creeley issue" of *Origin*, the same issue in which Levertov's work debuted in the United States, and *Origin* frequently published him thereafter. Olson noted that Blackburn had been born in Vermont and linked him with the other New Englanders who dominated the Black Mountain movement. Olson bestowed on him the dubious epithet of friendship "the Black—who burns my arse" yet nonetheless counted him with himself, Creeley, Corman, and others as "parts of a Landsgeist which has now, again, reasserted itself."[56] After the appearance of Blackburn's first book, a translation of troubadour poetry entitled *Proensa*, which Creeley's Divers Press published in Mallorca in 1953, Olson wrote a short poem of the same title dedicated to Blackburn and Creeley.[57] Blackburn's work also appeared regularly in *Black Mountain Review*. He, like Duncan before him, went to join Creeley on Mallorca, where a second book, *The Dissolving Fabric*, was also published by the Divers Press in 1955. These poems are written in a compact style that he retained.

Blackburn had begun writing in the late 1940s after reading Pound's translations of troubadour poetry. "What got me started on Provençal was reading squibs of it in the *Cantos* and not being able to understand it, which annoyed me."[58] He went to Europe to continue his studies in Provençal literature, to Toulouse in 1954 as a Fulbright scholar, returned the next year as *lecteur américain* at the University of Toulouse, and lived part of the time from 1954 to 1957 in Spain. But the important consequence of this travel lay more directly in his lyrical evocations of the French cities he stayed in, later collected in *The Cities* (1967). Among the poets we are dealing with here, Blackburn comes closest to employing Olson's breath principle: his lines compel the reader to take note of their duration, with their exact fulfillment of a thought in a moment of breath. Paul Carroll has described Blackburn's poetic skill in his essay "Five Poets in Their Skins":

> Over the Labor Day holiday that year [1953] I visited Paul in New York. While trucks and taxis clattered all night down 55th Street, and while his girl let out periodic yelps from the bedroom telling us to pipe down or come to bed, Paul took my poems apart, line by line, showing me how the line breaks according to its own breath and how a stanza should build only out of its own unique life.[59]

But in all his work is a dominant tone: Blackburn was a modern pastoral poet whose sensibilities experience easily bruised. He wrote often of his loneliness, of watching others, of his shy sexual longings, of fantasies arising out of the banality of daily life, always attempting to protect his vulnerability by affecting a certain toughness or indifference. His first poems are somewhat callow in their emotional simplicity:

> My thoughts
> are flowers in your dark hair
>   your proud adornments
> But you do not say any kind word to me
>   nor bow your head
> under their delicate insinuations [60]

In his later poetry he wrote as a man who ventured into the world with too much tenderness. Tone is the delicate nuance of his best verse, an innocence of mind that is forever dissolving and reemerging from a tough antilyric vocabulary. He is the pastoral poet set loose in the drab, impersonal streets of New York. In the poems of *Brooklyn–Manhattan Transit* (1960), he describes the slight possibilities of romance in the dreary compartments of the subway train:

> The tanned blond
>   in the green print sack

    in the center of the subway car
                                    standing
    tho there are seats
                        has had it from
    1 teen-age hood
    1 lesbian
    1 envious housewife
    4 men over fifty
    (& myself), in short
                    the contents of this half of the car.[61]

In "Clickety-Clack," he tells us he read aloud from Lawrence Ferlinghetti's "A Coney Island of the Mind" to a subway car full of passengers, themselves headed for Coney Island, and records their dismay.[62]

Blackburn died leaving a canon of work, including his last-written poems, *The Journals*, which Robert Kelly edited in 1975. In his editorial note, Kelly claims that *The Journals* are "Blackburn's quintessential work." As early as 1968 Blackburn had a premonition of his impending death by cancer, to which he succumbed in 1971, and from that date, Kelly says, "his work, especially *The Journals*, reads like a *carnivale*, a joyous farewell to the flesh of the world." Perhaps "joyous farewell" is more than the text of the poems would bear out; many of the individual entries in the poet's journal are touching and poignant, sometimes starkly lyrical.

In these last poems, too, there is a superb sense of visual placement of language on the page: Blackburn communicates half of the content of his words merely by their location. The objective, mundane content is lined up against the left margin, the moodier passages and subjective embellishments against the right, and the play of the mind ranges down the center in steep terraces. There is an exact sense of spacing in the lines, a keen ear-sense as well in the way he dangles the terminal word of a line or halts a line and then introduces the key word in full capitals. These typographical techniques, so bold and controversial fifteen years before, appear under Blackburn's hand as the new conventions of modern poetic speech; they do not shout or violate the reader's expectations, they simply occur with precise, satisfying effect.

The Journals are also Blackburn's successful effort at a long poem, in which he recorded his late travels through Europe and the final months of his life in Cortland, New York, where he was teaching. As the title implies, these poems constitute his daybook, the form many poets of the short lyric have imposed on themselves to achieve a work of length and continuity. But whereas other poets have used the daybook as a rhythmic device, Blackburn seizes upon the form with a richer intent: the days themselves are increasingly more valuable as he senses his approaching death.

He avoids making a deliberate plot of his death; rather, the thought of it erupts intermittently in the flow of his brief lyrics. The last poems are not final in any thematic sense; they continue to make records of daily life as though the process were to go on forever. For the contemporary poet, death is an intractable subject. Its final meaning is unclear, and the fuller the treatment of it, the more the poet feels required to address himself to its religious and philosophical implications. Blackburn succeeds in treating the theme by approaching it with naive inquisitiveness. Three months before his death he can observe

> How it turns
> in again, the pain
>   across my shoulders these mornings.
>
>   Possession of the mind
>   a fragile thing / when the pain
>   goes,
> then's the time to use it . what's left of it . (p. 135)

Or, in an earlier poem, he writes,

>   Joan moves
>   her legs against mine in the hall, goes down to
> start my egg . Carlos thumps in the lower stairs . We move.
>
> All our farewells al-
> ready prepared inside us . aaaall our
> deaths we carry inside us, double-yolked, the
> fragile toughness of the shell . it makes
> sustenance possible, makes love   possible
> as the red buds break against the sunlight
> possible green, as legs move against legs (p. 116)

More poignantly still, he observes his frail diseased body in the tub with disarming candor and surprise:

> . . . I feel
> the skinnyness of arms, the bony chest
> cavity, front & back, as I soap up .

> It's something else for the fingertips to remember
> I haven't had a body like this since I was   15 .
> What is it the ribs remember, the clavicles, the
>   wingbones so unfleshed?
>   To recognize the differences
> in the quality of flesh tho, something else . (p. 131)

As it was for Emily Dickinson before him, death is a shock into greater consciousness which the poet explores precisely, openly, using every resource of language and technique to map and understand it.

These four poets constitute the core of Olson's circle by virtue of their personal acknowledgments of indebtedness to Olson's ideas and the use they made of them in their poems. Their intimate friendships with one another further bound them together. Creeley's press had published their early work, and their voluminous correspondence—much of it still to be edited and published—reveals the extent to which they pursued the same ideal: to bring more of human response to experience into their writing, to make the poem the act of self-discovery. In a time of increasing social regimentation, each wished to reveal in fluid compositions the mystery of the human organism. The projective poem, as Olson had initially formulated it, was likened to a missile, a declaration of complex identity to be hurled against all the received notions of mass behavior and all the converging tendencies of American society to rationalize existence.

Poets on the Fringe

The Black Mountain poets were part of a larger reaction in the arts against the increasing uniformity of American social life. Other schools of poetry were equally involved. The sheer multiplicity of categories in Allen's anthology attests to this (but also carries an implication of divisiveness to which Olson objected).[63] The New York poets, whose works are represented in Ron Padget and David Shapiro's *An Anthology of New York Poets*, as well as in Allen's anthology, pursued freedoms of composition similar to those of the New York action painters. Their unique emphasis upon luxurious color and texture shows a pronounced painterly imagination which distinguishes this school. The San Francisco poets, and the renaissance that emerged from their public readings, comprise another facet of this larger reaction. All these movements are further diversified by the social class and political ideologies of the poets involved. Within the same general pursuit of freer forms of poetic composition, we can locate an elegant upper-class experience among the New York poets, a radical political consciousness among certain San Francisco poets, and a brooding sense of alienation from roots among the displaced New England poets of the Black Mountain school.

In the ferment of the postmodernist revival of the arts, a number of poets usually identified with various other schools (or factions) published their work in the Black Mountain journals and constitute an outer fringe. Olson showed particular interest in the work of Imamu Amiri Baraka (Leroi Jones) and Ed Sanders. In an interview with David Ossman, Baraka makes mention of his poetic transformation, from his "Eliot Period" to that of the "Imagist's poetry."[64] His magazine *Yugen,* which he edited during the late 1950s and early 1960s, published much of the later work of the Black Mountain poets.

Baraka is among the few black writers with whom Olson came in contact, and his struggle to deal with the situation of his race and the black consciousness in America naturally appealed to Olson's own concern for individual awareness. The oppressed circumstances of the black American made the possibility of direct perception much more difficult.

Since the late 1950s, when Baraka and Olson were closely associated through the journals of the poetic avant garde, Baraka has become one of the most compelling black writers in America. His career began in the company of white poets, and his volume of poems *Preface to a Twenty Volume Suicide Note* (1961) is divided between evocations of black experience and the expression of a more general sense of rebellion against the postindustrial American culture that the avant garde as a whole opposed. With *The Dead Lecturer* (1964) and his autobiographical novel *The System of Dante's Hell* (1965), his attention focused on the conditions of blacks in America, which he has since made his exclusive subject.

In *Home: Social Essays* (1968), particularly in his essay "Cuba Libre," Baraka has identified himself as a socialist writer whose allegiance is no longer to the white conscience in America but to America's racial minorities and the small nations he feels are oppressed by a white American empire. Baraka has explored the terrain and conditions of the black man with a vigor and comprehension similar to Olson's. Baraka has in recent years refused to be associated with white poets and to have his work presented in anthologies featuring their poetry, but such a step was perhaps a psychological necessity for a poet who sees his own race as suffering under the domination of white values, including prejudices.

By the mid-1960s, the beat movement was nearly spent, but young writers continued to emerge from this ferment and to make their mark on the decade. More tenacious than most, Ed Sanders expressed himself through a variety of media: as editor-publisher of Fuck You Press, which issued a mimeographed quarterly from 1962 to 1966 that included works by Robert Creeley, Allen Ginsberg, Norman Mailer, and William Burroughs; as poet and novelist; and as singer and musician for "The Fugs," a rock group which he organized and performed with as lead vocalist. Olson was attracted to Sanders' raw, raucous lyrics, his bawdy, energetic prose, and general mayhem of his activities in the bohemian subculture of New York, all of which confirmed Olson's belief that the vitality of poetry had not dissipated but was taken up by a new generation which in some ways was more madcap and inventive than the last. Although he does pay tribute to Olson when he writes, "I grew up on Ezra Pound, Allen Ginsberg, Hesiod, and my final form is governed by those great men, Pindar, Herodotus, and Charlie Olson," the Missouri-born Sanders is different from other writers we have been discussing in that he had been influenced by the works of the postmodernists long before he met them or joined the movement in his own right.[65]

Other poets on this fringe include Gilbert Sorrentino, who edited the journal *Neon*. He too has made clear the primary influences on him as a poet:

> Speaking of the great influential poets of our time, Olson is certainly Creeley's mentor, I would say. Everyone else in the world today who cares for poems has learned from Olson. Olson is our Ezra Pound, if you want to be very corny about it. He is the oldest of the group, and he is the one who has written a long poem which makes it—*The Maximus Poems*—a beautiful book in which, on every level, mastery is shown.[66]

Some of Sorrentino's best poems are collected in an early volume entitled *Black and White*, edited by Baraka. An epigraph from William Carlos Williams on the subject of love points to the major theme of the poems, but the techniques and the thoughtful modesty of the persona suggest Creeley's influence. The title of the book, with its immediate associations of snapshots and of unvarnished reality, expresses the attitude in the poems. The book is a series of short commentaries on affection and desire, in which the bland details of daily life take their place among the moments of passion. Sorrentino, although less gifted than Creeley, includes a wider range of feeling in his sober compositions. Sorrentino's work, although of minor quality, is an intelligent consolidation of Black Mountain techniques and attitudes.

Paul Carroll, as an editor first of *The Chicago Review* and then of

Big Table, also published Black Mountain poetry and has written about it in his critical book, *The Poem in Its Skin* (1968). Vincent Ferrini and Cid Corman, as we have seen, were both close friends of Olson, and Corman's interest in Black Mountain poetry cannot be overstated.

But the fringe dissolves into other movements, and the links and relationships fan out with increasing subtlety of connection. With the breakup of the college, the movement dispersed and became absorbed into the main currents of American poetry. Creeley entered into the New York ferment for a time with his patronage of the Cedar Bar, a new hub of artistic activity, and Duncan returned to San Francisco, where the young beat poets were beginning to emerge. Indeed, the final issue of *Black Mountain Review,* published in the autumn of 1957, was devoted to the new beat poets, perhaps in recognition of the fact that it was to them that the life and energy of poetry had naturally flowed at the time.[67]

"Black Mtneers"

Finally, we should not forget several poets who were Olson's students at Black Mountain College, whom he referred to once, affectionately, as the "Black Mtneers": Ed Dorn, for whom Olson wrote his *Bibliography on America;* Jonathan Williams, the energetic publisher of the Jargon Press; John Wieners; and Michael Rumaker. Olson's reputation as a teacher has provoked widely varying criticism, which Duberman summarizes in his book *Black Mountain*:

> Olson used Dostoevski's *Notes from the Underground,* for example, to drive home the point that "there are certain things which you hide from close friends and admit only to yourself; the task of the writer is to dig out those things which you will not admit to yourselves." Olson did *not* mean thereby to encourage what he called "wretched lyricism," a subjectivism merely self-indulgent. Rather, he wanted his students to become "personal revolutionaries," to learn that "the person is his or her own material"; wanted them to "more and more find the kinetics of experience disclosed—the kinetics of themselves as persons as well as of the stuff they have to work on, and by"; wanted, in short, "to release the person's energy word-wise, and thus begin the hammering of form out of content."
> But "wretched lyricism," and worse, was nonetheless a frequent

result. Olson, after all, was dealing with a group of mostly teen-agers/early adults, and in a highly charged, isolated community setting. Which meant, inevitably, a lot of noise—"pure messy noise," as Francine du Plessix Gray has called it. And Olson did encourage it—not the mess, but making noise, did so in the hope that something that might count would come out of it.[68]

The student writers I have mentioned, all of them now of established reputation, came under Olson's influence at a time when he was fully absorbed with the difficulties of writing the *Maximus* poems and solving the technical problems of composing a long poem. His classrooms were a context in which to explore the various possibilities of writing works of sustained attention, and each of his students took away with his experience of Olson the conviction that the writer must take up the precise conditions of his immediate existence and illuminate them in his work.

In the years of his rectorship at Black Mountain College, Olson exposed his students to the catalog of his eccentric interests and passions, which he treated as a curriculum of lore and disciplines necessary to anyone who worked in the medium of open poetry. He preached a doctrine of experience which insisted that even the most mundane detail of local terrain was invested with meaning and that earth, the cosmos, was the proper context in which to speak of any event or object. Hence the students who persisted under his tutelage were assaulted with myth, history, geography, astronomy, and whatever else Olson at the moment thought pertinent.

A considerable amount of their work has already been published by reputable presses, but some of it remains to be collected from the small magazines and ephemeral press books they first appeared in. Even with their careers in mid-stride, it is possible to discern Olson's mark on these writers: they have written with a deliberate attention to the local terrain, and each has created his own version of Maximus and placed him in new regions.

Edward Dorn (b. 1929) attended the University of Illinois and then had his education "corrected," as he put it in his note for Donald Allen, by the faculty at Black Mountain College. He attended the college in 1950 and again in 1954. In a long essay, "What I see in the Maximus Poems: Part I," he has written a sensitive and thoughtful appreciation of the method employed in *The Maximus Poems*, comparing Olson's rendering of his local terrain into a vital esthetic whole to the thin reality of his own residence, Santa Fe, New Mexico. Creeley has judged this

essay and Duncan's "Notes on Poetics Regarding Olson's 'Maximus'"
as "two works of exceptional critical reading."[69]

Dorn is the most prolific of the Black Mountain student poets and is
quickly proving to be the most talented and far-reaching in his work.
Even in his first collection of poems, *The Newly Fallen* (1961), a youthful and uneven book, he showed an understanding of the techniques of
open poetry. Many of the poems are breezy general commentaries on
the failings of American culture, but several of the poems, "Sousa" in
particular, display a sharply observant mind and a complex imagination.
"Sousa" is a fitful evocation of his Illinois childhood; memories of pa-
triotic parades and the marching tunes of John Philip Sousa are recalled
against the backdrop of the nuclear age and the threat of war. Dorn
moved to the Southwest after leaving Black Mountain College, and
"The Biggest Killing" and several other early poems are his preliminary readings of this region.

It is apparent from his second volume, *Hands Up!* (1964), that Dorn
requires a large, loosely structured format for his best work. His shorter
poems are either petulant in their attacks upon the cheapness of South-
western culture or blandly lyrical when he turns to the standard themes
of love, friendship, and having children. His genius is evident in his
long, rambling poem on the settling of this region entitled "Home on
the Range: February, 1962." In this humorous and compelling monologue, Dorn nicely observes that the homesteads were America's first sub-
divisions. In another long poem, "The Land Below," he articulates in
detail his thoughts about a small town in New Mexico in which he purchased a house. The issue of ownership raises the larger consideration
of its history of ruthless speculation. The drab town that survives the
age of profiteering is thrust within the grandeur of the natural landscape as a pathetic emblem of the exploitive will. A line from one of
his meditative poems, "A Fate of Unannounced Years," expresses the
theme and preoccupation of this book of poems: "I an American finding myself in America."

Most of Dorn's short poems have now been published by Four Seasons Foundation under the title *The Collected Poems: 1956–1974*. The
volume gathers up most of his earlier books, including *Geography* (1965)
and *The North Atlantic Turbine* (1967), his most distinguished group
of shorter poems. Of the younger Black Mountain poets, Dorn has done
work that comes closest to Duncan's lyrical richness and breadth of
learning. The poems in *Geography*, particularly the longer work entitled
"The Problem of the Poem for My Daughter, Left Unsolved," are

open-ended and frequently engage in bold political satire. *Geography* is dedicated to Charles Olson, whose stamp is everywhere in the volume.

Dorn's poems typically invoke seemingly closed events and "resist" them with a multiplicity of perspectives and perceptions. But the poems are deliberately rooted to a political awareness; like Duncan, Dorn is insistent that the quality of American life be examined with stern critical judgment. In his more strident poems, he inveighs loudly against the sterility of capitalism, as in "The Sense Comes Over Me, and the Waning Light of Man by the 1st National Bank." Although he frequently writes brief poems, Dorn pushes for the sustained narrative. His genius as narrator is already evident in this volume; his best poems narrate adventures in the landscape around him, as in "Idaho Out," a rambling travelogue dense with observation and mordant social commentary.

The North Atlantic Turbine is a rich narrative account of his travels through England. The speaker, conscious that he has simply drifted from one corner of Western civilization to another, finds the condition of England, both as a quaint reminder of the American past and as a somewhat desperate and dying nation, pretext for examining his attitude toward the American present. Throughout the long, often barbed discourse of the poem, Dorn struggles to come to terms with this civilization, to understand his existence amid all the politically contrived circumstances in which he finds himself. His discourse surveys, among many other things, the incompetent political leadership of Western nations over the past several decades, the ruthless aggression of America, the awesome spread of Western industrial technology and commerce to the rest of the globe: "Big system! China-and-the-East / is simply an amateur West."[70] Part of his poem describes the American traveler to Oxford who candidly admits his envy of the intellectual sophistication he finds there. The work is subtitled throughout with parodic headlines that promise but do not always deliver the sober reflections of a learned adventurer in a foreign land. Instead, Dorn's commentary runs the gamut of language and experience in a style that is unrestrained and critically acute. The drama of the book comes in the confrontation between the youthful, frank American and the look, sound, and feel of England, America's doddering but cultivated parent. At the end of the sequence the speaker is home again in the Southwest, and several of the final poems introduce the hero of Dorn's most ambitious poem, *Gunslinger*, a quixotic romance of American politics and popular culture.

Gunslinger (1975) is Dorn's boldest and most sustained effort at a long poem. It is open in construction, even langorous in its disheveled narrative style, and, like any profusive discourse, lives by its flashes of perception. But it is different from the long poems of Pound, Williams, and Olson. There is none of the halting progress of these earlier poems, where the difficulties of the subject are overcome slowly and with painful self-scrutiny. Dorn worked on the sequence sporadically over a period of seven or eight years; each of its parts appears to have been composed in one intense, uninterrupted effort. The language pushes forward without the kinds of resistance one finds in Olson's *Maximus*; as a consequence, the language lacks rough texture. And the subject becomes increasingly amorphous as the sequence moves on.

Gunslinger begins with extraordinary promise. A journey is planned by a cast of richly caricatured stock figures taken from western movie romances. The Gunslinger is himself a mystic and a demigod, and his horse, as quick-changing as a cartoon figure, is at times a wag, a gambler, a riddlesome philosopher, a sidekick, and a sort of rueful Jacques. Lil is the quintessential saloon girl. Another figure by the name of "I" comes and goes in the drama. The itinerary of this group is changed several times, but their progress is toward Las Vegas, the ultimate Western city. Part-way there, a new figure is picked up, Kool Everything, who carries with him his only fortune, a quantity of lysergic acid.

The poem proposes a stunning possibility at its opening: Dorn seems about to write a new *Canterbury Tales*, with this crew making a pilgrimage to a peculiarly American shrine. But in the ensuing books of the poem this plot disperses into rant. The Gunslinger himself is credited with more possibilities than he can embody. His purportedly mystical faculties and his semidivine potential are rendered as stuffy and half-private witticisms spread out in long digressive monologues.

But, as Robert Duncan observed, the poem creates the sense of a new era for poetry. And this may be its greatest significance: it points out the possibility of substantial subject matter for the long poems now to be written. His broad caricatures of "Hughes Howard," "Trustworthy Kaput" (Truman Capote), and other figures of popular culture give the poem weight and potentially high interest. The poem is bold in its grasp of contemporary experience, and the humor, often crude but effective, registers a new but as yet lightly treated aspect of life: the America that is projected through television, night club entertainment, and films. If the poem fails, the theme it attempts to treat is an important new direction for a long poem. With Dorn, the long poem has ceased to be a form to be discovered in every step of its making: it is now an available convention in which to gather in the reality of the moment.

Among the poets who attended Black Mountain College, only Jonathan Williams (b. 1929) was actually indigenous to the area. He was born in Ashville, North Carolina, and continues to live nearby in the family summer home in Highlands, where his Jargon Press is now located. After studying at the Chicago Institute of Design, Williams founded the press in 1951 and has since published the writing of a wide variety of poets working in the Pound/Williams/Olson tradition. In fact, while stationed with the army in Stuttgart, Germany, he and a local printer named Dr. Cantz brought out the first twenty-two letters of Olson's *The Maximus Poems.* Williams had attended a summer session at Black Mountain College in 1951, and in an interview with Martin Duberman he has recounted his first experience of Olson as a teacher:

> I couldn't write poems worth a damn. I wrote a sort of horrible cummings/Patchen pastiche—really hopeless, full of fog and gold singing snakes! When I met Olson he was antagonistic toward me because he didn't admire Patchen or cummings. He knew that this was a very idiosyncratic way to begin. So he was really very heavy with me. He ripped the stuff to pieces, with vast owlish distaste. It was a good thing to do so, but as a result, it took us about two months before we got friendly at all.[71]

He has since gone on to write a number of volumes of poetry, which have been collected in *An Ear in Bartram's Tree: Selected Poems 1957–1967* (1969).

Williams' poems, particularly those of his early volume *The Empire Finals at Verona* (1959), convey the local terrain of Black Mountain.[72] In a work in progress, *Blues & Roots/Rue & Bluets,* which forms the last section of his selected poems, he perceives the phenomena of language with fresh ears, noting the instances where the casually creative intellect flashes out in the most subliminal flourishes of southern dialect. He has a cheerful sensibility as a poet, which further distinguishes him from his colleagues; he has kept his work light and airy even when it has engaged themes of great seriousness: southern racism, bigotry, demagoguery, even death. The voice is undaunted; the punning phrase is, before death, a final defense, a solace for grief:

[An Epitaph for]*Bunk Johnson*

  he died
  like the moon

  fading out white
  before day[73]

He is best when he explores the vitalities of American speech and wherever his own immediate contact with his surroundings is worked into his witty, compressed commentaries. His other tendencies are not so entertaining, nor do they seem to engage his humor. Too often, for example, he indulges in bookishness.

His humor is in control in the beautifully witty poems of *Jammin' the Greek Scene*, where the imposing conceptions of Greek mythology are translated into American slang. Olson wrote a foreword to these poems, praising the frank, honest, and amusing use Williams had made of his subject and arguing that Williams' attitude was one that Americans had to acquire after so long a reverence for Europe.[74] Williams has written his own summary of his poetic in the prefatory note to the selections from *Sank-Aunt-Sank-Shows*: "Here the titles work as hinges to spring what follows loose. An ear is on the prowl, prying into the substance of words, finding things there while one eye watches and the other wanders about a bit amused."

The work of John Wieners (b. 1934) and Michael Rumaker (b. 1932), two other Black Mountain writers, is of varying quality. Olson lured Wieners to the college in 1954 during a poetry reading he gave in Boston to recruit students and financial support. He passed out copies of *Black Mountain Review*, and Wieners, who had graduated from Boston College with a B.A. in English, went to North Carolina to study under Robert Duncan and Olson.[75]

Much of Wieners' early poetry has been reissued in *Selected Poems* (1972), the dominant theme of which has been the frank and sometimes tedious exploration of his homosexuality. He is a poet of painful admissions, and there is a self-condemning urge in much of this work as he recounts the drab details of his sexual encounters. Stale bedrooms, naked light bulbs hanging over soiled cots, the dank corridors of cheap New York hotels, San Francisco drug parties, hustling in tap rooms, the occasional brief romance are the subjects of his short, tormented lyrics.

But Wieners has the most elegantly lyrical voice of the younger Black Mountain poets: he has a masterful control over the texture of his lines. In one poem, the voice is smooth and silken, as polished as the verses of Ernest Dowson; in another, he can jar and disrupt by the brute terseness of his sexual confessions. He is capable of sustaining this lyric music in longer poems, such as "The Magic of This Summer / June 23, 1963," a poem of several hundred lines of complex, interwoven meditation.

Wieners' persona is modest, unassuming, a poet of painful privacy of emotion, who whispers more than declaims. He brings to contemporary poetry a voice of precise musical perfection and conveys in his language and settings an amber world of regret, exhaustion, and pale moods, a past of bitter memories, and the gathering darkness of the present moment. Many of his poems are about all-night excursions or reveries at the windows of hotels as the sun rises or about uncompleted love affairs, longings, ineffectual contacts with new lovers. His essential voice is in these lines from "Acts of Youth" in *Selected Poems*:

> With great fear I inhabit the middle of night
> What wrecks of mind await, what drugs
> to dull the senses, what little there is left,
> what more may be taken away? (p. 50)

or in this superb concision of emotion from "Jive":

> Tomorrow some motel with a guy,
> Who'd have thought my dreams would come to this?
> It's better than junk.
> At least in a clean bed.
>
> Then movies with mother.
> The cycle goes on.
> It's two o'clock in the morning
> Rain on street. (p. 85)

or, more poignantly still, in these lines from "Some black man looms in my life":

> Some black man looms in my life, larger than life.
> Some white man hovers there too, but I am through with
>   him.
> Some wild man dreams through my day, smelling of
>   heroin.
> Some dead man dies in my arms every night. (p. 96)

In a more recent book entitled *Hotels* (1974), actually an informal talk which Larry Fagin and others transcribed and then published, Wieners may have invented a new subgenre of prose poem: the hotel reminiscence. The book is a series of recollections of rooms he has stayed in, in the United States, Canada, and Europe. He affects a tone of quiet seriousness as he recalls the details of each room, adding here and there brief commentaries on tipping, table service, the fare of certain dining rooms, the pleasure of lobbies and doormen. At every page the work threatens to collapse into trivia, but by some curious sense of humor and force of personality he urges the reader along to the last page, exasperated, puzzled, and amused at the whole strange effect that is achieved by this kind of absurd intimacy. Nowhere else in his writing does Wieners create this fragile humor.

Michael Rumaker was recruited to Black Mountain by Ben Shahn, who had given a talk at the Philadelphia Museum in 1952 and induced Rumaker to attend the college that same fall on a work scholarship; he remained for the next three years and was one of the few students besides Creeley to take a degree from the college. He has provided Martin Duberman with his own testimony about Olson:

> I was very drawn to Olson, and very repelled by him. I think so many people have that feeling. He's a very large man, and he's very dynamic; he's ruthlessly honest and great about detecting any kind of fraud or dishonesty in another person. . . . Charles would always say, "*You* are interesting, as a person, and you may have a feeling that what you have to say is not interesting, but this is not true. You as an individual are interesting."[76]

Rumaker has written very little poetry until recently, concentrating instead on a prose career. In 1962 he published a novel, *The Butterfly*, and *Gringos, And Other Stories* appeared in 1966. The novel is an elaborately written narrative about a young man's struggle to regain his bearings in society after a serious mental illness. The plot is thick with devices to show the stages of his difficult recovery, and Rumaker places unusual emphasis on the symbolism of certain flowers: each of the main characters toys meaningfully with a blossom each time the protagonist gains another foothold on the world. Rumaker's attempt to organize the minor events of the story into a vast symmetrical design seems heavy-handed. The first affair of the young man involves a somberly poetic Chinese girl, modeled after Yoko Ono, who represented the night side of life with her dark apparel and ascetic life in a New York loft. She is affectionate and open at first but is then seized with a sudden change of heart and dismisses the protagonist. That same evening, after much drinking and despair, he meets another woman, an Occidental with blond hair, blue eyes, and a fresh outlook on life. Their affair, even the minute details of their idle chat, is chronicled in the remaining chapters of the book. The sun must set, the unreality of love must be felt (the Chinese girl's name is Eiko!), before the dawn of a hard-earned reality arises. The most engaging moments of the book are the long, luxurious descriptions of gardens, autumnal landscapes, drunken meanderings through a wintry New York, in which his writing shows considerable skill.

Rumaker's short stories are technically more sophisticated. His typical characters are wanderers and misfits, and the situations he describes are unusually brutal. The tales are sketched with great economy of detail in contrast to the lyrical effulgence of his novel, although they have less subtlety than *The Butterfly*. There is no moralizing in any of the stories; the narrator is merely a lens through whom the reader peers to discover the lurid details of American low life. In "Exit 3," for example, we are given no more than the bare events of how a sailor is forced to care for a drunken, crazed marine bent on violence. In a brief scene before a drug store, the sailor watches as the marine taunts and is then beaten by three soldiers on leave. The sailor merely walks away from the crumpled figure as a patrol car approaches. In "The Pipe" several men wait for a river barge to begin dredging operations; they are scavengers of whatever the dredge pumps out on the marshy riverbank. The setting and situations are subtly enriched with archetypal significance. As the dredge erupts, one of the men strikes and kills another, and the group then scurries way. In all of the stories violence casually strikes and is just as casually dismissed by the perpetrator. The tales offend the reader with their documentary-style accounts of modern savagery, but their power lies in a deliberate spareness of technique.

These younger writers bear out what Olson's contemporaries also experienced in the presence—we might even say, under the pressure—of this dynamic individual: they were encouraged to look for their own feelings and to articulate them in ways true to their pulse beats and imaginations—these were the minimal demands Olson made of anyone who wished to write. Olson's poetic was an extension of his desire to register the pains of existence beneath the exploited superficial consciousness one lives in day by day. Olson believed the body had its own knowledge, which the psyche could only partly translate; in the field or open composition he formulated, perhaps he hoped that more of that knowledge would reveal itself as the content of the poem determined its own shape.

In Sum

Charles Olson was a product of the twentieth century and of the America that grew up in it. Life has been irreversibly transformed in the modern era, and we do not yet comprehend the result of these profound changes.

America is a different nation from the one that split and healed itself more than a century ago. Its new form is undefined. Modernism at the beginning of the century spread a cry of anguish across the genres of literature, as the past seemed to rip free of existence. The modernists grabbed history out of the fire and made man in the image of his dying remembrance.

The ideals of early modern poetry have a tarnished glow. The poems of Eliot and Pound are collages made from battered objects, in which the human figure is barely perceptible. He is seen in the distance, drifting through a world of discontinuities, which genius and eloquence cannot make beautiful. Their disconcerting vision drew few readers to them.

But the mass audience that turned to Charlie Chaplin, instead, saw much the same creature. The sad clown who shuffled through the canyon streets of the modern city, dressed in his quaint tails and derby, stirred the same metaphysical depths: his diminutive character ambled with poise and naive dignity into oblivion.

Olson emerged at the half-century, when the new world was fully manifest. The poetry of his time was divided between the agrarian poets' nostalgia for old technique and Robert Lowell's urge to confess the grimmest details of private agony.

The culture was streamlined. The new technology was turning society into a vast but simple mechanism. Human activity was swiftly rushing into two categories: mass production and mass consumption. What did not participate in either of these functions was considered eccentric to the whole design.

Small businesses dissolved; larger ones gave up their autonomy and became subsidiaries. Individuals sought the safety of employment in institutions. Personality was a right of occupation. The mid-century was enthralled by a new doctrine of cohesiveness: a mechanistic interlocking of parts. The village was annexed to the city; the individual worked in a team; the family by day was off to school or work. The age had seized too quickly upon a technique for order and had absolutized it into a faith.

It was against these tendencies that Olson created his stance and his art. The sound and look of his poems have no significance without this context. He released the disordered energies of his organism onto paper as a gesture of defiance. His life was the inverse of the social ideal.

Black Mountain College did not grow during his rectorship; it quite literally disappeared as parcels of its property were sold off. His students did not graduate; they drifted away to follow their own fortunes.

He never owned his own house. Even when he taught at the state university at Buffalo, he set his own rules for his classes and met them at his own convenience. The doctrines he preached in his essays and poems were useless to anyone who sought a place in the system's bureaucracies; they would only divert and confuse his ambitions.

Olson's canon has within it a potent utterance: life is strangled by systems. Existence has an order that cannot be isolated from nature; the order is continually changing and evolving. A system is a halting of change; it seizes upon a possible order and continues to duplicate it endlessly. As it entrenches in the midst of nature, its tyranny upon life grows, until the system is a prison of contradictions.

In his *Maximus* sequence, we are struck at once by the solitude of his protagonist. Olson portrayed himself as a lone adventurer in a world that other human beings have vacated. He celebrates the glory of direct experience, of awareness that is aroused by unmediated contact with nature beyond systematized thought. The poignance of this long, awesome poem comes from the sense that he cannot enjoy the splendor of earth alone; his words are the song that would lure humanity out of doors. Orpheus is one of his heroes. Fighters and redeemers are the gods of his personal mythology.

It may be difficult to accept Olson as a great poet. His poetic ideals were imperfection, the uncompleted, the process without the end, disordered vitality. He is a saboteur of the certainty that thrived in his era: his vision of man is that he is a wild and passionate creature who is being lured into a false Eden of systems and institutions and who barters the realms of nature and his own primal humanity for a few material possessions. As Olson argued throughout his writings, man only now wakes to the splendors of the real, still rubs from his eyes the primordial sleep, but already he is being driven back toward the dark again by a society that thrives on diminishing his awareness. Olson wanted the poet to be the measure of awareness, to be that lone human figure thrust deep into the uncertainty of the real, where he lives and expresses himself joyfully and is ultimately joined by others.

Notes

1. Charles Olson: An Introduction

1. *Boundary 2: A Journal of Postmodern Literature*, 2, nos. 1–2 (1973–74), is a special combined issue entitled *Charles Olson: Essays, Reminiscences, Reviews*, ed. Matthew Corrigan; the photographs are scattered among its 370-odd pages.
2. Guy Davenport, "Scholia and Conjectures for Olson's 'The Kingfishers,' " *Boundary 2*, 2 (1973–74), 250.
3. Albert G. Glover, ed., *Letters for Origin, 1950–1956*, p. 120 f. This edition, trimmed of scholarly apparatus and emended in certain other ways, is based on Glover's doctoral dissertation, "Charles Olson: Letters for Origin." In citations hereafter, I use the short titles *Letters* for the former and "Letters" for the latter.
4. Robert Duncan, "Nel Mezzo Del Cammin di Nostra Vita," in *Roots and Branches*, p. 21 f.
5. "The Advantage of Literacy Is that Words Can Be on the Page," in *Charles Olson: Additional Prose: A Bibliography on America, Proprioception, & Other Notes & Essays*, ed. George F. Butterick, p. 51.
6. Glover, *Letters*, p. 61.
7. Charles Olson, "This Is Yeats Speaking," in *Human Universe and Other Essays*, ed. Donald Allen, p. 100.
8. Quoted by Martin Duberman, *Black Mountain: An Exploration in Community*, p. 397.
9. George Butterick, "An Annotated Guide to *The Maximus Poems* of Charles Olson," pp. 168–172. Details and dates of Olson's life are taken directly from Butterick's "Chronology," but the interpretation is my own.
10. *Maps*, no. 4 (1971), p. 44.
11. Duberman, p. 354, says 6 feet 7 inches; Martin L. Pops, "Melville: To Him, Olson," *Boundary 2*, 2 (1973–74), 78, says 6 feet 8 inches; and Matthew Corrigan, "Materials for a Nexus," *Boundary 2*, 2 (1973–74), 203, says 6 feet 9 inches. Olson himself, in Glover, *Letters*, p. 1, says 6 feet 7 inches.
12. This observation was originally made by Pops, "Melville: To Him, Olson," p. 77; see also Butterick, "An Annotated Guide," pp. 4–5, 56.
13. It came to much less than the title might suggest. Duberman, p. 362, observes of the program, "The only institutes that resembled anything like their elaborate catalog descriptions were the summer sessions in the arts (and those of 1952 and 1953 were to be the most remarkable

ever held), and a 'crafts' institute reduced to the single category of ceramics and confined to a ten-day session."

14. Butterick, "An Annotated Guide," p. 169.
15. "Two OWI Aides Resign," *New York Times*, May 19, 1944, p. 14.
16. "People v. The Fascist, U.S. (1944)," *Survey Graphic*, 33 (1944), 368.
17. Butterick, "An Annotated Guide," p. 170; but he returns briefly to politics to support Senator Claude Pepper for president in 1948.
18. *Human Universe*, p. 100.
19. Ibid., p. 102.
20. Ibid.
21. "People v. The Fascist, U.S. (1944)," p. 356.
22. Ibid.
23. Donald Byrd, "Charles Olson's *Maximus*: An Introduction," p. 29, observes, "Although Olson had a continuing admiration for Roosevelt and, according to Fielding Dawson, spoke frequently of his 'Roosevelt days' while he was teaching at Black Mountain in the early 1950's, Olson might be considered one of the first post-liberals."
24. Olson recorded these meetings in various notes and journal entries after each visit; they have been published in *Charles Olson & Ezra Pound: An Encounter at St. Elizabeths*, ed. Catherine Seelye.
25. Butterick, "An Annotated Guide," p. 170. Notes for this project are in the Olson archives. Olson later planned a long poem to be entitled *West*, only part of which was ever completed. The text of this poem was published by Goliard Press in 1966 and features a frontispiece with the portrait of Chief Red Cloud. *Olson: The Journal of the Charles Olson Archives*, no. 5 (Spring 1976), contains most of the notes relating to the projected long poem, as well as the notes for his prose study, "Operation Red, White & Black," dated 1947.
26. The original manuscripts of Olson's letters are among the *Origin* papers filed in the Humanities Research Center, University of Texas at Austin; Corman's letters are in the Literary Archives of the University of Connecticut Library, informally referred to elsewhere herein as the Olson archives.
27. *Mayan Letters: Charles Olson*, ed. Robert Creeley, p. 5 f.
28. For Olson's return to Black Mountain College, see Duberman, pp. 354–355.
29. Ibid., p. 355.
30. The *Times* headline of January 11, 1970, p. 76, reads, "Charles Olson, Poet and Leader of Black Mountain Group, Died." He died of cancer of the liver, and the final months of his life are narrated in Charles Boer, *Olson in Connecticut*.

2. Toward a New Reality

1. Robert Creeley, *Contexts of Poetry: Interviews 1951–1971*, ed. Donald Allen, p. 36.
2. Ibid., pp. 36–38.
3. Here is Olson's view of the shift: ". . . it struck me that it was useful to be useful, to try to lay out to you this shift which I see as having happened right recently, and that I think is of such an order that poetry, as being written today, especially by or in our language, yields a future that is unknown, is so different from the assumptions that poetry has had, in our language, that the life that one lives in [sic] practically the condition of the poetry, rather than the poetic life being a thing in itself. And one could almost say that these two words today have practically flown together—*flowed*, I mean, flowed together" (*Poetry and Truth: The Beloit Lectures and Poems*, ed. George F. Butterick, p. 12).
4. George Lichtheim, preface to *The Phenomenology of Mind*, by G. W. F. Hegel, trans. J. B. Baillie, p. xx.
5. *Contexts*, p. 37.
6. Among the great number of books to appear in this ferment of the post–World War II period are David Riesman's *The Lonely Crowd* (1950), Paul and Percival Goodman's *Communitas* (1947), Herbert Marcuse's *Eros and Civilization* (1955), Erich Fromm's *The Sane Society* (1955), Erich Kahler's *The Tower and the Abyss* (1957), and Hannah Arendt's *The Human Condition* (1958). Each of these studies deals in some degree with the meaning of the term "alienation," a word that, as Walter Kaufman observed, "became so ubiquitous that it was no longer clear whether the myriad uses to which it was put allowed for any single definition" (Richard Schacht, *Alienation*, p. xxiii).
7. Max Horkheimer, *Eclipse of Reason*, pp. 18, 4. Further citations in this chapter will appear parenthetically in the text. For an excellent discussion of Horkheimer's life and ideas and of the activities of the Frankfurt school in America, see Martin Jay, *The Dialectical Imagination: A History of the Frankfurt School and the Institut of Social Research 1923–1950*.
8. Kenneth Rexroth, *American Poetry in the Twentieth Century*, p. 134.
9. Paul A. Robinson, *The Freudian Left: Wilhelm Reich, Geza Roheim, Herbert Marcuse*.
10. For a complete history of the emigration of German gestalt psychologists to America, see Jean and George Mandler, "The Diaspora of Experimental Psychology: The Gestaltists and Others," in *Perspectives in American History*, eds. Donald Fleming and Bernard Bailyn, II, 371–419. A 1933 *Manchester Guardian Weekly* article listing the professors expelled from German universities appears in *Perspectives*, II, 234.
11. *Gestalt Therapy*, pp. 367, 373.

12. Portions of this earlier text survive in the Olson archives in badly deteriorated condition. The book was originally divided into three broad sections entitled "In Adullam's Lair," "Exodus," and "Genesis." The text of "In Adullam's Lair" was edited by George Butterick and published by To the Lighthouse Press, Provincetown, Massachusetts, in 1975. The other two sections require restoration before they can be transcribed. It is interesting to note that in the text of "In Adullam's Lair," Olson refers to Melville as the "Catskill Eagle" but then directs this phrase to Ishmael in *Call Me Ishmael*. The prose in these texts is a deplorable imitation of the biblical rhythms of Dahlberg's style. Olson tries for the same cryptic concision he admired in Dahlberg, but to judge from the many notes Dahlberg scratched into the margins of Olson's manuscript, he was aware of the imitations and wisely counseled against them. Many good ideas in the texts were used later in *Call Me Ishmael*, and Dahlberg's critical eye caught and praised them. More often, Dahlberg's function was to advise deletions, recastings, and the like. Olson's criticisms of Christ are detailed and emphatic and are perhaps unique in American literature. In his summation of Western thought, Olson argued that Christ was at the heart of all the abstract tendencies of this culture: "From the Cross, perpendicular thing, Christ went up into the abstract sky." For most of these attacks on Christ, Dahlberg repeatedly cried, "omit," but some of this Christological criticism endures in "part IV is LOSS: CHRIST" of the published book.

13. *Charles Olson & Ezra Pound: An Encounter at St. Elizabeths*, ed. Catherine Seelye, p. 85.

14. Charles Olson, "Projective Verse," in *Human Universe and Other Essays*, ed. Donald Allen, p. 52.

15. *Call Me Ishmael*, p. 11. Further citations in this chapter will appear parenthetically in the text.

16. F. O. Matthiessen, *American Renaissance: Art and Expression in the Age of Emerson and Whitman.* Olson's name and work are brought up on pp. 209, 413, 415, and 457. Matthiessen remarks in a note on p. 457, "I have been stimulated by Olson's vigorous and imaginative essay to take issue with it on many other points of fact and interpretation, particularly concerning the relation between Ahab and Pip." Further citations appear in the text.

17. But see Olson's review "Materials and Weights of Herman Melville," in *Human Universe*, p. 109, where he refers to Matthiessen's study as one of "the bead-telling books of the last years . . . in other words, a rosary of praise which has (with some quietness and a little decency) been the private act of these men," meaning to praise artistry as distinct from explanations of the methods of that artistry.

18. Quoted by Ann Charters, *Olson/Melville: A Study in Affinity*, p. 10.

19. Ibid., p. 36.

20. Olson dramatized the character of Ahab and Ishmael in a short play "The Fiery Hunt," in which he asserted a father and son relationship. The death of Ahab leaves Ishmael an orphan to the world. It is hinted throughout the play that Olson identified himself with Ishmael, and his father with Ahab. This and a series of other short plays, including "Apollonius of Tyana," have been edited by Donald Allen and George Butterick and are to be published soon by The Four Seasons Foundation. Original typescripts are filed in the Olson archives.

21. Geoffrey Hartman, *Beyond Formalism: Literary Essays 1958–1970*, p. 12.

22. Hartman, p. 12.

23. James M. Edie, ed., *Phenomenology in America: Studies in the Philosophy of Experience*, p. 8: "Many of the contributors to this book would hesitate to apply [phenomenologist] to themselves in any form, and none would do so without qualification. There is, in this book, almost no phenomenological flag-waving, almost no trace of any desire to show how these studies are based on earlier European sources."

24. Listed in "Olson's Reading: A Preliminary Report," *Olson: The Journal of the Charles Olson Archives*, no. 3 (Spring 1975) and no. 4 (Fall 1975).

25. Marjorie Grene, *Martin Heidegger*, p. 12.

26. Ibid., p. 17.

27. Ibid., p. 99.

28. William A. Luijpen, *Phenomenology and Humanism: A Primer in Existential Phenomenology*, p. 77.

29. Alden L. Fisher, introduction to *The Essential Writings of Merleau-Ponty*, p. 8.

30. From "Man and Adversity," a lecture delivered in 1951, in *The Essential Writings of Merleau-Ponty*, p. 94.

31. The phrase appears in "Projective Verse," in *Human Universe*, p. 59. In this chapter, further citations of material reprinted in *Human Universe* will appear parenthetically in the text with the abbrevation HU.

32. Olson assures Corman on February 20, 1951, while in Lerma, that he will "lighten some of the emphasis on Waddell's book" and again on March 2, 1951, that "it now carries its weight (Waddell) much more lightly" (Glover, *Letters*, pp. 36, 42).

33. See Olson's pamphlet *Pleistocene Man: A Curriculum for the Study of the Soul*.

34. See letter dated June 10 [1951] in Glover, *Letters*, especially p. 90.

35. *Mayan Letters: Charles Olson*, ed. Robert Creeley, p. 68.

36. Creeley's stories were "Mr. Blue," "The Seance," "The Lover," "Three Fate Tales," and "In the Summer." Olson's "Introduction to Robert Creeley" is reprinted in *Human Universe*, pp. 127–128.

37. For a treatment of dance from a similar critical perspective, see Olson's "A Syllabary For A Dancer," in *Maps*, no. 4 (1971), 9–15.

38. Glover, *Letters*, p. 171.

39. Ibid.
40. Ibid., p. 104.
41. Ibid., p. 105.
42. Ibid., p. 106.
43. Ibid.
44. *The Special View of History*, ed. Ann Charters, p. 27. Further citations in this chapter appear parenthetically in the text with the abbreviation SV.
45. For the full text of the letter, see *Letters of John Keats, 1814–1821*, ed. Hyder E. Rollins, II, 192–194.
46. Henri Lefebvre, *Dialectical Materialism*, trans. John Sturrock, p. 31, et passim.
47. According to Robert von Hallberg, "Olson, Whitehead and the Objectivists," *Boundary 2: A Journal of Postmodern Literature*, 2 (1973–74), 86, "Olson read Whitehead's most systematic and difficult book, *Process and Reality*, in the spring of 1955, again in the spring of 1956, of 1957, and of 1958."
48. Charles Olson, *Additional Prose*, ed. George Butterick, p. 11.
49. *Additional Prose*, p. 18.
50. Charles Olson, *Poetry and Truth*, ed. George Butterick, pp. 57–58.

3. Projectivism and the Short Poems

1. Donald Byrd, "Charles Olson's *Maximus*," p. 38.
2. Charles Olson, "Projective Verse," in *Selected Writings*, ed. Robert Creeley, p. 17.
3. Olson's letters to Dahlberg are deposited in the Humanities Research Center, University of Texas at Austin; in particular, the letter dated September 29, 1950, shows Olson at some pains to both excuse and explain his long delay in writing an essay on Dahlberg's *Can These Bones Live*, which Olson tells him he has approached in the spirit he first confronted Melville. But the recurrent dilemma for Olson is that he is unsympathetic to Dahlberg's criticisms of Melville.
4. For example, Glover, *Letters*, p. 131. For additional critical comment on Williams and Pound, see *Mayan Letters: Charles Olson*, pp. 26–30. Marjorie Perloff, "Charles Olson and the 'Inferior Predecessors': 'Projective Verse' Revisited," *ELH*, 40 (1973), 295–296, virulently attacks Olson for his denunciation of writers who had contributed much to his concept of poetry and characterizes the "Projective Verse" essay as "a scissors-and-paste job, a clever but confused collage made up of bits and pieces of Pound, Fenollosa, Gaudier-Brzeska, Williams and Creeley," but her argument confuses the distinction between continuity in poetic tradition and slavish derivation.
    In the remainder of the article, she has cited out of context a variety

of Olson's critical observations of the work of Pound and Williams. Olson was frequently petulant in his remarks about Pound, less so about Williams, but, while it is true that he is unattractive in these moments, it is not a basis on which to judge Olson as poet and thinker. Pound's correspondence is equally charged with sarcasm and merciless critique of his contemporaries. Olson put it best when he wrote to Corman, "It is a crazy thing abt life that those we strike (or sometimes overpraise) are most likely to be those who matter more to us than those we let off!" (Glover, "Letters," p. 221).

5. Olson, *Selected Writings*, p. 16.

6. Olson, *Human Universe and Other Essays*, p. 79.

7. *Selected Essays of William Carlos Williams*, p. 286.

8. Even the look of Olson's sequential short poems and the first triad of *The Maximus Poems* bear striking similarities in typographical arrangement to Pound's *Cantos*. Pound's cautious experiments in typography derive from his enthusiasm for Cummings, a poet whose work in abstract painting led to innovative arrangements of semantic and orthographic spacing of his poems. The result was a format for poetry that often filled the page margin to margin and allowed for internal shifts and breaks that have since become conventions of much contemporary American poetry.

9. The poet Allen Ginsberg, in a recently televised interview with Edwin Newman, commented at length on a Buddhist breathing exercise as a discipline for meditation. The exhalation of the breath becomes a focus of concentration for the meditator, who allows his thought then to expand as he imagines the exhaled air to, and as the range of his thought spreads over an ever-widening area, the fresh inhalation of breath is a sign for the meditator's thought to suddenly contract again to the point of his nose, which begins the cycle once more. Ginsberg's comments, and the poetry of Pound's *Cantos,* together with Olson's remarks on breathing as a metrical system, suggest a model of organic consciousness central to modern poetry.

10. Ezra Pound, "A Retrospect," in *Literary Essays*, ed. T. S. Eliot, p. 3.

11. Ibid., p. 9.

12. Olson, *Selected Writings*, p. 19.

13. Pound, *Literary Essays*, p. 25.

14. Olson, *Selected Writings*, p. 19.

15. The source Olson refers to is Pound's brief note entitled "Condensare," here quoted in full from *Guide to Kulchur*, p. 369:

> If T. W. [sic] Hulme's latest editor hasn't quoted it I should like to conserve his "All a man ever thought would go onto a half sheet of notepaper. The rest is application and elaboration."

16. See especially Michael Reck, *Ezra Pound: A Close-Up*, and Noel Stock, *The Life of Ezra Pound*.

17. Olson, *Selected Writings*, p. 23.

18. Ibid., p. 22.

19. Olson, *Selected Writings*, p. 29.

20. See Harold Rosenberg's "The American Action Painters," in *The Tradi-tion of the New*, for a similar conception of self-projection in abstract expressionist painting. The ideas of the poetic can be found in the other arts, suggesting there is a broad rejection of formalism and a tendency toward the impulsive and spontaneous in American culture as a whole. But the interrelatedness of ideas in the arts lies beyond the scope of the present study.

21. *Archaeologist of Morning*, p. [13]. The pages in this volume are unnum-bered. Further citations in this chapter will appear parenthetically in the text with the abbreviation AM but, for convenience, without square brackets around my page numbers.

22. Robert Creeley, *Contexts of Poetry*, ed. Donald Allen, pp. 34–35.

23. Glover, *Letters*, pp. 170–178.

24. This idea has been richly confirmed by Miller Williams in an unpublished paper entitled "Intuition, Spontaneity, Organic Wholeness and The Redemptive Wilderness: Some (Old) Currents in Contemporary Poetry," read at the South Central Modern Language Association Con-vention, Houston, Texas, 1974.

25. *Mayan Letters*, p. 27.

26. "Letter to Elaine Feinstein," in *Human Universe*, p. 97; see also "Letter 23," *The Maximus Poems*, pp. 100–101.

27. *Maximus Poems, IV, V, VI*, Book IV, p. [46].

28. *The Maximus Poems*, p. 52.

29. Creeley's review of *Y & X* is reprinted in *A Quick Graph: Collected Notes & Essays*, ed. Donald Allen, pp. 151–153; although in other writings a critic of dazzling precision and judgment, Creeley is here at a loss to find concrete words to express his admiration for Olson's work.

30. *Partisan Review*, 15 (1948), 856–857.

31. Glover, *Letters*, pp. 113–114. *Archaeologist of Morning* includes the poems of *In Cold Hell, In Thicket* in the original order implied by Olson's comments in the *Origin* letters.

32. Background details about the poem are from a remark Olson made in his talk "Poetry and Criticism," delivered at the Northwest Writers Con-ference, University of Washington, Seattle, January 8, 1947. A draft of the talk is included in the Olson archives. George Butterick has informed me that the GI was the painter Corrado Cagli, who later illustrated the Black Sun edition of *Y & X*.

33. Olson, *Selected Writings*, p. 62.

34. Guy Davenport, "Scholia and Conjectures for Olson's 'The Kingfishers,' " *Boundary 2: A Journal of Postmodern Literature*, 2 (1973–74), 252, et passim.

35. See Glover, *Letters*, p. 109.

36. Carl Jung, *Symbols of Transformation*, trans. R. F. C. Hull, pp. 241–244.

37. In *Mayan Letters*, pp. 9–15, Olson identifies the bird as a "chii-mi"; see also "Tyrian Businesses," in *The Maximus Poems*, p. 37.

38. For example, in an unpublished letter of November 16, 1950, now filed in the Olson archives, Corman replies,

> You neither understand what I've been saying, nor do you want to. It would be so simple to refute, to be as insulting as you have been for the past few letters, that it would be insulting just to answer in kind.
>
> My belief is that, apart from genuine differences of Taste (which you lack the humility to accept), at this point anything I write you must backfire—regardless of motive or what have you. You have evolved in your mind an idea of what I am and whatever I say is adapted to that idea.

Corman's anger was justified in a number of instances where Olson had become ruthless in his impatience over printing details, selections for *Origin*, and other matters related to the magazine. Olson's shaping and refining influence on *Origin* closely parallels Pound's editorial influence on Harriet Monroe's *Poetry*. Both chief editors, Corman and Monroe, experienced similar exasperation with the often peremptory counsel they received from their major contributors.

39. See Charles Olson, "On Black Mountain," in *Maps*, no. 4 (1971), 24, 40, n.f.

40. Details of the Tanzler story were gleaned from telephone conversations with the staff of the *Key West Citizen*.

41. Robert Graves, *The Greek Myths*, I, Sec. 65, pp. 211–212. "The Distances" was originally given the title "Galatea," until Donald Allen persuaded Olson to think of the present one. Allen's correspondence to Olson is filed in the Olson archives.

4. The *Maximus* Poems

1. In this chapter, parenthetical citations in the text will refer to these volumes as M1, M2, and M3. Pages in M2 are unnumbered, but for convenience I omit square brackets around my page numbers.

2. For an account of the writing of *The Maximus Poems* and a full annotation of the poems, see Butterick, "An Annotated Guide."

3. See Marjorie Perloff's "Charles Olson and the 'Inferior Predecessors': Projective Verse Revisited," *ELH*, 40, (1973), 285–306, and my comments in chapter 3, note 4.

4. See especially Dembo's introduction to *Conceptions of Reality in Modern American Poetry*.

5. Robert Graves, *The Greek Myths*, I, Sec. 68.2.
6. Sherman Paul, "In and About the Maximus Poems: I, *The Maximus Poems 1–10*," *The Iowa Review*, 6, no. 1 (Winter 1975), 124, has cataloged the polarities found in the first ten *Maximus* poems:

> Of primary importance is the geographical pair, sea vs. land; to which one adds the directions, outward vs. inward; the occupations, fishing (and poetry) vs. capitalism (slaving, advertising, etc.): the polities, polis vs. pejorocracy; the economies, local vs. absentee; the stances, the "old measure of care" (of eyes, of ears) vs. carelessness (abstraction); the applications, work vs. sloth; and the goals, eudamia vs. euphoria.

See also his more recent survey of the final volume of the *Maximus* sequence, "Maximus: Volume 3 or Books VII and After," in *Boundary 2*, 6 (1977), 557–571.
7. Details are from Butterick, "An Annotated Guide," pp. 28, 30.
8. Paul, ibid., pp. 126–127.
9. Butterick, "An Annotated Guide," p. 35.
10. In a letter to Corman in September 1953, Olson reported that almost the entire book had been finished: "Actually," he wrote, "as I think I must have told you, [Letters] 11–23 got solid in August, and are sitting for final mss the moment I hear fr [Jonathan] Williams that he is ready to make Book #2" (Glover, *Letters*, p. 128).
11. Ibid.
12. Butterick, "An Annotated Guide," pp. vii–viii.
13. See Glover, *Letters*, p. 198.
14. See Glover, *Letters*, p. 128; also Sherman Paul, "In and About the Maximus Poems, II," *The Iowa Review*, 6, nos. 3–4 (Summer–Fall 1975), 81–83.
15. This copy is in the Olson archives. All quotations are transcribed from Olson's handwritten notations.
16. This essay is in the Olson archives, as are the other five unpublished prose works discussed immediately after it in this chapter: "Notes for Poetry & Art," "The Science of Mythology," "An Essay in the Direction of a Restoration of the act of MYTH," "THE AREA, and the DISCIPLINE of TOTALITY," and "The heart of the art of experience is the archetypes." Throughout, I quote from transcriptions made by the archives staff from the original holographs or typescripts.
17. *Olson: The Journal of the Charles Olson Archives*, no. 6 (Fall 1976), contains the drafts of canceled *Maximus* poems intended at one time as the last book of the first volume. Olson was attempting to widen the grasp of Maximus' commentary to include the early history of the South and the exploration and settling of the Far West. But as Butterick comments about the drafts, "In any case, the poem threatened to get out of hand—he felt there were no clear precedents, not even

Pound and Williams—and the sections included here, all numbered or designated as Maximus letters on the manuscripts . . . were set aside and not sent to Jonathan Williams for publication following *The Maximus Poems / 11–22*."

The poems begin with a new "Letter 23" and run to "A Note: (#35)" and a final poem "Maximus Part II." The loose progression of the poems and the broad reach of history included in them indicate Olson's desire to expand the development of the volume as a whole and to vary its content and approaches. The unshapeliness drove him back to his original focus on Gloucester, however, and he reoriented the final section to dwell on the Dorchester fishermen. The canceled drafts were hesitant efforts to originate a new direction for the poem.

18. See Joseph Fontenrose, *Python: A Study of Delphic Myth And Its Origins*, chap. 12, "Herakles," pp. 321–364.
19. The couplet rephrases a quotation from John Smith's *Advertisements for the Unexperienced Planters* used in the title of [Letter 27], "History is the Memory of Time," in *The Maximus Poems*, p. 112. See Butterick, "An Annotated Guide," p. 112.
20. Listed in "Olson's Reading: A Preliminary Report," *Olson: The Journal of the Charles Olson Archives*, nos. 1–6 (1974–1976).
21. Especially Part I: "The Mythological Stages in the Evolution of Consciousness."
22. See Byrd's excellent discussion of the mythic ego in *Maximus IV, V, VI* in his dissertation, "Charles Olson's *Maximus*," pp. 164–197.
23. See especially *Python*, chap. 10, "Chaos and Cosmos," pp. 217–273.
24. Noted in entry on Neumann in "Olson's Reading: A Preliminary Report," *Olson*, no. 4 (Fall 1975), 111–112.
25. Butterick reported this to me in conversation during the summer of 1976.

5. Olson and the Black Mountain Poets

1. Robert Creeley, *Contexts of Poetry: Interviews 1961–1971*, ed. Donald Allen, p. 14.
2. C. K. Stead, *The New Poetic: Yeats to Eliot*, pp. 179, 181.
3. Hugh Kenner, *The Pound Era*, p. 183.
4. Edmund Wilson, *Axel's Castle*, p. 292.
5. Ibid., pp. 297–298.
6. Kenner, p. 174.
7. For a thorough discussion of this friendship and its influence upon Williams, see Bram Dijkstra's *The Hieroglyphics of a New Speech: Cubism, Stieglitz, and the Early Poetry of Williams Carlos Williams*, pp. 82–107.
8. According to Stanley K. Coffman, Jr., *Imagism: A Chapter for the History of Modern Poetry*, Pound was driven to formulate a new concept of

the imagist poetic following a disagreement with Amy Lowell, the result of which was a deep schism between Pound and the other members of the original group, Richard Aldington, H. D., F. S. Flint, and J. G. Fletcher, who formed with Lowell a new group. From 1914 to 1917 Pound associated himself with the painter-poet Wyndham Lewis and the magazine *Blast*, a publication designed to launch the new movement called vorticism. Pound felt more or less deserted by the Lowell group, especially after having contributed to the movement's conception in the first place. Vorticism was an ill-defined movement, according to Coffman, as much a reaction to the futurist ferment then alive in England and France as it was a legitimate effort to extend the meaning of the image and to locate a similar energy in the other arts of the period. See especially Coffman's chapter "The Imagist Movement, 1914–1917," pp. 26–46.

9. *Mayan Letters: Charles Olson*, p. 30.

10. Ibid., p. 27.

11. "Notes on Poetics," in *The Poetics of the New American Poetry*, eds. Donald Allen and Warren Tallman, pp. 187–195.

12. "Robert Creeley: In Conversation with Charles Tomlinson," in *Contexts*, pp. 22–23.

13. Jonathan Schell, "The Nixon Years," *The New Yorker*, July 7, 1975, p. 40.

14. "Robert Creeley" (a radio interview), in *The Sullen Art*, ed. David Ossman, p. 10.

15. *Contexts*, p. 25.

16. Olson informed Corman of the new journal in blunt terms in his letter of December 14, 1953, which reads in part:

> The point is, 1 hope i am the first to tell you that Robt [Creeley] is coming here [Black Mountain] as of March 29th, not only as an addition to the faculty in writing, but as editor of a new quarterly, to be called "The Black Mt. Quarterly", 100 pages, big review section, and planned to compete with Kenyon, Partisan, NMQ (what else is there, are Hudson, & Sewanee, still in existence?). Anyway, that sort of thing. . . .
>
> Anyhow, there the damned betrayal is—or so pain to such as yrself always strikes me, as. And i want you to feel very damned free to dump me like a hotcake, if you wish: that is, if you are so sore you want to cut me to hell out of Origin like that (in other words, want to call off all that i am making up for you for #12) why just damn well poke me in the puss.
>
> I hope to christ you don't. As I figure it this is a mag of another order. And will catch us all into itself, as

well as a lot of ginks Origin wldn't have bothered with—as Bob
plans it, he wants a very wide base, so it won't fall on any small
number issue after issue, nor be one man's headache . . .
            ok. that's it. that's the bad news (Glover,
    Letters, p. 133).

17. Mary Novik, *Robert Creeley: An Inventory, 1945–1970*, p. xi.
18. This fact is borne out in many places in both Creeley's and Olson's writ-
    ings, but perhaps Creeley demonstrates it best when, in responding
    to an interviewer's question, he remarked, "I think that's a quote from
    Olson—or from myself. I can't remember which" (*Contexts*, p. 107).
19. *Contexts*, p. 52.
20. See Novik, *An Inventory*, pp. 45–46.
21. *Contexts*, p. 59. But by 1952 Golden Goose Press had issued his first
    book, *Le Fou*.
22. Curiously, however, Olson, Creeley, and Duncan were not all together in
    the same place until the Vancouver Poetry Conference held July 29–
    August 17, 1963. "I remember," Creeley remarked in an interview,
    "in Vancouver a couple of years ago, Charles or Robert [Duncan] or
    somebody said, gee, this is the first time that we've all been together.
    It was really the first time in our lives that the three of us were
    present at the same time"(*Contexts*, p. 68).
23. See *Contexts*, p. 121: "I had been trying to write in the mode of Wallace
    Stevens and it just hadn't worked. The period, the rhythmic period
    that he was using, just wasn't intimate to my own ways of feeling and
    speaking. And so, much as I respected him, I couldn't use him at all."
24. Robert Creeley, *A Quick Graph: Collected Notes & Essays*, ed. Donald
    Allen, p. 96.
25. Ibid., pp. 61–62.
26. Ibid., p. 69.
27. *A Quick Graph*, pp. 70, 71–72; see also *Contexts*, pp. 121–122.
28. *American Poetry in the Twentieth Century*, p. 164.
29. *Contexts*, p. 97.
30. Ibid., p. 115.
31. Ibid., p. 192.
32. According to Butterick, "Olson's Reading: A Preliminary Report," *Olson:
    The Journal of the Charles Olson Archives*, no. 2 (Fall 1974), 94–
    95, *Maximus Poems IV, V, VI* contains references to *The Greek
    Myths* on pp. 95, 102–103, and 104; additional references appear in
    The Maximus Poems: Volume Three. Four separate editions of *The
    White Goddess* are listed in "Olson's Reading," and it may have been
    referred to in *The Maximus Poems*, p. 97.
33. Included in *For Love: Poems 1950–1960*, pp. 56–57.
34. Olson reviewed *For Love* in *Village Voice*, September 13, 1962, pp. 4–5.

35. Terry R. Bacon, "How He Knows When To Stop: Creeley on Closure/A Conversation With the Poet," *The American Poetry Review*, 5, no. 6 (1976), 6.
36. *Contexts*, pp. 105, 106.
37. From Lerma, Yucatan, June 10, 1951, reacting to the bad prose narratives he had found in James Laughlin's *New Directions in Prose and Poetry 12* (1950), he wrote to Corman that by contrast "Creeley is the push beyond Lawrence. And Lawrence is the *only* predecessor who can carry narrative ahead" and that "Bob is the *only* narrative writer I know now at work who is doing just that [i.e., disclosing the conditions of the present time through a projective method], who is a responsible writer" (Glover, *Letters*, p. 60). See also Olson's "Introduction to Robert Creeley," a prefatory not to Creeley's stories in *New Directions in Prose and Poetry 13* (1951), reprinted in *Human Universe and Other Essays*, pp. 127–128. See also Warren Tallman's *Three Essays on Creeley*.
38. *A Quick Graph*, p. 16.
39. *Contexts*, pp. 108, 109–110.
40. Ibid., p. 113.
41. Ibid., p. 198.
42. Counting from the first page of text, the quotation is on p. [35].
43. *The Years as Catches*, p. i. See the impressive bibliography at the end of the book.
44. *Contexts*, pp. 141–142.
45. "near-far Mister Olson," in *Origin*, no. 12 (Spring 1954), 210.
46. *The Poetics of the New American Poetry*, p. 195.
47. Ibid., pp. 185, 195.
48. Robert Duncan, *The Truth & Life of Myth*, p. 38.
49. Ibid., p. 67.
50. Robert Duncan, "Rites of Participation: Parts I & II," in *The Caterpillar Anthology*, ed. Clayton Eshleman, pp. 23–69.
51. *The New American Poetry*, pp. 433–434.
52. *Bending the Bow*, p. 11.
53. *The New American Poetry*, p. 441.
54. *The Poet in the World*, p. 4.
55. Ibid., p. 9.
56. Glover, "Letters for Origin," p. 219.
57. "Proensa," in *Archaeologist of Morning*, pp. [130–131].
58. Ossman, *The Sullen Art*, p. 22.
59. *Big Table*, 1, no. 4 (1960), 135.
60. "Two Greeks," in *Early Selected y Mas*, p. 18.
61. "The Once-Over," ibid., p. 94.
62. Ibid., p. 95.
63. At the Berkeley Poetry Conference, July 23, 1965, Olson commented on the Allen anthology during his reading:

I mean, you know it never was true that San Francisco was the source of the revolution or the Evergreen Review. And I think it's only been made accurate—As in fact, if I may criticise my own editor and publisher, the divisions of The New American Poetry weren't accurate either. That, as Mr. Dorn carefully said to me (and I urged Mr. Allen in a sense, not to divide his book that way, not by places) has been divisive. (*Charles Olson: Reading at Berkeley*, p. 25).

64. Ossman, *The Sullen Art*, p. 80.
65. *Contemporary Authors*, ed. Clare D. Kinsman, p. 696.
66. Ossman, *The Sullen Art*, p. 49.
67. In letters to Cid Corman, toward the close of their correspondence in the winter of 1958, Olson scanned the literary horizon in an effort to make out what was to become of the movement to which he had been central. In one letter he cited Ginsberg and the other burgeoning beat poets who had been featured in the last issue of *Origin*, observing, "As you know, the last year [1957] it was Ginzy & Kerouac (Ginzy I find very lively, but they are all so dull & *social*. . . ." A year later, August 3, 1959, he wrote Corman, now residing in Kyoto, Japan, "The scene here (meaning the States) is scrabble now - with Ginzy making the sole public sense. And beautiful verse. Otherwise the world is presently* catching up with what was published by you in Origin! In fact there is (tho no one sees it) the two groups: Origin, and Beat, and Origin is only on the immediate scene. . . ." The asterisk refers to this interjection: "But [William] Burroughs is abt to land, & he's it too," meaning that Burroughs' own fiction was approaching the standards that writers for *Origin* had first established (Glover, "Letters," pp. 252, 255).
68. Duberman, *Black Mountain*, p. 393.
69. Charles Olson, *Selected Writings*, p. 280.
70. Ed Dorn, *Collected Poems*, p. 194.
71. Duberman, *Black Mountain*, p. 405.
72. In a prefatory note to the selections from this book in *An Ear in Bartram's Tree*, Williams mentions as mentors the poets Zukofsky, Olson, Creeley, and Duncan and two other figures related to this circle: Fielding Dawson, once a student at Black Mountain College and author of the short memoir *The Black Mountain Book*, and Edward Dahlberg, for whom Williams edited *Edward Dahlberg: A Tribute / Essays, Reminiscences, Correspondence, Tributes*.
73. From *50! Epiphytes, -Taphs, -Tomes, -Grams, -Thets! 50!*, in *An Ear in Bartram's Tree*, n.p.
74. Neither the poems nor Olson's foreword appeared in 1959 as intended; the poems were first published in *An Ear in Bartram's Tree*, and in his prefatory note to them there Williams quotes only this excerpt

from Olson's foreword: "What Brother Jonathan does in hyar is to keep up the velocity at the same time that things are let be. Ganymedes, or Echo, or that one Io, get back, by vulgarisms, their patent vector powers. . . . Barbarism, neologism, vulgarism, these London better have her old ear out for. . . . I'm sure we got askance from utter shyness" (n.p.).

75. Wieners later followed Olson to SUNY at Buffalo and remained there when Robert Creeley replaced Olson on the faculty in the fall of 1966. He wrote a brief memoir of this experience: "Hanging on for Dear Life," *Boundary* 2, 2 (1973–74), 22–23.

76. Duberman, *Black Mountain*, pp. 401–402. See also *New American Story*, eds. Donald Allen and Robert Creeley, for Rumaker's notes about himself and his fiction; in a brief essay there entitled "The Use of the Unconscious in Writing," pp. 274–276, and intended as a statement on poetics, he has elaborated very successfully on the projective stance as it applies to the prose writer and made clear that a substantial connection exists between the work of the new poets and that of the new fiction writers.

Works Cited

Alighieri, Dante. *The Divine Comedy*. Trans. Geoffrey L. Bickersteth. Cambridge: Harvard University Press, 1965.

Allen, Donald M., ed. *The New American Poetry: 1945–1960*. New York: Grove Press, 1960.

————, and Robert Creeley, eds. *New American Story*. New York: Grove Press, 1965.

————, and Warren Tallman, eds. *The Poetics of the New American Poetry*. New York: Grove Press, 1973.

Arendt, Hannah. *The Human Condition*. Chicago: University of Chicago Press, 1958.

Bacon, Terry R. "How He Knows When to Stop: Creeley on Closure / A Conversation With the Poet." *The American Poetry Review*, 5, no. 6 (1976), 5–7.

Baraka, Imamu Amiri [Leroi Jones]. *The Dead Lecturer*. New York: Grove Press, 1964.

————. *Home: Social Essays*. London: MacGibbon and Kee, 1968.

————. *Preface to a Twenty Volume Suicide Note*. New York: Totem Press / Corinth Books, 1961.

————. *The System of Dante's Hell*. New York: Grove Press, 1965.

Blackburn, Paul. *Brooklyn–Manhattan Transit*. New York: Totem Press, 1960.

————. *The Cities*. New York: Grove Press, 1967.

————. *The Dissolving Fabric*. Palma de Mallorca: Divers Press, 1955.

————. *Early Selected y Mas: Poems, 1949–1966*. Los Angeles: Black Sparrow Press, 1972.

————. *The Journals*. Ed. Robert Kelly. Los Angeles: Black Sparrow Press, 1975.

————. *Proensa*. Palma de Mallorca: Divers Press, 1953.

Boer, Charles. *Charles Olson in Connecticut*. Chicago: Swallow Press, 1975.

Butterick, George F. "An Annotated Guide to *The Maximus Poems* of Charles Olson." Diss. State University of New York at Buffalo, 1970; revised as *A Guide to The Maximus Poems*. Berkeley: University of California Press, forthcoming.

————, ed. *Olson: The Journal of the Charles Olson Archives*. Nos. 1–6. 1974–1976.

————, and Albert G. Glover, eds. *A Bibliography of Works by Charles Olson*. New York: Phoenix Book Shop, 1967.

Byrd, Donald J. "Charles Olson's *Maximus*: An Introduction." Diss. University of Kansas, 1971.

Carroll, Paul. *The Poem in Its Skin*. Chicago: Follet Publishing Co., 1968.

Charters, Ann. *Olson / Melville: A Study in Affinity.* Berkeley: Oyez, 1968.

Coffman, Stanley K., Jr. *Imagism: A Chapter for the History of Modern Poetry.* Norman: University of Oklahoma Press, 1951.

Contemporary Authors. Ed. Clare D. Kinsman. Volume 13–16, First Revision. Detroit: Gale Research Co., 1975.

Corrigan, Matthew. "Materials for a Nexus." *Boundary 2: A Journal of Postmodern Literature,* 2 (1973–74), 201–228.

————. Preface to *Charles Olson: Essays, Reminiscences, Reviews.* *Boundary 2: A Journal of Postmodern Literature,* 2 (1973–74), xi–xiii.

Crane, Hart. *The Bridge: A Poem by Hart Crane.* New York, 1930; rpt. in *The Complete Poems and Selected Letters of Hart Crane.* Ed. Brom Weber. New York: Doubleday, 1966.

Creeley, Robert. *Away.* Santa Barbara: Black Sparrow Press, 1976.

————. *Contexts of Poetry: Interviews 1961–1971.* Ed. Donald Allen. Bolinas, Calif.: Four Seasons Foundation, 1973.

————. *A Day Book.* New York: Scribner's, 1972.

————. *For Love: Poems 1950–1960.* New York: Scribner's, 1962.

————. *The Island.* New York: Scribner's, 1963.

————. *Le Fou.* Columbus, Ohio: Golden Goose Press, 1952.

————. *Pieces.* New York: Scribner's, 1969.

————. *Presences.* New York: Scribner's, 1976.

————. *A Quick Graph: Collected Notes & Essays.* Ed. Donald Allen. San Francisco: Four Seasons Foundation, 1970.

————. *Thirty Things.* Los Angeles: Black Sparrow Press, 1974.

————. *Words.* New York: Scribner's, 1967.

Dahlberg, Edward. *Can These Bones Live.* New York, 1941; rpt. Ann Arbor: University of Michigan Press, 1967.

Davenport, Guy. "Scholia and Conjectures for Olson's 'The Kingfishers.' " *Boundary 2: A Journal of Postmodern Literature,* 2 (1973–74), 250–262.

Dawson, Fielding. *The Black Mountain Book.* New York: Croton Press, 1970.

Dembo, L. S. *Conceptions of Reality in Modern American Poetry.* Berkeley: University of California Press, 1966.

Dijkstra, Bram. *The Hieroglyphics of a New Speech: Cubism, Stieglitz, and the Early Poetry of William Carlos Williams.* Princeton: Princeton University Press, 1969.

D[oolittle], H[ilda]. *Trilogy: The Walls Do Not Fall; Tribute to the Angels; The Flowering of the Rod.* New York: New Directions, 1973.

Dorn, Edward. *The Collected Poems: 1956–1974.* Bolinas, Calif.: Four Seasons Foundation, 1975.

————. *The Cycle.* West Newbury, Mass.: Frontier Press, 1971.

————. *Geography.* London: Fulcrum Press, 1965.

————. *Gunslinger Book I.* Los Angeles: Black Sparrow Press, 1968.

————. *Gunslinger Book II.* Los Angeles: Black Sparrow Press, 1969.

————. *Gunslinger Book III: The Winterbook: Prologue to the Great Book IIII Kornerstone*. West Newbury, Mass.: Frontier Press, 1972.

————. *Hands Up!* New York: Totem Press / Corinth Books, 1964.

————. *The Newly Fallen*. New York: Totem Press / The Paterson Society, 1961.

————. *The Rites of Passage: A Brief History*. Buffalo: Frontier Press, 1965; revised as *By the Sound*. Mt. Vernon, Wash.: Frontier Press, 1971.

————. *Slinger*. Berkeley: Wingbow Press, 1975.

————. "What I See in *The Maximus Poems*." *The Poetics of the New American Poetry*. Eds. Donald Allen and Warren Tallman. Pp. 293–307.

Duberman, Martin. *Black Mountain: An Exploration in Community*. New York: Anchor Press, 1973.

Duncan, Robert. *Bending the Bow*. New York: New Directions, 1968.

————. "From a Notebook." *Black Mountain Review*, no. 5 (Summer 1955), pp. 209–212; rpt. in *The Poetics of the New American Poetry*. Eds. Donald Allen and Warren Tallman. Pp. 185–187.

————. "near-far Mister Olson." *Origin: A Quarterly for the Creative*, no. 12 (Spring 1954), 210–211.

————. "Notes on Poetics: Regarding Olson's *Maximus*." *Black Mountain Review*, no. 6 (1956), 201–211; rpt. in *The Poetics of the New American Poetry*. Eds. Donald Allen and Warren Tallman. Pp. 187–195.

————. *The Opening of the Field*. New York: New Directions, 1960.

————. "Rites of Participation: Parts I & II." *The Caterpillar Anthology*. Ed. Clayton Eshleman. Garden City: Anchor Press, 1971. Pp. 23–69.

————. *Roots and Branches*. New York: Scribner's, 1964.

————. *Tribunals, Passages 31–35*. Los Angeles: Black Sparrow Press, 1970.

————. *The Truth & Life of Myth: An Essay in Essential Autobiography* Freemont, Michigan: Sumac Press / Soma Books, 1968.

————. *The Years as Catches*. Berkeley: Oyez, 1966.

Edie, James M., ed. *Phenomenology in America: Studies in the Philosophy of Experience*. Chicago: Quadrangle Books, 1967.

Eliot, T. S. *Collected Poems: 1909–1962*. New York: Harcourt, Brace, and World, 1963.

————. *Four Quartets*. London: Faber and Faber, 1943.

Ferrini, Vincent. "A Frame." *Maps*, no. 4 (1971), 47–60.

Fontenrose, Joseph. *Python: A Study of Delphic Myth and Its Origins*. Berkeley: University of California Press, 1959.

Fromm, Erich. *The Sane Society*. New York: Holt, Rinehart and Winston, 1955.

Garland, Joseph E. *The Gloucester Guide: A Retrospective Ramble*. Gloucester, Mass.: Gloucester 350th Anniversary Celebration, Inc., 1973.

Glover, Albert Gould. "Charles Olson: Letters for Origin." Diss. State University of New York at Buffalo, 1968; revised and published as *Letters for Origin, 1950–1956*. (See under Charles Olson.)

Goodman, Paul, and Percival Goodman. *Communitas: Means of Livelihood and Ways of Life*. New York: Vintage-Knopf, 1947; 2nd ed., rev., 1960.

————, Frederick Perls, and Ralph F. Hefferline. *Gestalt Therapy: Excitement and Growth in the Human Personality*. New York: Julian Press, 1951; rpt. Dell Press, n.d.

Graves, Robert. *Collected Poems: 1966*. Garden City: Anchor Press, 1966.

————. *The Greek Myths*. 2 vols. Baltimore: Penguin Books, 1955.

————. *The White Goddess: A Historical Grammar of Poetic Myth*. New York: Farrar, Straus, and Giroux, 1970.

Grene, Marjorie. *Martin Heidegger*. New York: Hillary House, Inc., 1957.

von Hallberg, Robert. "Olson, Whitehead, and the Objectivists." *Boundary 2: A Journal of Postmodern Literature*, 2 (1973–74), 85–111.

Hartman, Geoffrey H. *Beyond Formalism: Literary Essays 1958–1970*. New Haven: Yale University Press, 1970.

Hegel, Georg Wilhelm Friedrich. *The Phenomenology of Mind*. Trans. J. B. Baillie. New York: Harper and Row, 1967.

Horkheimer, Max. *Eclipse of Reason*. New York: Oxford University Press, 1947; rpt. Seabury Press, 1974.

Howorth, Beckett. "Dynamic Posture." *Journal of the American Medical Association*, 131 (1946), 1398–1404.

Jay, Martin. *The Dialectical Imagination: A History of the Frankfurt School and the Institut of Social Research 1923–1950*. Boston: Little, Brown, and Co., 1973.

Jung, Carl Gustav. *Symbols of Transformation. Collected Works of C. G. Jung*. Trans. R. F. C. Hull. Vol. 15. Bollingen Series XX. Princeton: Princeton University Press, 1970.

Kahler, Erich. *The Tower and the Abyss: An Inquiry into the Transformation of the Individual*. New York: G. Braziller, 1957.

Keats, John. *Letters of John Keats 1814–1821*. Ed. Hyder E. Rollins. 2 vols. Cambridge: Harvard University Press, 1958.

Kenner, Hugh. *The Pound Era*. Berkeley: University of California Press, 1971.

Laughlin, James, ed. *New Directions in Prose and Poetry 12*. New York: New Directions, 1950.

————, ed. *New Directions in Prose and Poetry 13*. New York: New Directions, 1951.

Lawrence, D. H. *The Escaped Cock*. Paris, 1929; reissued as *The Man Who Died* in *St. Mawr and The Man Who Died*. New York: Vintage Books, n.d.

————. *Psychoanalysis of the Unconscious and Fantasia of the Unconscious*. New York: Viking Press, 1962.

_____. *Studies in Classic American Literature*. Garden City, 1923; rpt. New York: Viking Press, 1964.

Lefebvre, Henri. *Dialectical Materialism*. Trans. John Sturrock. London: Grossman Publishers / Cape Editions, 1969.

Levertov, Denise. *The Double Image*. London: Cresset Press, 1946.

_____. *Footprints*. New York: New Directions, 1972.

_____. *Here and Now*. San Francisco: City Lights Books, 1957.

_____. *The Jacob's Ladder*. New York: New Directions, 1961.

_____. *O Taste and See*. New York: New Directions, 1964.

_____. *Overland to the Islands*. New York: New Directions, 1958.

_____. *The Poet in the World*. New York: New Directions, 1973.

_____. *Relearning the Alphabet*. New York: New Directions, 1970.

_____. *The Sorrow Dance*. New York: New Directions, 1967.

_____. *To Stay Alive*. New York: New Directions, 1971.

_____. *With Eyes at the Back of Our Heads*. New York: New Directions, 1959.

Lévi-Strauss, Claude. *The Raw and the Cooked. Introduction to a Science of Mythology*. Trans. John and Doreen Weightman. Vol. 1. New York: Harper and Row, 1969.

_____. *From Honey to Ashes. Introduction to a Science of Mythology*. Trans. John and Doreen Weightman. Vol. 2. New York: Harper and Row, 1973.

Lowell, Robert. *Life Studies*. New York: Farrar, Straus, Cudahy, 1959.

Luijpen, William A. *Phenomenology and Humanism: A Primer in Existential Phenomenology*. Pittsburgh: Duquesne University Press, 1966.

Mandler, Jean M., and George Mandler. "The Diaspora of Experimental Psychology: The Gestaltists and Others." *Perspectives in American History*. Eds. Donald Fleming and Bernard Bailyn. Cambridge: Charles Warren Center for Studies in American History, 1968. II, 371–419.

Marcuse, Herbert. *Eros and Civilization: A Philosophical Inquiry into Freud*. Boston: Beacon Press, 1955.

Matthiessen, F. O. *American Renaissance: Art and Expression in the Age of Emerson and Whitman*. New York: Oxford University Press, 1941; rpt. 1968.

Melville, Herman. *Moby-Dick or, The Whale*. Ed. Charles Feidelson, Jr. Indianapolis: Bobbs-Merrill Co., 1964.

Merleau-Ponty, Maurice. *The Essential Writings of Merleau-Ponty*. Ed. Alden L. Fisher. New York: Harcourt, Brace, and World, 1969.

Neumann, Erich. *The Origins and History of Consciousness*. Trans. R. F. C. Hull. Bollingen Series XLII. Princeton: Princeton University Press, 1970.

Novik, Mary. *Robert Creeley: An Inventory, 1945–1970*. Kent, Ohio: Kent State University Press, 1973.

Olson, Charles. *Additional Prose: A Bibliography on America, Proprioception,*

& Other Notes and Essays. Ed. George F. Butterick. Bolinas, Calif.:
Four Seasons Foundation, 1974.

_____. *Archaeologist of Morning.* New York: Grossman Publishers, 1973.

_____. "THE AREA, and the DISCIPLINE OF TOTALITY." Unpublished manuscript. Literary Archives of the University of Connecticut Library.

_____. *Call Me Ishmael.* New York: Reynal and Hitchcock, 1947; rpt. San Francisco: City Lights Books, n.d.

_____. *Causal Mythology.* Ed. Donald Allen. San Francisco: Four Seasons Foundation, 1969.

_____. *Charles Olson: Reading at Berkeley.* Transcribed by Zoe Brown. San Francisco: Coyote, 1966.

_____. *The Distances.* New York: Grove Press, 1960.

_____. "An Essay in the Direction of a Restoration of the Act of MYTH." Unpublished manuscript. Literary Archives of the University of Connecticut Library.

_____. "The Growth of Herman Melville, Prose Writer and Poetic Thinker." Master's thesis. Wesleyan University, 1933.

_____. *Human Universe and Other Essays.* Ed. Donald Allen. San Francisco: Auerhahn Society, 1965; rpt. New York: Grove Press, 1967.

_____. *In Adullam's Lair.* Ed. George F. Butterick. Provincetown: To the Lighthouse Press, 1975.

_____. *In Cold Hell, In Thicket.* Palma de Mallorca: Divers Press, 1953; rpt. *Archaeologist of Morning.*

_____. "Lear and Moby Dick." *Twice A Year,* 1 (Fall–Winter 1938), 165–189.

_____. *Letters for Origin, 1950–1956.* Ed. Albert G. Glover. New York: Cape Goliard Press / Grossman Publishers, 1970.

_____. *The Maximus Poems.* New York: Jargon / Corinth Press, 1960.

_____. *The Maximus Poems / 1–10.* Stuttgart: Jonathan Williams, 1953.

_____. *The Maximus Poems / 11–22.* Stuttgart: Jonathan Williams, 1956.

_____. *Maximus Poems IV, V, VI.* London and New York: Cape Goliard Press / Grossman Publishers, 1968.

_____. *The Maximus Poems: Volume Three.* Eds. Charles Boer and George F. Butterick. New York: Grossman Publishers, 1975.

_____. *Mayan Letters by Charles Olson.* Ed. Robert Creeley. Palma de Mallorca: Divers Press, 1953; rpt. *Mayan Letters: Charles Olson.* London: Grossman Publishers / Cape Editions, 1968.

_____. "Notes for a lecture at Pacific Northwest Writers Conference." Unpublished manuscript. Literary Archives of the University of Connecticut Library.

_____. "Notes for Poetry & Art." Unpublished manuscript. Literary Archives of the University of Connecticut Library.

_____. "On Black Mountain." *Maps,* no. 4 (1971), 16–41.

_____. "People v. The Fascist, U.S. (1944)." *Survey Graphic*, 33 (1944), 356–357, 368.

_____. *Pleistocene Man: A Curriculum for the Study of the Soul*. Buffalo: Institute of Further Studies, 1968.

_____. *Poetry and Truth: The Beloit Lectures and Poems*. Ed. George F. Butterick. San Francisco: Four Seasons Foundation, 1971.

_____. *The Post Office*. Ed. George F. Butterick. Bolinas, Calif.: Grey Fox Press, 1975.

_____. "The Science of Mythology." Unpublished manuscript. Literary Archives of the University of Connecticut Library.

_____. *Selected Writings of Charles Olson*. Ed. Robert Creeley. New York: New Directions, 1967.

_____. *The Special View of History*. Ed. Ann Charters. Berkeley: Oyez, 1970.

_____. "A Syllabary for a Dancer." *Maps*, no. 4 (1971), 9–15.

_____. *West*. London: Goliard Press, 1966; rpt. *Archaeologist of Morning*.

_____. *Y & X*. Washington, D.C.: Black Sun Press, 1948; rpt. *Archaeologist of Morning*.

_____, and Ben Shahn. *Spanish Speaking Americans in the War*. Washington, D.C.: Office of the Coordinator of Inter-American Affairs, 1943.

Ossman, David, ed. *The Sullen Art*. New York: Corinth Press, 1963.

Padgett, Ron, and David Shapiro, eds. *An Anthology of New York Poets*. New York: Vintage Press, 1970.

Paul, Sherman. "In and About the Maximus Poems, I & II." *The Iowa Review*, 6, no. 1 (Winter 1975), 118–130, and nos. 3–4 (Summer–Fall 1975), 74–96.

_____. "Maximus: Volume 3 or Books VII and After." *Boundary 2: A Journal of Postmodern Literature*, 6 (1977), 557–571.

Perloff, Marjorie. "Charles Olson and the 'Inferior Predecessors': 'Projective Verse' Revisited." *ELH*, 40 (1973), 285–306.

Pops, Martin L. "Melville: To Him, Olson." *Boundary 2: A Journal of Postmodern Literature*, 2 (1973–74), 55–84.

Pound, Ezra. *ABC of Reading*. London, 1934; rpt. New York: New Directions, 1960.

_____. *The Cantos of Ezra Pound*. New York: New Directions, 1973.

_____. *Guide to Kulchur*. London, 1938; rpt. New York: New Directions, 1970.

_____. *Instigations of Ezra Pound with an Essay on the Chinese Written Character by Ernest Fenollosa*. New York, 1920; rpt. *The Chinese Written Character as a Medium for Poetry*. Ed. Ezra Pound. San Francisco: City Lights Books, 1968.

_____. *Literary Essays*. Ed. T. S. Eliot. Norfolk, Conn.: New Directions, 1954; rpt. New York, 1968.

————. *Personae: The Collected Shorter Poems of Ezra Pound.* New York: New Directions, n.d.

Reck, Michael. *Ezra Pound: A Close-Up.* New York: McGraw-Hill, 1973.

Rexroth, Kenneth. *American Poetry in the Twentieth Century.* New York: Seabury Press, 1973.

Riesman, David. *The Lonely Crowd.* New Haven: Yale University Press, 1950.

Robinson, Paul A. *The Freudian Left: Wilhelm Reich, Geza Roheim, Herbert Marcuse.* New York: Harper and Row, 1970.

Rosenberg, Harold. *The Tradition of the New.* 2nd ed. New York: McGraw-Hill, 1965.

Rumaker, Michael. *The Butterfly.* New York: Scribner's, 1962.

————. *Gringos, and Other Stories.* New York: Grove Press, 1966.

Schacht, Richard. *Alienation.* New York: Doubleday and Co., 1971.

Schell, Jonathan. "The Nixon Years." *New Yorker,* 51, nos. 15–20 (June 2–July 7, 1975); revised and published as *The Time of Illusion.* New York: Knopf, 1976.

Seelye, Catherine, ed. *Charles Olson & Ezra Pound: An Encounter at St. Elizabeths.* New York: Grossman Publishers, 1975.

Sorrentino, Gilbert. *Black and White.* Ed. Leroi Jones [Imamu Amiri Baraka]. New York: Totem Press / Corinth Books, 1964.

"The State of American Writing, 1948: Seven Questions." *Partisan Review,* 15 (1948), 855–894.

Stead, C. K. *The New Poetic: Yeats to Eliot.* New York: Harper and Row, 1966.

Stock, Noel. *The Life of Ezra Pound.* New York: Pantheon Books, 1970.

Tallman, Warren. *Three Essays on Robert Creeley.* Toronto: The Coach House Press / Beaver Kosmos, 1970.

Weaver, Mike. *William Carlos Williams: The American Background.* Cambridge: Cambridge University Press, 1971.

Whitehead, Alfred North. *Process and Reality: An Essay in Cosmology.* New York, 1929; rpt. Harper and Row, 1960.

Whitman, Walt. *Leaves of Grass.* Ed. Emory Holloway. New York: Doubleday and Co., 1948.

Wieners, John. *Hotels.* New York: Angel Hair Books, 1974.

————. *Selected Poems.* New York: Grossman Publishers, 1972.

Williams, Jonathan. *An Ear in Bartram's Tree: Selected Poems 1957–1967.* Chapel Hill: University of North Carolina Press, 1969; rpt. New York: New Directions, 1972.

————, ed. *Edward Dahlberg: A Tribute. / Essays, Reminiscences, Correspondence, Tributes.* New York: David Lewis Press, 1970.

Williams, Miller. "Intuition, Spontaneity, Organic Wholeness and the Redemptive Wilderness: Some (Old) Currents in Contemporary Poetry." Paper delivered at the South Central Modern Language Association convention, Houston, Texas, December 1974.

Williams, William Carlos. *In the American Grain*. Rpt. New York: New Directions, 1956.

———. *Kora in Hell*. Boston, 1920; rpt. San Francisco: City Lights Books, 1960.

———. *Paterson*. New York: New Directions, 1963.

———. *Pictures from Brueghel and Other Poems: Collected 1950–1962*. New York: New Directions, 1962.

———. *Selected Essays of William Carlos Williams*. New York: New Directions, 1969.

———. *The William Carlos Williams Reader*. Ed. M. L. Rosenthal. London: MacGibbon and Kee, 1966.

Wilson, Edmund. *Axel's Castle: A Study in the Imaginative Literature of 1870–1930*. New York: Scribner's, 1931; rpt. 1969.

Zukofsky, Louis. *"A" 1–12*. Garden City: Doubleday and Co., 1967.

———. *"A" 13–21*. Garden City: Doubleday and Co., 1969.

———. *"A" 22 & 23*. New York: Grossman Publishers, 1975.

———. *"A" 24*. New York: Grossman Publishers, 1972.

———, ed. *An 'Objectivists' Anthology*. Le Beausset, France, 1932.

Index